The RENAISSANCE

AN ENCYCLOPEDIA FOR STUDENTS

The RENAISSANCE

AN ENCYCLOPEDIA FOR STUDENTS

Paul F. Grendler, Editor in Chief

PUBLISHED IN ASSOCIATION WITH THE RENAISSANCE SOCIETY OF AMERICA

Volume **3**

KEPLER—PRINCES AND PRINCEDOMS

CHARLES SCRIBNER'S SONS®

THOMSON

GALE

New York • Detroit • San Diego • San Francisco • Cleveland • Boston • New Haven, Conn. • Waterville, Maine • London • Munich

The Renaissance An Encyclopedia for Students

Paul F. Grendler, Editor in Chief
Copyright © 2004 Charles Scribner's Sons.
Developed for Charles Scribner's Sons by
Visual Education Corporation, Princeton, N.J.
For Scribners

PUBLISHER:
Frank Menchaca

EDITORS:
John Fitzpatrick, Sharon Malinowski

COVER AND INTERIOR DESIGN:
Jennifer Wahi

IMAGING AND MULTIMEDIA:
Lezlie Light, Robyn Young, Mary Grimes, Dave
Oblender, Leitha Etheridge-Sims, Dan Newell,
Christine O'Bryan

COMPOSITION:
Evi Seoud

MANUFACTURING:
Rhonda Williams

For Visual Education Corporation

PROJECT DIRECTORS:
Darryl Kestler, Amy Livingston

WRITERS:
John Haley, Mark Mussari, Charles Roebuck,
Rebecca Stefoff

EDITORS:
Tobey Cloyd, Cindy George, John Kennedy

ASSOCIATE EDITOR:
Sarah Miller

COPYEDITING SUPERVISOR:
Helen Castro

ELECTRONIC PREPARATION:
Fiona Shapiro

For more information, contact
Charles Scribner's Sons
300 Park Avenue South
New York, NY 10010
Or visit our Internet site at
http://www.gale.com/scribners

Since this page cannot legibly accommodate
all copyright notices, the acknowledgments
constitute an extension of the copyright
notice.

For permission to use material from this
product, submit your request via Web at
http://www.gale-edit.com/permissions, or you
may download our Permissions Request form
and submit your request by fax or mail to:

Permissions Department
The Gale Group, Inc.
27500 Drake Rd.
Farmington Hills, MI 48331-3535
Permissions Hotline:
248-699-8006 or 800-762-4058

LIBRARY OF CONGRESS CATALOG-IN-PUBLICATION DATA

The Renaissance : an encyclopedia for students / Paul F. Grendler.
    p. cm
        Summary: An encyclopedia of the Renaissance with articles on various
        aspects of social, cultural, and political history such as literature, gov-
        ernment, warfare, and technology, plus maps, charts, definitions, and
        chronology.
        Includes bibliographical references and index.
        ISBN 0-684-31281-6 (set hardcover : alk. paper) — ISBN 0-684-31282-4
        (v. 1) — ISBN 0-684-31283-2 (v. 2) — ISBN 0-684-31285-9 (v. 3) — ISBN
        0-684-31284-0 (v. 4) — ISBN 0-684-31424-X (e-book)
        1. Renaissance—Encyclopedias, Juvenile. [1. Renaissance—
        Encyclopedias.] I. Grendler, Paul F. II. Encyclopedia of the Renaissance.
        III. Title.

CB361.R25 2003
940.2′1′03—dc22

This title is also available as an e-book
ISBN 0-684-31424-X (set)

Contact your Gale sale representative for ordering information

Printed in the United States of America
10 9 8 7 6 5 4 3 2 1

Table of Contents

VOLUME 1

Academies—Cromwell

VOLUME 2

Daily Life—Julius II

VOLUME 3

Kepler—Princes and Princedoms

VOLUME 4

Printing and Publishing—Writing

Maps

Genealogical Charts

Color Plates

Kabbalah

See *Magic and Astrology.*

1571–1630
German astronomer

* **duchy**   territory ruled by a duke or duchess

* **astrological**   relating to astrology, the study of the supposed influences of the stars and planets on earthly events

German astronomer Johannes Kepler was a key figure in Renaissance science. He made groundbreaking discoveries in the fields of ASTRONOMY, mathematics, and optics (the study of the properties of light). One of his most important achievements was explaining the physical laws that govern the motions of the planets. His discovery provided support for Nicolaus COPERNICUS's theory that Earth and the other planets revolve around the Sun.

Early Career. Kepler was born to a Lutheran family in Weil der Stadt, a Catholic city in what is now Germany. In the mid-1570s his family moved to the Protestant duchy* of Württemberg, where Kepler began his education. A scholarship enabled Kepler to study at a Latin school, and from there he moved on to the University of Tübingen to prepare for the Lutheran ministry. He also studied mathematics and astronomy. One of his teachers introduced him to the theories of Copernicus, and Kepler became convinced that the Sun stood at the center of the universe.

After Kepler had spent three years at the university, school officials gave him a position teaching mathematics in Graz, Austria. In addition to teaching, Kepler served as district mathematician, a job that required him to produce astrological* calendars of coming events. In Graz, Kepler wrote his first book, *Secret of the Universe* (1596). It discussed the Copernican system and set forth many major ideas that Kepler pursued in his later work, such as the belief that simple mathematics could describe the nature of the universe.

Kepler's book established his reputation as an astronomer and prompted the Danish astronomer Tycho BRAHE to invite Kepler to work with him. Kepler was eager to accept, as he hoped to use Tycho's excellent collection of astronomical data to support his theories about the structure of the solar system. In 1600 Kepler joined Tycho and other intellectuals at the court of RUDOLF II in Prague, where Tycho served as court mathematician.

Kepler's years in Prague were the most productive of his life. During this period, he discovered the first two laws of planetary motion. The first describes the shapes of planetary orbits as ellipses, or ovals. The second describes the area traced out by a line drawn between the Sun and an orbiting planet. Kepler showed that this area is always equal for a given period of time. He also began to study optics. After learning about Galileo GALILEI's pioneering work with telescopes, Kepler wrote two books about the use of lenses in telescopes. In addition, he wrote about astrology, trying to reform the subject in ways that would make it fit in with his new discoveries about the physics of space.

Later Career. Kepler left Prague in 1612 and found work as district mathematician in the city of Linz in Austria. Trouble arose when his

Johannes Kepler changed the face of astronomy with his works describing the motion of the planets. He also made important contributions to the fields of mathematics and optics, the study of the properties of light.

IOANNIS KEPPLERI, Mathematici Cæsarei hanc Imaginem, ARGENTORATENSI BIBLIOTHECÆ Confecr.

mother was accused of being a witch, but Kepler used his contacts to protect her from torture during her arrest, and she was eventually released.

Despite his problems, Kepler continued to make useful discoveries. In 1615 he conducted a study of the quantity of wine that a barrel could hold. This work later proved useful in the development of calculus, a form of advanced mathematics. In 1619 Kepler published *Harmony of the World,* which he saw as the climax of his studies. It contained the third law of planetary motion, which laid out the relationship between planets' average distance from the Sun and the time it takes them to

orbit the Sun. Around this time Kepler also wrote a textbook on Copernican astronomy.

After a brief stay in the duchy of Sagan, Bohemia, Kepler died while on his way to collect some money owed to him for his astronomical work. Four years after his death, his final work was published. Called *Dream,* it was a forerunner of modern science fiction, describing how the solar system would look to a traveler to the Moon. (*See also* **Science.**)

Kings and Kingship

See *Monarchy.*

Knox, John

ca. 1514–1572
Scottish Protestant preacher

* **Protestant Reformation** religious movement that began in the 1500s as a protest against certain practices of the Roman Catholic Church and eventually led to the establishment of a variety of Protestant churches

* **theologian** person who studies religion and the nature of God

* **regent** person who acts on behalf of a monarch who is too young or unable to rule

* **depose** to remove from high office, often by force

A powerful preacher, John Knox had a major impact on the course of the Protestant Reformation* in Scotland and England. Born near Edinburgh, Scotland, Knox became a Catholic priest in 1536. He converted to Protestantism in the early 1540s and became an associate of George Wishart, a well-known Protestant preacher. Although reluctant at first to become a minister himself, Knox eventually became convinced that God called him to serve.

In 1547 French forces attacked Scotland and took Knox prisoner. He spent most of the next two years as a slave on French ships. Released in 1549, he chose to settle in Protestant England rather than return to Catholic Scotland. His powerful preaching earned him an appointment as a royal chaplain. Knox became known for his strict interpretation of the Bible—a view that often placed him at odds with English religious leaders such as Thomas CRANMER.

When the Catholic Mary Tudor took the throne of England as MARY I in 1554, Knox fled to mainland Europe. He eventually reached Geneva, Switzerland, home of the Protestant theologian* John CALVIN. A year later Knox went on a secret mission to Scotland and reestablished contact with leaders of the Protestant movement there. In 1558 Knox wrote a series of pamphlets justifying armed resistance against "ungodly" rulers. In one of these works, he attacked female rulers as "monstrous." As a result, the new Protestant queen of England, ELIZABETH I, prevented Knox from reentering England. He returned to Scotland instead.

In 1559 Knox's preaching triggered a Protestant rebellion against the queen regent* of Scotland, Mary of Guise, whose daughter MARY STUART had married a French Catholic prince. Under Knox's influence, Scotland briefly adopted Protestant doctrines. In 1561, however, Mary Stuart regained power. Knox spoke out against the queen's Catholic beliefs and tried unsuccessfully to convert her to Protestantism. However, his influence gradually declined, and he played no significant role in the rebellion that deposed* and exiled the queen. Knox spent the last years of his life writing a history of the Scottish Reformation, which appeared in print in 1586, 14 years after his death. (*See also* **Protestant Reformation.**)

Ladino Language and Literature

See *Jewish Languages and Literature.*

Language

See *individual languages.*

Las Casas, Bartolomé de

1474–1566
Spanish author and activist

* **Dominican** religious order of brothers and priests founded by St. Dominic

Bartolomé de Las Casas, a Spanish friar, is best known for his criticism of Spain's colonial policies in the Americas, particularly its cruel treatment of Native Americans. His role in bringing this injustice to the attention of the world has earned him a place in the struggle for human rights.

In 1502 Las Casas settled on the Caribbean island of Hispaniola, Spain's first American colony. Ten years later he took part in the conquest of Cuba. The Spanish friar soon recognized the unjust nature of Spain's *encomienda* system, which forced Indians to labor for colonists who were supposed to Christianize them. He gave up his own *encomienda,* freed his Indians, and claimed that the Spanish conquest was wiping out the Native American population. He joined forces with the Dominican* order, which had also been protesting the treatment of the Indians. In 1515 Las Casas and other friars met with the Spanish king to plead for a more just and peaceful way of converting the Indians to Christianity.

During the 1520s Las Casas began writing *In Defense of the Indians* and *History of the Indies.* In 1530 he set out for Mexico, Guatemala, and Nicaragua, criticizing Spanish officials wherever he found the Indians unjustly treated. He achieved some success. In 1537 Pope Paul III declared that Native American lives and property deserved protection, and soon afterward Las Casas established a peaceful mission community in Guatemala. Back in Spain, he persuaded Emperor CHARLES V to pass laws outlawing Indian slavery. Later, however, the emperor canceled some sections of the laws, fearing a revolt by angry colonists. Some Spanish intellectuals opposed Las Casas, arguing that it was proper to use war to bring the Indians to Christianity. Las Casas spent his final years in a Dominican convent.

Critics have accused Las Casas of writing inaccurate history and exaggerating Spain's cruelty to the Indians. However, recent studies of the decline of the Native American population have largely supported him. Las Casas has also been attacked for recommending the use of African slaves instead of Indian laborers, but in *History of the Indies* he stated that African slavery was as unjust as Indian slavery. (*See also* **Spain.**)

Łaski Family

The Łaski family produced a number of outstanding churchmen, diplomats, and supporters of humanism* in Poland. Jan Łaski (1455–1531) was the leading Polish diplomat of the early 1500s, becoming the kingdom's grand chancellor under King Aleksander

Jagiellonczyk. He also served as archbishop of Gniezno and head of the church in Poland. An expert in political affairs and a champion of legal reform, Łaski was largely responsible for publication of the set of Polish laws known as the *Statut Laskiego*. He fought the spread of the Lutheran faith in Poland and was a patron* of humanist scholars and writers.

Jan Łaski provided for the education of his three nephews. Hieronim (1496–1542) played a key political role in Poland, and Stanisław (ca. 1500–1550) served two Polish kings as a diplomat. Perhaps the most accomplished of the nephews was Jan Łaski the Younger (1499–1560), a scholar who traveled widely and held several church offices during his life. Jan attracted a circle of young humanists devoted to the ideas of ERASMUS.

In the 1520s Jan Łaski the Younger became interested in Protestantism, preferring the moderate approach of Philipp MELANCHTHON to the more radical ideas of Martin LUTHER. Jan moved for a time to Louvain in Belgium. In 1541 he returned to Poland and swore to be faithful to the Catholic Church. He soon broke his promise, however, and went to England to help archbishop Thomas CRANMER set up the Protestant Church of England. Łaski fled England in 1553 when MARY I, a Catholic, became queen. Returning to Poland again, he became actively involved with the Protestant movement there and translated the Calvinist* version of the Bible into Polish. He also helped establish an academy for non-Catholics. In addition, he had great influence on other Protestant reformers in Poland, especially his nephew, Olbracht. (*See also* **Poland.**)

Lasso, Orlando di

ca. 1530–1594
Flemish composer

One of the most admired composers of the Renaissance, Orlando di Lasso was the first great composer whose fame spread through printed music. A master of many musical forms, Lasso wrote more than 1,000 compositions ranging from religious Masses to secular* songs.

Lasso grew up in the Flemish* town of Mons and received his earliest musical training there. His original name was probably Roland de Lassus. As a boy he was kidnapped three times for his beautiful voice. Between 1544 and 1554 Lasso traveled through Italy, staying in Milan, Naples, and Rome, where he became choirmaster of a major church. His years in Italy played a crucial role in his musical development, so much so that he permanently changed his name to its Italian version.

Lasso returned home in 1554 to find that his parents had died. He then moved to Antwerp, where he lived until 1556. He left when the duke of Bavaria hired him to sing in the court chapel. The duke named him head of his chapel in Munich, one of Europe's leading musical establishments, in 1562. Lasso held the position for the remainder of his life, becoming the most famous and admired composer in Europe during his time. Critics hailed him as the "prince of music" and "the divine Orlando."

Lasso excelled in all types of vocal music of his day. His work included more than 500 motets (songs written for several voices), about 60 Masses, and hundreds of other musical works. While he set most of his

compositions to sacred texts, some celebrated secular occasions or individuals. The most essential aspect of Lasso's music was his ability to express the meaning of the words in a song through rhythm, melody, harmony, and other musical elements. (*See also* **Music; Music, Vocal.**)

Lateran V, Council of

See *Councils.*

Latin Language and Literature

* **humanist** Renaissance expert in the humanities (the languages, literature, history, and speech and writing techniques of ancient Greece and Rome)

* **classical** in the tradition of ancient Greece and Rome

Latin was the most important language in Europe during the Renaissance. Throughout the Middle Ages, Latin had been essential to learning, religion, and government. During this period the language had changed considerably from the Latin spoken and written in ancient Rome. It had also taken different forms in different parts of Europe and in different fields of study. Renaissance scholars sought to restore a consistent, elegant Latin based strictly on the work of ancient authors.

In the early 1300s, a small group of learned people in northern Italy began a movement to revive the language, literature, and history of ancient Greece and Rome. These scholars, known as humanists*, sought to return the Latin language to its Roman roots. Authors such as the Italian poet PETRARCH studied ancient works and used them as models for their own writing. Their efforts gave rise to a tradition of writing new Latin works in a classical* style. Such "Neo-Latin" literature flourished throughout Europe in the Renaissance.

Studying Latin. As the humanist movement spread, schools began to focus on the study of ancient poets, orators, and historians. Students at humanist schools read works by such famous Roman poets as VIRGIL, Ovid, and Horace. Renaissance readers took these classical writers as examples, both for writing Latin and for living a moral life.

Schoolbooks from the Renaissance provide evidence about the ways that students approached classical works. In some cases, they read books straight through from beginning to end. In others, they skipped around, searching the text for well-turned phrases. Teachers often instructed their students to keep "commonplace books," in which they recorded their favorite lines from classical writings. They might copy well-written passages to use as models for their own writing, as well as lines that illustrated moral virtues.

While humanists agreed on the value of imitating classical authors, they disagreed about which authors were the best models. Some, such as the Italian scholar Lorenzo VALLA, favored learning from a wide variety of ancient writers. In the 1440s Valla wrote one of the most influential books on the use of Latin, *Six Books of the Elegances of the Latin Language.* Based on Valla's careful study of ancient Roman literature, this work taught Renaissance scholars how to use an eclectic Latin—that is, a style that combined the best elements of many ancient authors. However, other scholars focused heavily on the works of the Roman orator CICERO, whom they considered the finest writer of the ancient world.

Some took this view to extremes, claiming that Cicero was the only model Renaissance authors should imitate.

Nonetheless, Renaissance authors turned to many classical writers for models and inspiration. One of the most influential was the Roman poet Virgil, whose works took a central place in Renaissance schools. Virgil's great epic* the *Aeneid* described the travels of the hero Aeneas, the legendary founder of Rome. Petrarch used this work as a model for his own epic poem, *Africa,* which praised the ancient Roman warrior Scipio Africanus. Virgil's works also inspired such celebrated authors as Ludovico Ariosto in Italy, Clément Marot in France, and Edmund Spenser in England.

* **epic** long poem about the adventures of a hero

Authors drew on the works of the ancient writers Ovid, Plautus, Terence, and Seneca as well. Ovid's love stories served as models for the tales in the *Decameron,* a collection of stories by Italian author Giovanni Boccaccio. Plautus and Terence, two Roman playwrights, inspired many comedies by the English dramatist William Shakespeare. Seneca was a major source for Shakespeare's tragedies.

Writing in Latin. Neo-Latin literature based on the classics spread across Europe much the same way that humanism did. It was already flourishing in Italy in the 1400s, and Italian humanists helped spread it to other areas. By the end of the century it had spread to northern Europe, eastern Europe, and Britain, and in the mid-1500s it took root in the Scandinavian countries.

Authors used Latin for many types of written works. Scholarly writings, including works on philosophy, theology*, and science, made up a large part of the body of Neo-Latin texts. Renaissance writers also adopted Latin for poetry, dialogues, and essays published in the form of letters. Many Neo-Latin works of this type were studied in schools alongside the writings of ancient authors. Other important genres* of Neo-Latin writing include speeches, drama (both comedy and tragedy), travel accounts, and satire*.

* **theology** study of the nature of God and of religion

* **genre** literary form

* **satire** literary or artistic work ridiculing human wickedness and foolishness

Educated writers chose to write in Latin for a variety of reasons. Most importantly, the use of Latin made their works understandable to readers across Europe. Many writers who did not aim to reach an international audience still chose Latin because it had been the accepted language of scholarship since the time of ancient Rome. Writing in Latin gave their works weight and authority. Another advantage of classical Latin was its stability. While local languages were constantly changing, Latin provided a secure and well-defined medium for ideas—one that future generations would be likely to understand.

Writers could not keep classical Latin completely pure. During the Middle Ages, writers had needed to create new words to describe new things not found in ancient Rome. Neo-Latin writers had little choice but to use these terms when discussing new political, religious, and scholarly concepts. They also gave new meanings to some words that had existed in ancient Rome.

Latin remained the language of learning and science throughout the Renaissance. Toward the end of the period, vernacular* languages began

* **vernacular** native language or dialect of a region or country

to take its place in some parts of Europe. In northern and eastern regions, however, scholarly Latin lasted well into the 1700s. In addition, Latin remained the official language of the Roman Catholic Church, used in ceremonies and spoken at gatherings of high church officials.

Speaking Latin. Neo-Latin was mostly a literary language. It took its form from a particular body of texts, not from the speech of people in the streets. However, in some circles Latin also served as a spoken language. In many parts of northern Europe, students in Latin schools were required to speak only Latin in school once they had acquired a basic knowledge of the language. Latin was also the teaching language at Renaissance universities. Thus, students needed to be able to read textbooks, understand lectures, and answer questions in Latin. Latin could also serve as a common language among educated people throughout Europe, enabling them to communicate without the aid of interpreters. (*See also* **Classical Scholarship; Education; Humanism; Literature.**)

Law

* **humanism** Renaissance cultural movement promoting the study of the humanities (the languages, literature, and history of ancient Greece and Rome) as a guide to living

* **jurist** person with a thorough knowledge of the law

* **papal** referring to the office and authority of the pope

* **medieval** referring to the Middle Ages, a period that began around A.D. 400 and ended around 1400 in Italy and 1500 in the rest of Europe

Renaissance Europe inherited a variety of legal codes and procedures from the Middle Ages. Much of this legal tradition remained intact throughout the period. However, the Renaissance also saw the spread of ancient Roman law to parts of northern Europe, as well as the development of new legal systems based on humanism*. By the 1600s, the foundations of modern international law had begun to emerge.

Law in the Middle Ages. The 1100s marked a turning point in the development of law in Europe. During that century, the study of ancient Roman law revived in Italy. At the same time, the related study of canon law, or church law, developed. The Italian city of Bologna became one of the most important early centers for legal study, which focused on written texts.

The texts of Roman law had been assembled in the 500s by order of the Roman Emperor Justinian. They included the *Codex,* a collection of existing laws; a textbook on law; and a collection of writings from Roman jurists*. Roman civil law focused on such matters as kinship and status, inheritance, property, and obligations. Criminal law and judicial procedure received much less attention. Canon law, however, developed those areas further.

The central text of canon law was the *Decretum,* assembled in the 1100s by a monk named Gratian. Unlike Roman law, canon law was used, interpreted, and applied in courts throughout Christian Europe. When problems arose with canon law, the pope in Rome would settle the disputed point. These papal* rulings on legal issues such as marriage became part of the body of canon law.

Learned jurists in Bologna saw these unrelated ancient and medieval* legal codes as forming a single body of law, based on a basic, unchanging standard of reason and justice. They made no attempt to find or correct errors in legal texts. Instead, they studied the texts and instructed

others in the law, chiefly by preparing comments that explained legal terms, highlighted principles, and referred to other sections within the legal code. These comments became the basis from which students learned how to apply and extend the *ius commune*—the body of common law.

By the mid-1200s, many Italian cities and states had books of their own local laws on such matters as government offices, public places, crimes, and inheritance. Similar sets of laws appeared in France, Spain, and Portugal. These laws and customs made up the *iura propria*—a set of laws peculiar to a specific place, in contrast to the *ius commune*. However, the *ius commune* served as a secondary source of rules on the local level. Local laws changed frequently, but common law provided a fixed body of rules and principles.

Counsels and Commentaries. Legal scholars of the 1300s and 1400s developed new types of legal writing that had a major impact on the study of law. The two chief forms were *commentaria* (commentaries on legal texts) and *consilia* (advice on legal cases or problems).

The *commentaria* were the personal views of jurists on how to interpret medieval legal texts. Many of them sought to identify connections between different legal principles and to give reality to the body of law. *Consilia*, by contrast, were written opinions that jurists had given in actual cases. These texts often focused on the question of which law, within the body of common law or local laws, applied in a given case. *Consilia* first appeared in the 1100s, and by the late 1300s they had became a regular feature of judicial practice. They could serve to aid a judge or to support the arguments of one of the parties in a lawsuit.

Many *consilia* by famous jurists were collected and published in the 1400s. Other jurists referred to them for arguments to use in their own *consilia*. In Italian cities, the production of legal opinions became a major activity and a source of income for jurists. As the century progressed, *consilia* became longer, including more and more notes on each point of law. The material in the *consilia* served as a body of *communes opiniones* (common opinions) on legal points—in essence, a form of judicial precedent*.

In some cases, jurists used these precedents to overturn existing laws. Rulers came up with various strategies to avoid this problem. The city of Florence set up a court called the *ruota*, staffed by trained jurists, both local and foreign. The decisions of this court, rather than the precedents established in common opinion, were the final authority in matters of law. In other cases, rulers simply used their authority to rewrite laws or overturn decisions.

One of the most important authors of *commentaria* and *consilia* was the Italian jurist Bartolus of Sassoferrato, who lived in the 1300s. During his life, Bartolus produced hundreds of *commentaries, consilia,* and treatises* based on his study of legal texts. His work helped make the law more flexible, adapting ancient legal principles to the realities of his day. Another Italian jurist of the 1300s, Baldus of Ubaldis, expanded on Bartolus's work, seeking to adapt the law to the standards of his time.

Women and the Law

Renaissance women did not have nearly as many rights as men did, either as individuals or as members of family groups. Local customs and laws limited women's control of property and their access to the courts. Many of these laws dictated that if a man died without a will, his money went to his nearest male relatives. In some parts of Europe, however, a woman could own and sell property in her own name, and when she died her dowry (the money she had brought to her marriage) went to her heirs. The different legal codes of the Renaissance left a confused pattern.

* **precedent**   legal decision that serves as an example in deciding similar cases

* **treatise**   long, detailed essay

Lawyers and judges of the Renaissance often turned to collections of earlier legal opinions, known as *consilia,* for help in arguing or deciding cases. This illustration of a law professor teaching a class appeared in a volume of *consilia* published in 1537.

The works of Bartolus and Baldus became key references for later jurists, who often quoted them in their own legal writings.

Humanist Ideas on Law. The humanistic approach to law had its roots in the 1300s, when scholars such as PETRARCH and Giovanni BOCCACCIO criticized legal practice and teaching because it lacked a sense of history. They began to question the role of law in human knowledge. Humanist criticism of medieval legal ideas increased in the 1400s. A number of humanist scholars strongly attacked the work of earlier jurists, such as Bartolus, on the grounds that they contained errors in their language and in their interpretation of ancient texts.

The work of these humanist scholars turned the common view of Roman law on its head. They saw Roman law as the product of a specific social and political environment, rather than as a universal standard. They rejected the idea of Bartolus and Baldus that ancient laws could be adapted to modern societies. Humanists presented Roman law as a leftover from the past—useful in some ways, but not essential.

Law Across Europe. Like other Renaissance ideas, the different views of law spread from Italy to other parts of Europe during the 1400s and early 1500s. The English king HENRY VIII established faculties of civil law at Oxford and Cambridge Universities. The Holy Roman Empire* also adopted the practical methods of Italian law. One example was a new means of conducting trials, in which judges questioned witnesses directly rather than listening to the evidence presented by the opposing parties. The law faculties of German universities also adopted Italian methods of teaching law. A new class of jurists arose who helped spread Italian legal ideas to the courts of cities and rulers.

The jurists of France, however, rejected both Roman law and Italian legal methods as foreign and unsuitable. They adopted their own method of humanist study of law, creating a "French style" to counter the "Italian style" of Bartolus and Baldus. Spain, by contrast, continued to cling to the legal ideas of the Middle Ages. Spanish scholars believed in an eternal standard of justice contained in "natural law"—a code of

* **Holy Roman Empire** political body in central Europe composed of several states; existed until 1806

rules and behavior inspired by God, which applied to all human societies.

Natural Law. Debate over natural law deepened in the 1600s. By that time, humanistic views on law had undermined Roman law, which could no longer serve as a universal standard. Similarly, the Protestant Reformation* had made it impossible for traditional canon law to provide a universal standard, as there was no longer a single, unified church. Legal publications began focusing on existing laws, customs, and court rulings, and many proposals appeared for creating a modern code of law.

In 1625, Dutch humanist Hugo GROTIUS launched the modern era of international law with the publication of his book *The Law of War and Peace*. Grotius based his ideas on the principles of natural law, rather than on ancient Roman codes. Grotius, however, saw natural law not as inspired by God but as an extension of human reason. His work inspired legal reform through much of Europe, and international law grew throughout the 1600s. (*See also* **Crime and Punishment; Humanism; Ideas, Spread of; Universities.**)

* **Protestant Reformation** religious movement that began in the 1500s as a protest against certain practices of the Roman Catholic Church and eventually led to the establishment of a variety of Protestant churches

Leiden

By the late 1400s Leiden was the most populous town in the county of Holland, with about 14,000 inhabitants. Its prosperity depended chiefly on the cloth industry, which employed nearly half the town's population. Good times came to an end in 1477, when a century-long period of economic decline and social unrest began.

Leiden's history took a turn in the 1500s during the Dutch revolt against Spanish rule. In 1575, after a yearlong siege of the town by Spanish troops, Dutch leader William of Orange founded a Protestant university there. The town also began welcoming Protestant refugees from the southern Netherlands, who helped modernize the cloth industry.

Cultural life in Leiden was fairly regional. Two monasteries produced manuscripts, and Dutch literature flowered in local literary societies. Many of Leiden's leading literary figures sympathized with Protestantism, and the town adopted Calvinism* in 1572. However, a controversy over theology* that began in Leiden grew into a political and religious conflict that divided the Dutch republic.

In general, though, the religious climate in Leiden was very tolerant. In 1609 the town allowed English exile John Robinson to found his Separate Church, which had about 300 English members. In 1620 William Bradford, one of the leaders of this English community, organized the departure from Leiden of the first group of Pilgrims bound for New England.

Leiden's university gained fame throughout Europe, especially for its literary studies. Many renowned scholars taught there. Intellectual life also flourished outside the university, but Leiden played only a secondary role in the Golden Age of Dutch painting and literature that began in the late 1500s. The Dutch translation of the Bible, first published in

* **Calvinism** Protestant church founded by John Calvin

* **theology** study of the nature of God and of religion

Leiden in 1637, had a major influence on the Dutch language. Leiden also produced many talented painters, but most of them settled elsewhere. Renaissance architecture arrived in the town only in the late 1500s. A notable example can be seen in the facade of Leiden's town hall. (*See also* **Art in the Netherlands; Netherlands.**)

1475–1521
Pope

* **patron**   supporter or financial sponsor of an artist or writer

* **humanist**   Renaissance expert in the humanities (the languages, literature, history, and speech and writing techniques of ancient Greece and Rome)

* **papal**   referring to the office and authority of the pope

* **Papal States**   lands in central Italy under the authority of the pope

* **Holy Roman Empire**   political body in central Europe composed of several states; existed until 1806

* **conspiracy**   plotting with others to commit a crime

Pope Leo X played a strong role in efforts to protect the church and its lands. He worked to promote the spread of Catholicism and keep foreign invaders out of Italy. In addition, Leo was an important patron* of artists and humanists*. During his years as pope, Rome experienced a "golden age" of Renaissance culture.

Early Life.   Leo was born in Florence as Giovanni Romolo Damaso de' Medici, son of the head of Florence's powerful MEDICI family. Destined for a career in the church, Giovanni had a well-rounded education that included studies in Latin and Italian literature as well as Greek and music. At only 14 years of age he became a deacon in the church, and within a month he had gained appointment to cardinal. Giovanni then traveled to Pisa, where he studied under some of the most famous legal minds of the time. He received a degree in church law from the University of Pisa in 1492.

Shortly after earning his degree, Giovanni went to Rome to join the College of Cardinals—a select body of bishops, priests, and deacons who advised the pope. After a period of travel, he settled in Rome. In 1506 he served as governor of Perugia, and five years later he became an official papal* representative to part of the Papal States* and to the papal army under Pope JULIUS II. When Julius died in 1513, Giovanni became pope, taking the name Leo X.

Leo As Pope.   As ruler of the Papal States, Leo continued many of Julius's policies. He asserted greater control over his territory by reducing the influence of powerful families and by forcing lesser rulers to surrender to papal control. In foreign affairs, Leo presented himself as the promoter of peace among Christians. Behind the scenes, however, he worked to lessen foreign influence in Italy. He joined Spain and the Holy Roman Empire* to drive the French out of Italy in 1513. Two years later, however, the French returned. Leo accepted their presence until 1521, when he allied himself with the HABSBURG dynasty in order to drive the French from Milan and restore papal authority in the cities of Parma and Piacenza.

Leo also sought to promote his own family's interests. He aimed to control Florence through his brother and nephew and arranged marriages for them with members of the French royal family. Even though their untimely deaths frustrated Leo's efforts, he kept control of Florence through his cousin, Giulio de'Medici. Leo's interference in the affairs of Siena provoked a conspiracy* to poison him, but the conspirators were discovered and executed or forced to pay enormous fines.

* excommunicate to exclude from the church and its rituals

In 1517 Protestant reformer Martin LUTHER attacked the Catholic Church in his Ninety-Five Theses. Unable to silence Luther, Leo excommunicated* him. Shortly after, he named HENRY VIII of England "Defender of the Faith" for his stance against Luther. Leo made additional efforts to encourage the spread of Catholicism by allowing a native of Africa to become a bishop. He also promoted a number of his own relatives to important church positions as archbishops and cardinals. When Leo died, his cousin Giulio succeeded him as Pope Clement VII.

In addition to ruling the Papal States, Leo was one of the leading artistic and humanistic patrons of the Renaissance. He made the University of Rome an intellectual center by appointing famous professors and adding a Greek college and press. He also patronized great Italian artists. MICHELANGELO BUONARROTI carved several tombs for members of Leo's family, and RAPHAEL painted Leo's portrait and took charge of the construction of the church of St. Peter. (*See also* **Popes and Papacy.**)

Leonardo da Vinci

1452–1519
Italian artist and scientist

Leonardo da Vinci, one of the best-known figures of the Renaissance, is remembered for his achievements as a painter, sculptor, architect, scientist, and engineer. Because of the broad range of his interests, he has come to be seen as the supreme example of the universal genius, curious and knowledgeable about many things. A pioneer in both art and science, Leonardo left a body of work that stretches from the famous painting of *Mona Lisa* to drawings of birds in flight and designs for flying machines.

ARTISTIC CAREER

Although Leonardo completed relatively few artworks, he played a key role in shaping Renaissance art. Other major artists of the time, such as RAPHAEL and MICHELANGELO, recognized Leonardo's mastery in painting. They learned from his insights into the arrangement of figures, the use of light and shade, and the distinct personalities of individuals. Many painters, especially those who worked with him, copied his designs.

* guild association of craft and trade owners and workers that set standards for and represented the interests of its members

* apprentice person bound by legal agreement to work for another for a specified period of time in return for instruction in a trade or craft

Early Career. Leonardo was born in Anchiano, near the city of Vinci in the Tuscan region of Italy. By the age of 20 he was living in Florence, where he had joined the painters' guild*. As an apprentice* in the workshop of artist Andrea del VERROCCHIO, he had opportunities to practice sculpture, metal-casting, drawing, and nature study as well as painting.

Leonardo's earliest surviving painting, the *Annunciation,* dates from 1473. His desire to understand and reproduce elements of nature appears in many aspects of this work, from the effect of light on human faces to the fine details of plants. Around 1476 Leonardo also worked on Verrocchio's *Baptism of Christ,* contributing the face of one of the angels and the landscape. The scene—a body of water framed by rock in a misty atmosphere—reveals Leonardo's interest in nature and his ability to portray it.

ARTISTIC CAREER

THE RENAISSANCE

13

Although the great Renaissance artist Leonardo da Vinci completed relatively few paintings and sculptures, his work had a significant influence on other artists of the time. *Lady with the Ermine*, painted around 1490, shows Leonardo's skillful use of light and shadow to make figures appear more lifelike.

The masterpiece of Leonardo's early years was the *Adoration of the Magi* (1481), painted for a monastery outside Florence. He placed the figures in the picture in a new and unusual arrangement, with a pyramid-shaped group of individuals in the foreground surrounded by a circle of onlookers. Leonardo paid great attention to every gesture and facial expression in the scene, making each figure distinct. He also used chiaroscuro—the interplay of light and shadow—to give objects a sense of form and weight. However, the artist moved away from Florence about 1482, leaving the *Adoration* unfinished.

Leonardo went to Milan and eventually worked for Ludovico Sforza, the ruler of the duchy* of Milan. In a letter to Ludovico, Leonardo described himself as a civil and military engineer and a sculptor. In

* **duchy** territory ruled by a duke or duchess

Milan, the artist painted portraits, designed costumes and stage sets for theatrical presentations at court, helped decorate the Sforza palace, and developed architectural plans for churches. He also designed a massive statue of a man on horseback as a monument to Ludovico's father, Francesco Sforza. However, this work was never completed because Ludovico Sforza was driven from Milan in 1499.

Leonardo's greatest project of the 1490s was the fresco* of the *Last Supper,* painted for a Milanese convent. The fresco deteriorated badly over the centuries, but a 1999 restoration brought back much of the original color and light. The *Last Supper* is notable for its carefully balanced arrangement of figures, the skillful use of perspective*, and the individuality of the characters around the table.

Later Career. Leaving Milan in 1500, Leonardo spent time in Venice, Mantua, and Florence. He also served as architect and engineer to the nobleman Cesare BORGIA. By 1503 Leonardo had returned to Florence, where he was invited to paint a large fresco in the newly built council chamber. The result was the *Battle of Anghiari,* celebrating a 1440 Florentine victory. Unfortunately, Leonardo used an experimental painting technique that proved unsatisfactory because the paint did not dry. When artist Giorgio Vasari tried to restore the fresco's central section in 1565, he destroyed it. The work is known only from drawings and copies made by other artists. In the *Battle of Anghiari,* Leonardo used details such as distorted human faces and horses with gnashing teeth to show the extreme physical strain of battle. The fresco's design was a complex interplay of many parts, studied by numerous later artists. Italian sculptor Benvenuto CELLINI called the *Battle of Anghiari,* along with a fresco by Michelangelo in the same chamber, "the school for the world."

While working on the *Battle of Anghiari,* Leonardo painted his best-known work, the *Mona Lisa.* A portrait of the wife of a prominent Florentine citizen, *Mona Lisa* harmoniously blends human and natural elements. Leonardo painted the subject's head and torso in sfumato, a style that uses gentle variations of tones to show the outlines of shapes. The shadowy landscape creates a mood that perfectly matches the woman's mysterious smile.

By 1508 Leonardo had returned to Milan, which had been taken over by the French. He worked on several projects there, including plans for a monument to include a group of horses on an elaborate base. Although the work was never completed, the drawings for it show Leonardo's ongoing interest in the movements of horses and riders. Leonardo also worked on several paintings, including *St. John the Baptist,* in Milan.

After 1513 Leonardo spent some time in Rome. Compared with such artists as Michelangelo, Raphael, and Donato BRAMANTE, he contributed little to the city's artistic life. However, he did work on the painting *Virgin and Child with St. Anne and a Lamb,* another composition featuring tightly packed figures arranged in a pyramid. In 1517 Leonardo went to France at the invitation of the new king, FRANCIS I. The artist may have taken some paintings with him to work on, including the *Mona*

---

* **fresco**   mural painted on a plaster wall

* **perspective**   artistic technique for creating the illusion of three-dimensional space on a flat surface

---

Leonardo the Mathematician

Leonardo da Vinci is remembered as an artist and an inventor, but he was also a mathematician. In fact, the study of mathematics was central to many of his activities. He used mathematics to analyze the structure of elements in nature. He also expressed his theories of vision and his study of optics, the science of light, in mathematical terms. As an artist, Leonardo used mathematics to create the illusion of perspective, making an image seem three-dimensional. By following the principles of geometry and proportion, he created a sense of order and harmony in his works.

Lisa and *St. John the Baptist.* At the French court, Leonardo drew up plans for a huge royal palace. However, it was never built because he died in 1519. Long after Leonardo's death, a collection of his writings on art were published as a *Treatise on Painting* (1651).

SCIENCE AND ENGINEERING

Leonardo believed that art theory and scientific investigation were closely linked. He thought that artists were better equipped than anyone else in society to observe reality and communicate their perceptions of it to others. He embraced scientific investigation, basing ideas and theories on his own experience and keen observation.

As an artist, Leonardo wanted to understand the human form so that he could paint it. This led him to a passionate interest in anatomy and to dissecting human corpses to find out how muscles worked. Between the 1490s and about 1515 he made many notes on the subject, including drawings to illustrate a scientific work on anatomy (never written).

Leonardo was also interested in machines. He designed a number of devices, such as a gun with three racks of barrels and an armored vehicle. As an inventor, though, he is best known for his work in the field of human-powered flight. Drawings in Leonardo's notebooks show that he carefully studied bird flight and air movements and that he made numerous designs for flying machines.

Geology, the study of the earth's history and features, also captured Leonardo's attention. Using his astonishing powers of observation, he investigated questions such as the origin of fossils and the role of water in shaping the land. (*See also* **Art; Art in Italy; Mathematics; Science; Technology.**)

See color plate 8, vol. 4

R enaissance libraries were important centers of learning and culture. More than just collections of books, they gave scholars a place to study languages and to explore ancient ideas. Many libraries treated books and manuscripts as works of art, prized as much for their beauty as for their content. They often displayed volumes alongside cabinets of interesting objects—ancient artifacts*, natural wonders, or scientific instruments. From the private collections of individuals to the glorious libraries of royal courts, libraries formed the focus of Renaissance scholarship.

Early Humanist Libraries. During the Renaissance, humanist* scholars kept some of the finest book collections in Europe. The Italian poet PETRARCH, the scholar most associated with the birth of humanism, called book collecting his "passion." His private collection contained about 200 volumes. Most of them were ancient works in Latin and writings by the early leaders of the Roman Catholic Church. Petrarch carried his books with him in his travels throughout Italy.

Other humanists also kept notable libraries. One of the most impressive private collections belonged to the Italian scholar Giovanni PICO

* **artifact** ornament, tool, or other object made by humans

* **humanist** referring to a Renaissance cultural movement promoting the study of the humanities (the languages, literature, and history of ancient Greece and Rome) as a guide to living

Pope Nicholas V founded the Vatican Library around 1450. The richest library in Rome, it housed collections of works contributed by popes. This wall painting of the library shows Pope Sixtus IV with librarian Bartolomeo Platina among the stacks of books and manuscripts.

DELLA MIRANDOLA. His thousand-volume library contained more than 100 Hebrew manuscripts—one of the largest such collections in all of Italy. Pico's other volumes ranged from literature of his day to ancient Latin texts on religion, philosophy, and science.

Church Libraries. Since the Middle Ages, religious houses had served as centers of learning in Europe. Catholic monasteries often held rich collections of manuscripts. During the Protestant Reformation*, many Protestant states broke up the monasteries. Their holdings fell into the hands of courts, universities, and private individuals. In Catholic lands, however, monastic* libraries became tools for renewing the church.

The cardinals of the Roman Catholic Church kept some of the most impressive private collections in Europe. Many cardinals associated with humanist scholars and took an interest in recovering ancient texts from both pagan* and Christian traditions. Some cardinals kept quite small collections, while others had as many as a few hundred volumes. The largest library belonged to Bessarion, a Greek monk who had moved to Italy in the 1400s and become a cardinal in the Catholic Church. He owned more than 1,000 volumes, with a strong focus on Greek manuscripts.

Cardinals' libraries increased in size and splendor as the Renaissance progressed. Founded in the early 1600s, the library of Cardinal Federico Barberini (the nephew of Pope Urban VIII) became one of the richest in Rome. It was second only to the Vatican Library, founded around 1450 by Pope NICHOLAS V. Although popes had kept collections of books and documents for centuries, Nicholas wanted to open a library "for the common convenience of the learned." His own collection became the

* **Protestant Reformation** religious movement that began in the 1500s as a protest against certain practices of the Roman Catholic Church and eventually led to the establishment of a variety of Protestant churches

* **monastic** relating to monasteries, monks, or nuns

* **pagan** referring to ancient religions that worshiped many gods, or more generally, to any non-Christian religion

core of the new library, which occupied three rooms in the Vatican. By the late 1500s it had expanded to several thousand texts and required a building of its own. However, the popes of the early 1600s no longer made the collection open to the public. Only those with special permission could enter for a few hours at a time on certain days.

Court Libraries. Kings, queens, and other nobles kept some of the finest libraries in Europe. Developed partly to house accounts and legal documents, court libraries became important centers of scholarship. Naples was home to the oldest major court library in Italy. Started in the 1200s, it grew dramatically in the mid-1400s under the patronage of Alfonso, the king of Aragon and Naples. Other major libraries in Italy included the collections of the GONZAGA family in Mantua, the Visconti in Milan, and the ESTE in Ferrara. Each of these noble families possessed hundreds of manuscripts.

In 1520 the humanist scholar Guillaume Budé established the new royal library of the French king FRANCIS I at Fontainebleau. Within 25 years, the collection had grown to about 2,686 volumes. By the end of the 1500s the library had been moved to Paris. One of the largest court libraries of the Renaissance was the Escorial near Madrid in Spain. In addition to its books, this library housed a large collection of mathematical and scientific instruments. It also served as a personal spiritual retreat* for Spain's king PHILIP II.

The court library had its greatest impact in Germany and central Europe. In the German city of Augsburg, the wealthy merchants and bankers of the FUGGER FAMILY created a library based on Italian models and even hired an Italian architect to design it. The Fugger collection later became part of the court library of Duke Albrecht V of Bavaria. In the late 1500s, books taken from Catholic monasteries enriched the court libraries of Protestant Germany. The library at Wolfenbüttel, in northern Germany, eventually became the largest in all of Europe. By the middle of the 1600s, it held more than 100,000 volumes.

Private and Public Libraries. Private book collections grew throughout the Renaissance. Many professionals, such as lawyers and doctors, kept large private libraries of books about their areas of interest. Especially in northern Europe, such private libraries were used for both teaching and study in a number of fields.

Some private collections helped to promote new ideas. For example, physician Nicolò Leoniceno, who taught medicine at the University of Ferrara in the late 1400s, kept a large collection of scientific texts. Among them were over 100 Greek works covering every major area of science. Libraries such as his helped to revive interest in ancient Greek medicine. Similarly, collections of Greek mathematical manuscripts led the rebirth of mathematics in the 1500s.

During the Renaissance many "private" collections became semipublic, providing places for scholars to meet, study, and exchange ideas. A few libraries took on a form similar to the modern public library. In 1444 the library of the monastery of San Marco in Florence opened its doors to the public. Like later public libraries, it began as a private col-

* **retreat** quiet, private, or secure place

lection, originally belonging to humanist Niccolò Niccoli. Another important public library opened at Oxford University in 1602. English politician and writer Francis BACON said that he hoped the new library would serve as "an ark of learning." (*See also* **Books and Manuscripts; Brunswick-Wolfenbüttel; Humanism; Medicine; Popes and Papacy.**)

L isbon, the capital of Portugal, played a key role in the sudden rise and fall of that nation's economy and culture during the Renaissance. Improvements to Lisbon's seaport in the 1300s increased trade with northern and Mediterranean cities, and the enlargement of the city's walls helped unify Lisbon.

In the 1400s and early 1500s, Portuguese voyages of exploration and conquest in Africa and Asia had a considerable impact on Lisbon. Gold, exotic goods, and African slaves flowed into Lisbon and led to a reorganization of the city. In 1505 King Manuel I moved the royal residence from an old hilltop fortress to a newly built palace along the banks of the Tagus River. This change signaled a shift in the city's outlook to a broader perspective focused on empire and commerce.

The monarchy, noble families, and newly prosperous bankers and merchants erected many public and private buildings in Lisbon. The population surged as peasants arrived from the countryside in search of work and opportunities. However, public services were poor and unreliable in this rapidly growing urban center. As the slave population increased and the promise of quick riches drew many to Lisbon, critics wrote mournfully about the decay of society.

The fortunes of Lisbon and Portugal took a turn for the worse in the 1500s. The city led the nation into economic decline, and the Portuguese monarchy collapsed in 1578. These developments opened the door for Spanish king PHILIP II to take control of the country. Although Lisbon kept its status as a capital, it owed taxes to Spain's rulers. Portugal's independence was not restored until 1640.

* **humanist** referring to a Renaissance cultural movement promoting the study of the humanities (the languages, literature, and history of ancient Greece and Rome) as a guide to living

* **Gothic** style of architecture characterized by pointed arches and high, thin walls supported by flying buttresses; also, artistic style marked by bright colors, elongated proportions, and intricate detail

During the years of prosperity, literature and humanist* writing thrived in Lisbon, stimulated by contact with Italy, France, Spain, and northern European countries. However, Portuguese painters and architects tended to resist the new styles of the Renaissance. Until the mid-1500s, most architects continued to build Gothic* structures, such as the Tower of Belém fortress. (*See also* **Art in Spain and Portugal; Exploration; Portugal; Portuguese Language and Literature.**)

T he term *literacy,* generally speaking, refers to the ability to read and write. However, scholars do not agree on a precise definition of the word or on how to determine literacy rates. One common measure of literacy is the ability to sign one's own name. Others focus on reading ability. In addition, historians distinguish between functional literacy—the ability to carry out everyday tasks—and scholarly or religious literacy.

For all these reasons, it is difficult to say just how literacy rates in Europe changed during the Renaissance. However, a few generalizations are possible. For one, literacy rates varied by region, language, social status, and gender. Second, various factors had an impact on literacy in the Renaissance. These included the scholarly use of books, new methods of teaching, and the arrival of the printing press. However, scholars have not found any direct relationship between the spread of Renaissance ideas and the growth of literacy.

Literacy Rates. At the beginning of the Renaissance, European males had a literacy rate of about 5 to 10 percent. However, this number varied based on social class and location. In some urban areas, for example, merchants might have a literacy rate as high as 40 percent. In the Italian city of Florence, the overall literacy rate may have been 25 to 35 percent in the 1330s. However, there were sharp differences based on sex, wealth, social status, and occupation. In England literacy rates in males may have reached as high as 25 percent by 1530—perhaps even higher within London.

Many factors contributed to the growth of literacy during the Renaissance. Books became more widely available, and the number of schools, universities, and libraries increased. In addition, it became increasingly common to use vernacular* languages, rather than Latin, for business and legal purposes. A healthy economy may also have been a factor in rising literacy rates.

Literacy rates often differed from region to region, both within a country and throughout Europe. In Italy, the city of Florence educated between 28 and 33 percent of boys in 1480, but Venice did not educate that many males until 1586. In Spain during the 1500s, reading spread to the lower classes, and literacy rates were higher than in other parts of Europe. By 1650, 62 percent of all men in Toledo, Spain, could sign their names.

Reading and writing ability also varied based on occupation or profession. At the end of the 1500s, in the French city of Languedoc, almost all merchants were literate. Yet, in the same city, only two-thirds of all artisans*, one-tenth of all farmers, and one in a hundred laborers could sign their names. Over the centuries following the Renaissance, these social differences evened out. In Sweden, for example, the entire population could read by 1800.

The Impact of Schools. A variety of schools taught reading and writing skills during the Renaissance. Small children learned the alphabet and beginning prayers at "petty" or ABC schools. Some children then moved on to elementary schools—sometimes called grammar schools—where they learned everyday language skills. Some elementary schools, and most secondary schools, focused on teaching Latin. Only after the Renaissance did vernacular languages replace Latin in many secondary schools.

Various organizations ran schools during the Renaissance, including towns, cathedrals, parishes, and guilds*. Some schools operated by

* **vernacular** native language or dialect of a region or country

* **artisan** skilled worker or craftsperson

* **guild** association of craft and trade owners and workers that set standards for and represented the interests of its members

charging tuition, while others received funding from the state or from religious institutions. Some schools were boarding schools, and others were located within walking distance of the students' homes. Wealthy students might be educated privately, by tutors, whereas apprentices* studying with tradesmen learned their literacy skills on the job. In dame schools, women used their homes to teach basic skills to young children.

Some people became literate without receiving a formal education. Many learned to read and write on their own or from relatives and friends. In the 1500s and 1600s, the Protestants known as Lutherans encouraged parents to teach their children at home.

Books and Reading. As learning grew in importance during the Renaissance, reading became a more valued skill than speaking. The Renaissance scholars known as humanists* played a major role in promoting reading skills. In Italy, for example, humanists aimed to educate boys in the wisdom of the ancient Latin and Greek classics. They believed this type of education would help boys to become useful citizens and good Christians.

The Renaissance and the printing press grew up together, each supporting the other. The increased availability of books promoted the growth of libraries, both private and public. Libraries, in turn, contributed to the growth of private reading and study—although reading in groups remained a popular activity. In general, increasing literacy during the 1500s and 1600s owed less to the Renaissance and humanism than to other changes in religion, government, and the economy. However, humanists did shape the tools that brought about the rise in literacy: schools, teachers, and books. (*See also* **Books and Manuscripts; Education; Humanism; Latin Language and Literature; Libraries; Printing and Publishing.**)

* **apprentice**   person bound by legal agreement to work for another for a specified period of time in return for instruction in a trade or craft

* **humanist**   Renaissance expert in the humanities (the languages, literature, history, and speech and writing techniques of ancient Greece and Rome)

The Renaissance was an extremely fruitful period for European literature. Much of the writing of the time reflected a renewed interest in the literary works of ancient Greece and Rome. Scholars studied these classical* texts and used them to form theories about writing. Authors also drew on classical works as inspiration for their own writings. Combining ancient ideas with literary styles from the Middle Ages, they left the world some of its finest and most enduring literary achievements.

* **classical**   in the tradition of ancient Greece and Rome

LITERARY THEORY

Literary theory and criticism blossomed during the Renaissance. Scholars turned to classical texts to help them understand the literary trends of their day. Based on these texts, they developed new theories about such topics as the use of language and the value of poetry.

Rediscovering Ancient Texts. Beginning in the late 1300s, Italian humanists* uncovered many ancient Latin and Greek texts that had been unknown to scholars of the Middle Ages. These discoveries, which

* **humanist**   Renaissance expert in the humanities (the languages, literature, history, and speech and writing techniques of ancient Greece and Rome)

Painter Sandro Botticelli created this picture for the *Decameron,* a famous collection of stories by Italian author Giovanni Boccaccio. The painting illustrates the story of a scornful maiden who is sentenced after her death to be hunted endlessly by the ghost of her rejected lover.

* **rhetoric**   art of speaking or writing effectively

continued throughout the 1400s, had a major influence on Renaissance literature. Classical studies received a boost in 1450 when Johann GUTENBERG developed the printing press, which made it possible to print books on a large scale. His invention helped spread classical texts, both in their original languages and in translation.

The most influential ancient text on the writing of poetry, drama, and fiction was *Poetics,* by the Greek philosopher ARISTOTLE. A Latin translation of this work was published in 1498, and the Greek original appeared in print ten years later. Renaissance scholars embraced Aristotle's views about the importance of plot, the need for realism and unity in a literary work, and the use of literature to transmit moral values. Scholars also drew ideas about writing from the *Art of Poetry,* by the ancient Roman poet Horace. This work, less formal than Aristotle's, emphasized the value of rhetoric* in making an impact on the reader.

A Question of Language. The discovery and translation of ancient works helped fuel an ongoing debate about whether authors should write in Latin or in their own native tongues. Throughout the Middle Ages, most educated writers in Europe had used Latin for their works. Around 1300, however, some authors began to produce works in ver-

* **vernacular**   native language or dialect of a region or country

nacular* languages. As distinct national literatures emerged, various writers defended the use of their native tongues as superior to Latin.

Many authors, however, continued to support the use of Latin. They believed that the Latin language provided the best tool for capturing the elegance of classical styles. They attempted to return the language, which had changed over the course of the Middle Ages, to its ancient Roman roots by imitating classical writers, especially the Roman orator CICERO. Their works created a flourishing Neo-Latin literature that crossed all national and social borders. However, today this literature is almost unknown because so few people read Latin.

In Defense of Poetry. Renaissance authors also devoted their attention to poetics, the study of poetry. Throughout the Middle Ages, poets and scholars had admired the works of classical poets and had drawn many of their ideas about verse writing from ancient Greece and Rome. Over the years, however, theories about poetry had moved away from their classical roots. As the humanists of the Renaissance revived the ideas of ancient writers, they placed a particular emphasis on poetry writing.

* **pagan**   referring to ancient religions that worshiped many gods, or more generally, to any non-Christian religion

* **allegory**   literary or artistic device in which characters, events, and settings represent abstract qualities, and in which the author intends a different meaning to be read beneath the surface

Some scholars opposed the study of pagan* poetry. Certain religious leaders, for example, attacked poets as liars whose works tended to inspire immoral behavior. Humanist scholars, in response, published defenses of poetry. The great Italian poet PETRARCH claimed that poems were not lies but allegories* for great moral truths. Author Giovanni BOCCACCIO agreed, noting that pagan verse reflected many of the ideas in the Bible. He also declared that poetry played an important role in civilization. Educator Guarino GUARINI argued that ancient poetry was not only useful but necessary to support religious teachings.

* **treatise**   long, detailed essay

Bartolomeo della Fonte of Florence published *On the Art of Poetry,* the first Renaissance treatise* on poetics, around 1490. His book explored such topics as the moral value of poetry and the use of classical models for verse writing. In the 1500s ideas about poetics began to spread from Italy to other parts of Europe. In 1583 English poet Philip SIDNEY published a *Defense of Poetry* that blended some of the best ideas of ancient writers and Renaissance critics.

DEVELOPING LITERARY STYLES

As Renaissance scholars learned more about the ancient literature of Greece and Rome, they revived many of the literary forms of the ancient world. They also modified genres* from the Middle Ages, such as the romance*. Some Renaissance writers brought back the classical tradition of celebrating sexuality in literature. Their openness about sexual matters earned them the disapproval of many religious leaders.

* **genre**   literary form

* **romance**   adventure story of the Middle Ages, the forerunner of the modern novel

Allegory. Writers of the Renaissance made frequent use of allegory, a device in which people and events serve as symbols, so that a story carries a hidden meaning. Allegory appeared in drama, poetry, and other literary forms. In some cases, a single extended allegory made up an entire work.

* **medieval**   referring to the Middle Ages, a period that began around A.D. 400 and ended around 1400 in Italy and 1500 in the rest of Europe

* **explicit**   presented in a clear and direct way

Authors used allegory in several different ways. Sometimes their human characters represented abstract qualities. In *The Faerie Queene*, Edmund SPENSER of England created a character called Disdain, who walked on tiptoes and had knees that did not bend. Objects could also serve as symbols. For example, a crown could represent rulership.

Other forms of allegory were more complex. In some cases, an entire work retold events from history, using different characters to represent real people. Spenser told the English queen ELIZABETH I that his *Faerie Queene* reflected Elizabeth and her realm "in mirrors more than one." Events and figures within a story could also serve as religious symbols, turning the story into a reflection of Christian beliefs. Both Spenser and Philip Sidney claimed that story writing had value because it could present moral truths through allegory.

Satire.   Another literary device popular with Renaissance authors was satire—the use of writing to expose human wickedness or foolishness. Early in the Renaissance, writers began reviving classical satire, as practiced by such ancient Roman authors as Horace, Juvenal, and Martial. They followed the lead of these ancient writers in praising the virtues and mocking the vices of their own societies. Famous satirists included Ludovico ARIOSTO in Italy, François RABELAIS in France, Thomas MORE in England, and Desiderius ERASMUS in the Netherlands.

Like allegory, satire appeared in a variety of literary forms. The shortest was the epigram, a brief poem or witty saying. Short allegorical stories, known as fables, were another popular mode of satire. Writers also produced longer satires in the form of verse or dialogue. They used satire to attack all aspects of Renaissance culture, including the church, the law, and the life of the court. Appropriate subjects included, in the words of Juvenal, "whatever men do."

Romances.   The romance form dates back to the 1100s, when French writers adopted ancient Latin stories of war and adventure. The romance tradition reflected the ideals of chivalry, a code of honor for medieval* knights. Legends of the Welsh king Arthur and his Knights of the Round Table played a major role in the development of this literary form.

Romances gained favor with readers during the Renaissance. The most popular romances came out of Italy, where writers such as Ludovico Ariosto and Torquato TASSO adapted the conventions of the genre to create finely crafted masterpieces. In England, the romance of chivalry became the most popular form of fiction during the Renaissance. Philip Sidney's *Arcadia* and Edmund Spenser's *The Faerie Queene,* both published in the 1590s, drew on the Arthurian tradition. Toward the end of the Renaissance, Spanish author Miguel de CERVANTES both adopted and mocked the romance tradition in his famous novel *Don Quixote.*

Pornography.   Although the word *pornography* did not exist during the Renaissance, sexually explicit* writings certainly did exist at that time. Renaissance humanists actively studied the sexual customs of

ancient Greece and Rome, where poetry and statues had openly celebrated nudity and sexual desire. These ancient works embraced a variety of sexual behaviors that Christian churches condemned. As a result, they challenged the humanists' view that there was no conflict between ancient literature and Christian belief.

Some scholars simply ignored the ancient literature that focused on sex. Others censored ancient works, removing indecent passages to protect young readers. Many humanists, however, studied these works as seriously as other forms of ancient literature. Some authors, in fact, pointed to the sexual writings of the ancient world to justify their own works on similar topics.

Sexual literature provoked criticism from many readers. In 1425, for example, Italian writer Antonio Beccadelli published a poem called *Hermaphroditus*. The title refers to an ancient Greek god who had both male and female sexual organs. Preachers and the pope condemned the poem, and copies of it were burned publicly in several cities. Many humanists, however, viewed the work as a witty imitation of ancient writing.

One of the most popular writers of pornography in the Renaissance was Pietro Aretino. In his *Lewd Sonnets** (1527), Aretino described 16 sexual positions, based on drawings by a Roman artist. The book created a scandal, yet it also became hugely popular. Many historians see it as the first true work of pornography in the modern sense of the word. (*See also* **Drama; Drama, English; Drama, French; Drama, Spanish; English Language and Literature; French Language and Literature; German Language and Literature; Italian Language and Literature; Jewish Languages and Literature; Latin Language and Literature; Literacy; Poetry; Poetry, English; Portuguese Language and Literature; Religious Literature; Spanish Language and Literature.**)

* **sonnet**   poem of 14 lines with a fixed pattern of meter and rhyme

---

Liturgy

See *Christianity.*

Logic

* **humanist**   Renaissance expert in the humanities (the languages, literature, history, and speech and writing techniques of ancient Greece and Rome)

* **classical**   in the tradition of ancient Greece and Rome

Logic is the study of the formal principles of reasoning. It focuses on how to attain knowledge and how to determine whether statements are true or false. Renaissance humanists* contributed to this science in two ways. First, they studied and taught the ideas of classical* writers, especially the Greek philosopher ARISTOTLE, on the subject of logic. Second, they developed new theories about the purpose of logic.

Traditional Logic. The basis of Renaissance logic was Aristotle's *Organon*. This important work came to the West in three stages. During the 500s the Roman scholar Boethius translated part of it into Latin, along with an introduction written by another Greek scholar. By about 1280, scholars had translated the rest of the text from Greek and Arabic into Latin. Then, in the 1490s, a new edition of the complete *Organon*

appeared in the original Greek. Around the same time, commentaries on Aristotle's logic by scholars of the late Middle Ages also appeared in print. The recovery of these texts led to a burst of scholarship on the subject of Aristotelian logic. Jacopo Zabarella produced the most extensive works on this topic in the mid-1500s.

Aristotelian logic had a great influence on education. The lectures of the Jesuit* Ludovicus Rugerius show how important logic was to Renaissance scholars. Rugerius taught a three-year course in philosophy in Rome in the 1590s. He devoted the entire first year of this course to logic. Rugerius covered Aristotle's text in detail and also made use of commentaries by Greek, Arab, and Latin scholars, including Zabarella and other researchers of his time.

Scholars at the University of Padua in Italy played a major role in the study of Aristotelian logic. For more than a century, they analyzed and debated a section of the *Organon* that dealt with scientific reasoning. They focused on the problem of how to use facts to prove conclusions and achieve scientific knowledge. Zabarella provided the essential Renaissance solution to this problem in his *Book on the Regress* (1578).

Spanish scholars at the University of Paris pursued a different line of study in the early 1500s. They focused on mathematics and on the use of logic in philosophy and theology* rather than in science and medicine. One of these scholars, Domingo de Soto, later taught at the University of Salamanca in Spain, where he published commentaries on Aristotle's logic. His student Franciscus Toletus became a Jesuit and organized the philosophy course at the order's Collegio Romano in Rome. In 1572 Toletus published *Commentaries, with Questions, on All of Aristotle's Logic*. This work formed the basis of Jesuit teaching in logic until the end of the 1600s.

Humanist Logic. Some Renaissance scholars rejected traditional logic and its formal arguments as sterile and not useful. In its place they created a new logic that emphasized persuasion. They sought to link logic to grammar and rhetoric*.

One of the first scholars to pursue this program was Lorenzo VALLA, a noted Italian humanist of the 1400s. He rejected Aristotle's concern with formal proof, instead claiming that a sound argument rested on good use of language. However, few philosophers accepted Valla's new system of logic. The work of Dutch humanist Rudolf AGRICOLA was more influential. In his *Three Books on Dialectical Invention* (1479), Agricola proposed a form of logic based on topics rather than on terms. He argued that the formal proofs of Aristotelian logic were of limited use in debate. Instead, he advised his readers to practice the art of influencing others, to involve opponents in debates, and to aim at likelihood rather than certainty.

In the 1500s French humanist Petrus RAMUS proposed another alternative to Aristotelian logic. He divided logic into two parts: invention and arrangement. Invention meant finding the best arguments to use in addressing a particular problem or question. Ramus defined an argument as a relationship between a subject and the facts that can be stat-

*** Jesuit** refers to a Roman Catholic religious order founded by St. Ignatius Loyola and approved in 1540

*** theology** study of the nature of God and of religion

*** rhetoric** art of speaking or writing effectively

ed about that subject. For example, in the sentence "Cold causes shivering," the word "causes" lays out the relationship between cold and shivering. The process of arrangement, in turn, involved laying out arguments in a useful order. Ramus proposed using outlines to organize subject matter, with headings moving from general concepts to specific ones. This technique became very popular in textbooks on all subjects through the end of the 1500s. (*See also* **Classical Scholarship; Philosophy; Rhetoric.**)

See color plate 9, vol. 3

London was the principal city of England during the Renaissance. At the time, it consisted of the City of London, Westminster, and some suburbs. The City of London was a small, densely populated area originally developed by the Romans. By the Renaissance, the City boasted St. Paul's Cathedral, the Guildhall, the shops of rich merchants, docks, and warehouses. London Bridge connected the City with Southwark and other areas across the Thames River.

Several miles upstream a second center of population grew up around Westminster Abbey and the Palace of Westminster. Once a royal residence, the Palace of Westminster housed law courts and St. Stephen's Chapel during the Renaissance. The chapel served as a meeting place for the House of Commons, Parliament's lower house. Smaller buildings for other government offices crowded up against the palace. Most of England's business was conducted in this administrative complex.

Westminster and the City of London were linked by the Strand, the main street that paralleled the Thames River. Along the Strand stood the palaces or town houses of a number of bishops, including York Place. This was the home of Cardinal Thomas WOLSEY, a key adviser of HENRY VIII. After Wolsey fell from power, the king had York Place converted into Whitehall Palace, which became a royal residence.

Across the Thames from the City of London, Southwark contained many theaters and other entertainment sites. These included the Bear Garden and the Globe Theater, which offered plays by William SHAKESPEARE and others. Lambeth Palace, across the river from Westminster, had been the residence of the archbishops of Canterbury since the 1100s. Ferries and barges provided regular passage across the Thames, linking Lambeth and Westminster.

Henry VIII's break with the Roman Catholic Church brought many changes to England in the 1500s. He seized many monasteries and other religious buildings, but Westminster Abbey was too important to be touched. The site of royal coronations and funerals and the tombs of most of England's medieval* monarchs, it remained a national shrine. Most other religious buildings fell, becoming commercial sites or residences for members of the aristocracy*.

Many bishops lost their town houses at this time as well. A number of them were demolished to make space for Somerset House. A wealthy aristocrat's home, Somerset House was one of the earliest English structures to show the influence of the Renaissance and to incorporate elements of classical* architecture.

* **medieval**   referring to the Middle Ages, a period that began around A.D. 400 and ended around 1400 in Italy and 1500 in the rest of Europe

* **aristocracy**   privileged upper classes of society; nobles or the nobility

* **classical**   in the tradition of ancient Greece and Rome

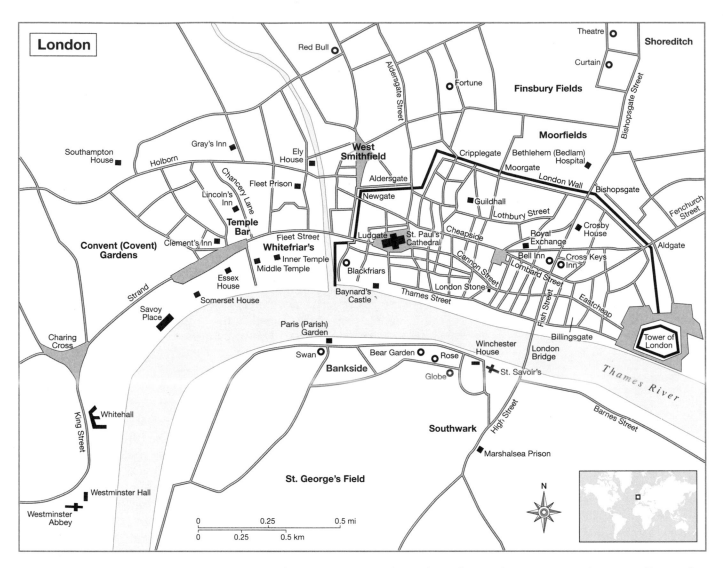

London

The appearance of London changed even more dramatically in the 1600s under the STUART DYNASTY. Development along the Thames River and the Strand continued and increased. The earl of Bedford hired the famous English architect Inigo JONES to build a great public square based on those in France and Italy. In his design, Jones surrounded the square with elegant town houses for members of the aristocracy who wanted houses in London as well as estates in the countryside. Jones produced some of the finest houses in London. His designs established a pattern that would be widely copied in later centuries.

Jones also worked for the royal family, and his love of classical and Renaissance architecture became most apparent in his designs for the Stuarts. He drew plans for a reconstruction of Whitehall Palace, but because of a lack of finances, only one part of it was actually completed. Jones's design for this structure, known as Banqueting House, helped establish a pure classical style of architecture in England.

The population of London increased dramatically during the course of the Renaissance. With perhaps 100,000 residents in 1500, it was

smaller than European cities such as Paris, Milan, Venice, and Naples. However, by 1600 London had grown to 200,000 inhabitants, and the population reached about 400,000 in 1650. This growth, the result of continuing immigration from the countryside, occurred despite very high mortality in London. By the mid-1600s, London had become the largest city in western Europe. (*See also* **Architecture; Cities and Urban Life; England.**)

During the Renaissance, Europeans saw love and marriage as two important, but very different, parts of life. Poets described love as an overpowering force, both spiritual and sexual. For most people, however, marriage was a more practical matter. As the basic building block of society, it involved the expectations of families and communities, not just the wishes of two individuals. Although marriage was the normal state of life for most people, many remained unmarried for either practical or religious reasons.

Renaissance Ideas About Love. The idea of romantic love took shape in the centuries leading up to the Renaissance. The literature of the Middle Ages developed the concept of courtly love, which treated the beloved as a pure ideal. Two Italian writers of the 1300s, Dante Alighieri and PETRARCH, drew on this tradition in their poetry. Each of them presented a beloved woman as a source of inspiration and a symbol of female perfection. European poetry in the following centuries followed their lead, treating love as an experience above and beyond ordinary life. Some poets saw sexual desire as a vital part of love, while others presented love as a pure and selfless emotion.

Renaissance thinkers viewed "platonic" love as the highest and noblest form of love. This concept of love was based on the ideas of the Neoplatonists, a group of philosophers who had given new interpretations to the works of the ancient Greek thinker PLATO. They saw love as a path to the divine, which was the source of the beloved's beauty. Italian writer Baldassare CASTIGLIONE discussed Platonic love in the fourth part of *The Book of the Courtier* (1528).

Another idealized view of love appeared in pastoral* poetry, which focused on the loves of shepherds and nymphs*. Poets presented the countryside as a place of simple pleasures and honest feelings, far removed from the ambitions and deceptions of urban life. However, not all Renaissance literature portrayed love as idealized or romantic. Opposing views appeared in bawdy* stories, which focused on crude sexuality, and in writings that attacked women as wicked temptresses who led men astray.

Sometimes, various conflicting views of love appeared in a single work of literature. The *Decameron,* a collection of short stories written by Italian author Giovanni BOCCACCIO around 1350, contains many tales about love, ranging from stories of deep devotion to lively accounts of sexual affairs. In a similar collection from the 1500s called the *Heptameron,* by MARGARET OF NAVARRE, the storytellers reflect on the

* **pastoral**   relating to the countryside; often used to draw a contrast between the innocence and serenity of rural life and the corruption and extravagance of court life

* **nymph**   in ancient mythology, a nature spirit who takes the form of a beautiful young woman

* **bawdy**   indecent; lewd

Most marriages between ruling families had a political rather than romantic basis. This mural by Taddeo Zuccaro shows Pope Paul III presiding over the arranged union of his grandson Ottavio Farnese of Italy and Margaret of Austria in 1539.

OCTAVIVS · FARNESIVS · CAMERINI · DVX
MARGARITAM · CAROLI · V · IMP · FILIAM
PAVLO · III · PONTIFICE · MAX · AV SPICE
SIBI · DESPONDET · ANNO · SAL · ᴐᴐ BXXXIX

meaning of love, its effect on Christian virtue, and its relationship to marriage.

Making Marriages. The Renaissance view of marriage had little to do with love. Most people believed that the perfect love of the poets could not exist alongside the everyday concerns of marriage. The reality, of course, was more complicated. Although practical matters played a major role in marriage, some rebels insisted on marrying for love.

At the highest levels of society, a marriage was not just a bond between two people but a union of two families and their fortunes. Marriages between ruling families could seal political alliances and even unite empires. Therefore, among the upper classes, parents took the lead in arranging marriages. The feelings of the bride and groom were rarely considered unless one of them very strongly opposed the marriage. Families might spend weeks or months negotiating over such matters as the bride's dowry* and what would happen to the couple's property after one of them died. Marriage contracts spelled out these details.

Arranged marriages also occurred among peasant families, especially when power or property was at stake. In general, though, members of the lower classes mingled fairly freely, and courtship arose out of the contacts of daily life. Parents could veto their children's choices, but they rarely did so. Although society generally frowned on sex before marriage, many women of the lower classes were pregnant at the time of their weddings. Communities tolerated sexual contact between couples if they seriously intended to marry—and if they were well matched. Local youth groups discouraged what they viewed as mismatches, such

* **dowry** money or property that a woman brings to her marriage

as unions between people of very different ages or between locals and outsiders.

Courtship led to betrothal, which until the late 1600s was an important step in the process of getting married. Betrothal bound a couple in a relationship that could only be broken if both parties agreed. Couples often pledged themselves to each other in a formal ceremony, which might take place in front of a priest at the church door. The legal difference between betrothal and marriage was not entirely clear, and church lawyers wrestled with cases in which one party wished to break a betrothal. In some cases, women claimed that men had promised to marry them and then had sex with them, and authorities had to decide whether the couple was legally married. Eventually both Protestants and Catholics tried to do away with formal betrothals, focusing instead on the public exchange of vows at the wedding.

The legal requirements for a marriage were a confusing mix of church law, local rules, and custom until the mid-1500s. After that time, the church became a legal part of the marriage ceremony. Most Protestant governments passed laws requiring weddings to take place in churches with ministers, and Catholics defined legal marriages as those in which the couple exchanged vows before a priest and other witnesses. Other wedding customs, however, remained unchanged. Couples typically exchanged vows and signed a marriage contract, if there was one. Marriage celebrations often included processions to or from the church, traditional foods, music, and dancing.

Married Life. After marriage, couples were expected to abandon the romantic behaviors of courtship. The relationship between a husband and wife focused on companionship, rather than passion. Most people saw sexual relations in marriage as a "debt" that the partners owed to each other. Some people even brought their spouses before church authorities to complain that they were not paying this debt. However, religious writers warned that an excess of sex within marriage was sinful.

Renaissance society gave husbands authority over their wives. Married women generally could not act for themselves in law or commerce. However, women did have some rights in marriage. Although husbands controlled their wives' property, they also had to support, protect, and provide for their wives. Moreover, many husbands admired their wives and secretly relied on their judgment. In some cases, a husband's will left considerable power in the hands of his widow.

Divorce was not a real option for most couples, even where it was technically legal. Couples could legally separate, and occasionally marriages were annulled, or declared invalid. An annulment might take place if one partner had never consented to the marriage, if the couple had never had sexual relations, or if there was some legal reason why the marriage should not have taken place at all. Most marriages did not end until one partner died, but the high death rate meant that many marriages were short. As many as 25 percent of all brides and grooms were marrying for the second or third time because death had ended earlier unions.

Runaway Lovers

A few Renaissance couples, faced with opposition from their parents, ran away to be married in secret. The Roman Catholic Church did not require the parents' consent for a marriage to be legal; until 1563 it did not even require that a priest perform the ceremony. Protestant couples faced greater obstacles to elopement because many Protestant communities required parental consent, especially for couples below certain ages. No matter how strict the rules, however, there were always some clever couples who managed to bypass them.

* **chaste** sexually pure

Celibacy and Virginity. A fairly large portion of the population of western Europe was celibate, or unmarried. Roman Catholic priests, who were forbidden to marry, made up the largest group of celibates. However, many priests who were celibate according to the letter of the law openly kept concubines, women who were their wives in all but name.

Other people remained celibate for only part of their lives. Although early marriage was common among the upper classes, especially for women, Europeans in general tended to marry later than people elsewhere. Late-marrying adults, along with widows and widowers who hoped to marry again, were temporary celibates. So were soldiers and servants, who generally could not marry while they held those professions. The younger sons of wealthy families often had to live unmarried lives because the oldest son inherited all the family's property, leaving his brothers to enter careers in the church or the military. Similarly, parents of daughters sometimes splurged on large dowries for one or two girls and sent the others into RELIGIOUS ORDERS.

Celibacy was a matter of public knowledge. Virginity, the state of sexual innocence, was a more private matter but one of considerable importance to society. Western Christianity placed a high value on lifelong virginity. Many Catholic saints were men and women who had preserved their virginity in the face of temptation or threats. For most Christians, however, the way to observe the ideal of virginity was to remain chaste* until marriage. Single women, in particular, had to be virgins in order to be suitable for marriage. On the other hand, church law allowed a man who had sex with a virgin to make up for his fault by marrying her. A young woman who wanted to marry a man against her family's wishes might force them to allow the marriage by announcing that she had lost her virginity to him. This legal loophole provided a strategy for couples who wanted to marry for love. (*See also* **Family and Kinship; Sexuality and Gender.**)

Luther, Martin

1483–1546
German religious reformer

* **Protestant Reformation** religious movement that began in the 1500s as a protest against certain practices of the Roman Catholic Church and eventually led to the establishment of a variety of Protestant churches

* **classical** in the tradition of ancient Greece and Rome

Martin Luther was the first and most important leader of the Protestant Reformation* in Europe. Though he was born during the Renaissance, Luther's life and work rejected many of the values of that time, including the appreciation for classical* ideas, creativity in art and literature, and the willingness to trust human reason.

Luther and the Catholic Church. Luther was born in the German state of Saxony. His father, a restless miner who moved often, recognized that Martin had a brilliant mind and made sure that his son went to good schools. Martin graduated from the University of Erfurt in 1505, and his father expected him then to study law. However, in July 1505, while returning to Erfurt from a visit home, Martin was knocked down by lightning during a storm. Terrified, he vowed to become a monk. Against his father's will, Luther entered a monastery in Erfurt and became a Roman Catholic priest in 1507. The following year he went to the University of Wittenberg to teach.

In 1510, Luther traveled to Rome to represent his monastery in a religious dispute involving the Augustinian RELIGIOUS ORDER. He later said that the immorality and unbelief that he found among church officials there shocked him. The sale of indulgences especially angered Luther. Indulgences promised the lifting of all or part of the punishment for a sin in return for a good action (such as giving money to the church), so long as the person was sorry for the sin. At the time, Pope LEO X permitted the sale of indulgences as a way to raise money for the construction of the church of St. Peter in Rome.

Luther returned to Wittenberg in 1512 and began lecturing on the Bible. In 1517, his anger at the papacy* erupted when a seller of indulgences came to a nearby town. Luther wrote a letter of protest to the archbishop of Mainz, who shared in the profits from the sale of indulgences. Along with the letter he sent a list of 95 theses, or issues for debate, which questioned the value of indulgences and criticized the papacy for its financial mistreatment of Germany. Contrary to legend, Luther did not nail these 95 theses to the door of the castle church.

Luther soon found himself in a battle with the Catholic Church over the issue of papal authority. In one of his works he asked German princes* to take over the duty of church reform. In another he claimed that the sacraments* of the church were part of a papal plot to enslave Christians. He rejected most of the sacraments, accepting only baptism and communion*. Luther also wrote that the true Christian performed good deeds not out of a desire for reward but out of gratitude to God for salvation. Many of his ideas contradicted Catholic teachings, and the church came to regard him as a dangerous heretic*.

In 1520, Pope Leo X threatened to excommunicate* Luther if he did not forsake his views. The next year, the pope formally excommunicated Luther from the Roman Catholic Church. However, CHARLES V, leader of the Holy Roman Empire*, gave Luther a hearing at a political assembly called the Diet of Worms. Luther expected a chance to debate his ideas, but the emperor asked only if he would abandon them. Luther's powerful defense of his books and views failed to persuade the emperor, and the Edict of Worms declared Luther an outlaw.

Luther and the Protestant Movement. Frederick the Wise, the leader of the German state of Saxony, helped Luther escape to Wartburg Castle, where he hid for almost a year. During that time, he wrote many works on religious beliefs and issues. He also began translating the New Testament of the Bible into German. His complete Bible, finished about a decade later, was not the first German translation, but it was so well done and Luther so important that it shaped the modern German language.

In 1522 Luther returned to Wittenberg, drawn there by unrest caused by people who had taken his ideas on religious authority to an extreme. These people wanted to destroy all religious images, and the violence and destruction they caused threatened the social order. With Frederick's help, Luther put a stop to the violence. Recognizing the need

* **papacy**   office and authority of the pope

* **prince**   Renaissance term for the ruler of an independent state

* **sacrament**   religious ritual thought to have been established by Jesus as an aid to salvation

* **communion**   ritual sharing of bread and wine in memory of Jesus Christ, with different meanings for different Christian churches

* **excommunicate**   to exclude from the church and its rituals

* **heretic**   person who rejects the doctrine of an established church

* **Holy Roman Empire**   political body in central Europe composed of several states; existed until 1806

See color plate 12, vol. 4

* **oppress**   to exercise power over others in an unjust or cruel way

* **humanist**   Renaissance expert in the humanities (the languages, literature, history, and speech and writing techniques of ancient Greece and Rome

* **patron**   supporter or financial sponsor of an artist or writer

* **elite**   privileged group; upper class

* **secular**   nonreligious; connected with everyday life

* **coat of arms**   set of symbols used to represent a noble family

* **retreat**   quiet, private, or secure place

for a framework to contain the movement he had begun, Luther started to organize his own church and spread his new religious doctrine.

In the mid-1520s, Germany experienced a series of uprisings known as the PEASANTS' WAR. Oppressed* by the nobility, peasants combined demands for social justice with the language of religious reform. At first, Luther supported the peasants, but he later reacted to their armed resistance by siding with the German authorities and condemned the peasants. Increasing conflict with other reformers marked Luther's last years. He attacked those who opposed him and argued with humanists* such as Desiderius ERASMUS, who criticized Luther's views on free will. (*See also* **German Language and Literature; Protestant Reformation; Religious Thought.**)

Renaissance Europeans held contradictory views about luxury. On one hand, they placed a greater value than ever before on the quality and number of their material possessions. The objects people owned helped define their identity as consumers, collectors, and patrons* of the arts. On the other hand, there remained an undercurrent of religious and moral suspicion about excessive displays of wealth. Most places had laws governing how much money people could spend on such luxuries as jewelry and fine clothing.

Material Culture.   The Renaissance gave birth to a new cultural trend that focused on the pursuit of worldly goods. This "material culture" first arose in the city-states of Italy, which had been centers of European economy and trade for several centuries. Italy's urban elites* displayed their wealth, power, and taste by investing in splendid buildings, clothing and ornaments, books and art objects, and lavish public celebrations.

Italy experienced a building boom during the Renaissance. Churches grew larger, creating a demand for murals, paintings, and sculptures to decorate them. Secular* urban architecture also reflected a new concern with magnificence. Cities built public buildings and monuments to reinforce their new roles as political, economic, and cultural centers. Wealthy families built residences that advertised their wealth and social standing. For instance, the palace of Cosimo de' MEDICI in Florence, built in the 1400s, displayed the family's coat of arms* on the front. While most of the poor continued to live in single-room, single-bed dwellings, the wealthy began dividing their homes into more rooms, offering greater privacy to those who lived there.

One of the most important rooms in the house was the study. Many men regarded their studies as retreats* where they could keep their private papers out of the hands of women. The study also provided a place to display collections of books, maps, scientific instruments, or artworks. The urge to collect became a passion in the Renaissance. Many intellectuals kept a *Kunstkammer,* or cabinet of curiosities, in which they stored such interesting natural objects as plants, skeletons, and animal specimens. These collections gave rise to the first museums of natural history.

Renaissance gentlemen had a passion for collecting. Many intellectuals kept "cabinets of curiosities" in which they stored natural items such as plants, skeletons, and animal specimens.

* **gilded** coated with gold

By the late 1400s, home furnishings accounted for a larger percentage of overall household expenses than in earlier times. Owners kept their most precious treasures, such as jewels and silver, locked up, often in their private studies. Other luxury items, such as gilded* leather, fine fabrics, and decorative sculptures, became more common throughout the house. Artworks also made up part of the home's furnishings. New artistic techniques helped lower the price of paintings, making them a major consumer product.

Over time, the material culture of Italy spread to other areas. Foreign travelers to the Netherlands—which overtook Italy as Europe's leading economic center in the 1600s—noted the abundance of country mansions, lavish gardens, and specialty shops bursting with wares, especially in the city of Amsterdam. The Dutch became deeply fond of decorative objects, including mirrors from Venice and silks from Persia (now Iran). This passion reached its height in the 1600s, when tulips became the object of a collecting craze.

Sumptuary Laws. Many parts of Europe had laws designed to prevent extravagance in dress, food, and other goods. Known as sumptuary laws, these regulations focused on fancy clothing, jewelry, and other ornaments. Governments had two main reasons for passing sumptuary laws. First, from a moral standpoint, many people saw luxuries as signs of sinful pride. On a more practical level, these laws helped prevent peo-

* **dowry**   money or property that a woman brings to her marriage

ple from overspending and falling into debt. Some sumptuary laws restricted the amount people could spend on events, such as weddings and funerals. In some cases, laws limited the size of girls' dowries* for fear that large dowries would lead to late marriages and a low birthrate.

Sumptuary laws helped reinforce the boundaries of class and social standing. For example, they often placed limits on who could wear certain furs and fabrics, with the finest goods reserved for royalty. In Germany, strict dress codes established visible differences between servants and their employers. Prostitutes throughout Europe also had to follow dress codes. The city of Florence used its sumptuary laws to generate income by requiring women to register all garments above a certain value and pay taxes on those that were considered too fancy. The city even hired inspectors to examine women's clothes chests. Sumptuary laws also sought to enforce decency by closely regulating the depth of women's necklines.

Punishment for breaking the sumptuary laws usually took the form of a fine. The enforcement of the laws varied widely, with Switzerland particularly strict in its punishments. From 1541 to 1564, when Protestant reformer John CALVIN held power in the Swiss city of Geneva, there were more than 800 arrests, 76 banishments, and 58 death sentences for moral offenses, including violations of the sumptuary laws. In England, by contrast, records show few punishments for breaking these laws. During the reign of JAMES I in the 1600s, the country did away with its sumptuary laws altogether. (*See also* **Architecture; Books and Manuscripts; Châteaus and Villas; Clothing.**)

Lyon

Lyon, the greatest money market and commercial hub of France during the Renaissance, was a major center of printing and of literary and intellectual activity. The city's prosperity came mainly from its location at the intersection of key land and water routes. Also important were Lyon's annual trade fairs, which attracted merchants from throughout Europe. By the early 1500s, dozens of Italy's most influential merchant and banking families, including the house of MEDICI of FLORENCE, had representatives in the city.

The richest part of Lyon's commerce involved the import of fine cloth from Italy. The city's trade fairs, started between 1420 and 1463, were occasions not only for exchanging cloth and other goods but also for financial dealings. French kings came to rely on Lyon's merchant-bankers to finance military operations, particular for wars with Italy.

French king FRANCIS I encouraged the establishment of a silk industry in Lyon in 1536. Taking root rapidly, the industry employed thousands by the mid-1500s. Lyon's first printing press began operating in 1473, and enterprising printers soon made the city a leading center of European book production. However, the rapid growth of industry in Lyon resulted in considerable social unrest. Tensions were particularly high in the printing industry, where workers went on strike in 1539.

The government of Lyon was composed of 12 officials, elected by representatives of the city's crafts and a group of wealthy citizens. Major

* **humanist** referring to a Renaissance cultural movement promoting the study of the humanities (the languages, literature, and history of ancient Greece and Rome) as a guide to living

decisions were made by town assemblies made up of all those with voting privileges. In 1527 the city established an important secondary school, the College of the Trinity, which adopted a humanist* course of study. A number of leading humanists lived in Lyon, and the city's literary circles were enriched by several great French poets, including François RABELAIS. In 1534 the city created the General Charity, which became a model in France for the reform of assistance to the poor.

Lyon became a center of Protestant reform, based on the ideas of John CALVIN. The Protestant Reformed Church, established in the 1550s, grew rapidly. Protestants seized control of Lyon in 1562, but Catholics regained control the following year. A massacre of Protestants in August 1572 claimed hundreds of lives and led many Protestants to leave the city or return to the Catholic faith.

In the late 1500s, the WARS OF RELIGION caused great economic hardship in Lyon. As warfare paralyzed trade, many leading Italian banking families fled. Moreover, between 1592 and 1594, the city fairs ceased as well. After peace returned to Lyon, some commercial activity came back. However, most of those engaged in finance preferred to live in Paris, which replaced Lyon as the banking and financial capital of France. (*See also* **Fairs and Festivals; France; Money and Banking; Printing and Publishing.**)

1469–1527
Italian statesman and political philosopher

* **humanist** referring to a Renaissance cultural movement promoting the study of the humanities (the languages, literature, and history of ancient Greece and Rome) as a guide to living

Niccolò Machiavelli was a keen observer of political affairs, with experience both as a participant in government and as a writer of books on politics. He held various positions in the government of FLORENCE, which allowed him to meet powerful rulers and study their behavior. An accomplished writer, he produced histories, plays, and poems as well as political works. In his most widely read book, *The Prince,* he described how rulers should act to gain and keep power. Machiavelli's ideas attracted considerable attention in his own day and have continued to influence political theorists in modern times.

Early Life and Political Career. Niccolò Machiavelli grew up in Florence at a time when Lorenzo de' MEDICI (also known as Lorenzo the Magnificent) ruled the city. Niccolò was a friend of Lorenzo's youngest son, Giuliano. Machiavelli received a humanist* education and probably met some of the great intellectual and literary figures active in Florence.

In 1498 Machiavelli began a political career. He was appointed to coordinate Florence's relations with its possessions, visiting cities and towns and advising the government on various problems. In addition, Machiavelli served as secretary to the foreign policy office of one of Florence's ruling councils. In this position, he represented the city on missions throughout Europe. During the next 14 years, Machiavelli spent much of his time negotiating agreements, delivering messages, gathering information, and reporting his observations to the members of the council.

Machiavelli's official travels took him to many regions that were experiencing political crises. He visited the city of PISA, which rebelled

* **papal**   referring to the office and authority of the pope

* **Holy Roman Emperor**   ruler of the Holy Roman Empire, a political body in central Europe composed of several states that existed until 1806

* **mercenary**   hired soldier

against Florentine rule in 1494, and Imola and Cesena, where Cesare BORGIA (1475–1507) struggled to maintain control. The Borgia government made a particularly vivid impression on Machiavelli, who later wrote about Cesare's characteristics as a ruler. In the early 1500s, Machiavelli was sent to the papal* court of JULIUS II and to the courts of Louis XII of France and MAXIMILIAN I, the Holy Roman Emperor*.

Machiavelli's reports to the Florentine government sometimes caused controversy. Instead of just gathering information, he often expressed his own opinions. For example, he criticized Florence's reliance on foreign mercenaries* rather than a homegrown military force. Yet Machiavelli had the support of Florence's political leader, Piero Soderini, who placed him in charge of planning, recruiting, and training an army to put down the rebellion in Pisa. When the Florentine forces reconquered Pisa in 1509, Machiavelli's political reputation reached its peak.

From Politics to Writing. After the triumph in Pisa, Machiavelli's political career began to decline. In 1512 Spain joined with the pope against Florence, and Machiavelli's forces proved no match for the Spanish troops. Soderini resigned and the Medici returned to power. Because of his close association with Soderini, Machiavelli lost his government position, had to pay a heavy fine, and was not allowed to travel outside Florence or its territories for a year. Then, in early 1513 he was accused of plotting against the Medici and arrested. Machiavelli appealed to his friend Giuliano de' Medici for help. However, he did not gain his freedom until a large number of prisoners were released in celebration of the election of another Medici family member as Pope LEO X.

By the middle of 1513 Machiavelli's political career was finished. He retreated to his family's country home outside Florence and corresponded with his friend Francesco Vettori, the Florentine ambassador to the papal court. From their letters emerged many of the themes found in *The Prince,* which Machiavelli wrote in the second half of 1513. He dedicated the work to Giuliano de' Medici's nephew (Lorenzo), the new ruler of Florence, probably in an attempt to regain favor with the Medici. However, the Medici made it clear that they had no intention of employing him.

Over the next decade Machiavelli completed a remarkable number of projects. Between 1515 and 1517 he wrote a book about the work of the ancient Roman historian Livy. He also completed a theatrical comedy, *The Mandrake Root* (ca. 1518), which was modeled partly on ancient Roman plays. In addition, Machiavelli wrote poetry, other plays, and various political texts.

Between 1520 and 1524 Machiavelli produced his greatest historical work, *Florentine Histories.* This project helped him regain the support of the Medici and opened the door to opportunities for public service. In 1526, Pope Clement VII (the former Giulio de' Medici) appointed Machiavelli to a new position in which he traveled around central Italy inspecting fortifications and troops. However, the following year, the Florentine people drove out the Medici and restored the republic*. Machiavelli's connections with the Medici now worked against him and

* **republic**   form of Renaissance government dominated by leading merchants with limited participation by others

led the new leaders of Florence to mistrust him. Before he could clear his name, he fell ill and died.

Political Philosophy. During his years of public service, Machiavelli showed interest in a number of philosophical issues related to politics and government. One of his basic ideas involved the link between people's actions and the times. He argued that nature provides each person with a different temperament and imagination. While these never change, times and circumstances vary. Machiavelli believed that success depends on matching actions to the needs of the times and that failure results when a person's behavior does not fit the circumstances.

Machiavelli was especially concerned with military strength. He urged the Florentine government to recruit and train its own troops instead of depending on foreign mercenaries. He also declared that citizens could not be expected to remain loyal to a government that was unable either to defend or to punish them.

Machiavelli expressed his political theories most fully and clearly in *The Prince.* In the early chapters of the book, he reviews different types of principalities and the qualities of great rulers. He argues that the most successful princes possess a quality known as *virtù,* the ability to act effectively and to inspire others with spirit and discipline. This quality gives princes the power they need to secure their positions and to take major steps, such as carrying out reforms.

Machiavelli used the career of Cesare Borgia as an example in his discussion. Borgia, the ruler of the region of Romagna in central Italy, gained power through the influence of his father, Pope ALEXANDER VI. Cesare then worked to consolidate his power—he brought peace to a lawless region, ruthlessly eliminated his rivals, and shifted the blame for his harsh rule onto others. Nevertheless, despite his skillful attempts to strengthen his position, he eventually lost control of his territory. In Machiavelli's view, Borgia's failure occurred because he had relied on his father's influence rather than on his own *virtù* to seize power. In addition, Borgia did not have a large military force under his control to defend his state. Machiavelli repeatedly points out that a homegrown military is essential to a prince's power. He emphasizes that strong states must have their own armies and that successful princes must devote all their attention and energy to the art of war and to organizing and training their troops.

Machiavelli goes on to discuss the ways in which a prince should conduct himself with regard to his subjects, advisers, and other princes. This portion of *The Prince* is very controversial because Machiavelli argues that a prince may use any means to maintain his power. If necessary, a prince should be ruthless, cruel, cunning, and willing to disregard accepted standards of behavior and morality. While a reputation for a good character may be useful, it is less important, according to Machiavelli, than maintaining power.

The conclusion of *The Prince* is a call to action. Machiavelli declares that the time is ripe for a "new prince" to emerge in Italy. This prince would provide the necessary *virtù* to drive out the foreigners occupying

Niccolò Machiavelli observed the actions of powerful rulers while he served in various positions in government. His most famous work, *The Prince,* argued that rulers should use any means—even cruel and immoral ones—to keep power.

Swirl of Controversy

Machiavelli's *The Prince* became one of the most controversial political works ever written. Debates about the book erupted even before its publication in 1532, several years after Machiavelli's death. In 1559 Pope Paul IV placed *The Prince* on the Index of Prohibited Books, which nearly ended further publication of the work in many Catholic countries. Responses to the text were overwhelmingly negative, and by the late 1500s the term *Machiavellian* had taken on a sinister meaning. Today, the term continues to mean crafty, deceitful, ruthless, and willing to do anything to gain power.

the country and to introduce reforms. He goes on to suggest that this new prince might come from the House of Medici, who could win the gratitude of all Italians by accomplishing this great task.

Machiavelli's Influence. Machiavelli ranks as one of the most influential Western political writers. He raised many important issues about the relationship between politics, religion, and morality and revived political debates that originated in ancient times and continue today.

Machiavelli made politics more secular* by separating it from Christian thought and values. He claimed that the goal of politics was the foundation and maintenance of a powerful state. Moreover, he argued that it was not possible for a person to be successful in politics without giving up traditional Christian and moral principles.

Machiavelli also influenced the nature of political writing. He analyzed historical examples to discover how political forces operate. Using ancient Rome as a model, he defended the republic as the form of government best suited to protecting citizens' liberties and preserving the state. Although some writers objected to Machiavelli's ideas, many others have come to value the clarity of his observations and his analysis. (*See also* **Medici, House of; Political Thought; Princes and Princedoms.**)

* **secular** nonreligious; connected with everyday life

In 1561 the king of Spain, PHILIP II, made Madrid the capital of the Spanish empire. Before then, Madrid had been a small, unimportant market town in the kingdom of Castile. The Renaissance appeared late in Madrid and the rest of Castile, and its styles and ideas were never fully accepted. In Madrid, the Renaissance consisted mostly in the use of ancient Greek and Roman themes in religious architecture, which remained essentially Gothic*.

Between 1560 and 1630, the population of Madrid increased dramatically, rising from 20,000 to 130,000 inhabitants. Most city residents worked as servants or suppliers for a small group of nobles and church and public officials. The royal court, housed in the Alcázar, became the center of intellectual life, and the monarchy was the most important patron* of the arts. The royal collections of Philip II included more than 1,500 paintings by Flemish* and Italian masters, especially TITIAN.

Painters, poets, and playwrights flocked to Madrid in search of patrons. The playwrights Pedro CALDERÓN DE LA BARCA and Lope Félix de VEGA CARPIO created a golden age of drama in the late 1500s and early 1600s. The first printing press was established in 1566, and by 1600 Madrid led the publishing business in Spain. For the most part, however, Madrid became a center of Baroque* rather than Renaissance culture. Baroque spectacles dominated city life, from religious processions and pageants to bullfights and other celebrations. Because Spanish kings preferred to build palaces and hunting parks in the countryside, relatively few Renaissance-style buildings or public spaces appeared in Madrid. (*See also* **Architecture; Art in Spain and Portugal; Spain.**)

* **Gothic** style of architecture characterized by pointed arches and high, thin walls supported by flying buttresses

* **patron** supporter or financial sponsor of an artist or writer

* **Flemish** relating to Flanders, a region along the coasts of present-day Belgium, France, and the Netherlands

* **Baroque** artistic style of the 1600s characterized by movement, drama, and grandness of scale

See color plate 13, vol. 3

Madrigals

See *Music, Vocal.*

ca. 1480–1521
**Portuguese navigator
and explorer**

See color
plate 5,
vol. 4

Perhaps the greatest navigator of Europe's age of discoveries, Ferdinand Magellan was the first European to sail from the Atlantic Ocean into the Pacific. The route he followed around the southern tip of South America is now called the Strait of Magellan in his honor. The explorer continued his voyage westward across the Pacific, landing in the Mariana Islands and the Philippines, which he claimed for Spain.

Born in northern Portugal, Magellan grew up during the years when the voyages of Christopher COLUMBUS and Vasco da GAMA were changing the map of the world. In 1505 Magellan sailed to Asia with the fleet of Dom Francisco de Almeida, first ruler of Portugal's Indian colony. He spent several years in southern Asia, where he heard of the Spice Islands or Moluccas (now part of Indonesia), the source of cloves and other precious spices.

By 1513 Magellan had returned to Portugal. Dissatisfied with service in the Portuguese court, he began planning an ambitious voyage. Magellan believed that he could reach the Spice Islands by sailing west across the Atlantic, finding a route past South America, and crossing the unexplored sea that was known to lie west of the Americas. Spain sponsored his voyage, and in August 1519 he set out with five ships and about 240 men.

By December the fleet had arrived near the present site of Rio de Janeiro, Brazil. Magellan spent nearly a year searching for a westward passage through or around South America. During this time, he put down a mutiny and lost one vessel to shipwreck. But by late November 1520, he had found and sailed through a long, winding passage at the tip of South America that ran between the mainland and nearby islands. One ship abandoned the fleet and returned to Spain, but the remaining three emerged into the Pacific Ocean.

Magellan's fleet spent nearly 100 days on the open Pacific, far longer than he had expected. The expedition landed on one of the Mariana Islands, probably Guam, and reached the Philippines soon afterward. Magellan became involved in a war between two local groups and was killed in a battle on the island of Mactan in April 1521. Around the same time, one of his three ships was burned. The ship's survivors reached the Spice Islands, loaded the remaining two ships with cloves, and set off for Spain. One of the ships, the *Trinidad*, started to return the way it had come but was captured by the Portuguese. The other, the *Victoria*, bore westward, through the Indian Ocean to the Atlantic, and reached Spain in 1522 with 17 Europeans and three East Indians aboard. It was the first vessel to sail around the world. Although historians do not know whether Magellan planned to complete his voyage this way or to return from the Spice Islands by way of the Pacific and South America, he is credited with having captained the first voyage across the immense, unknown Pacific. (*See also* **Exploration.**)

Magic and Astrology

* **astrology** study of the supposed influences of the stars and planets on earthly events

* **alchemy** early science that sought to explain the nature of matter and to transform base metals, such as lead, into gold

* **mystical** based on a belief in the idea of a direct, personal union with the divine

* **pagan** referring to ancient religions that worshiped many gods, or more generally, to any non-Christian religion

* **theologian** person who studies religion and the nature of God

See color plate 9, vol. 2

Renaissance Europeans used the term *magic* to refer to a set of beliefs and practices that had been known under that name since the 400s B.C. Theories of magic attempted to explain unusual or hard-to-believe physical events; the practice of magic sought to control such events. Renaissance thinkers saw links between magic and other practices such as astrology*, alchemy*, and WITCHCRAFT. Jewish traditions also played a major role in the Renaissance understanding of magic. Many Jewish scholars linked the practice of magic to the Kabbalah, a mystical* religious system that involved reading encoded messages in the text of the Hebrew Scriptures. Jewish thinkers shared their knowledge of Kabbalah with Christian scholars. As a result, Jewish and Christian theories of magic developed along similar lines during the Renaissance.

Magical Practices. According to Renaissance belief, an expert in magical theory—known as a magus—could predict the future, attract unearthly powers, summon angels, and drive away demons. There were strong links between Renaissance magic and astrology, which rested on the idea that movements in the heavens could influence events on earth. Renaissance magicians believed that they could cause changes in the heavens by arranging material objects—stones, plants, animals, and the like—based on qualities such as color, shape, texture, and taste. They thought that various features would attract or repel similar features in heavenly bodies, enabling them to draw the planets and stars into desired positions.

Heavenly bodies, however, were more than just material objects. They were also linked to the ancient gods and other figures of pagan* religions. The planet Mars, for example, bore the name of the Roman god of war. The Christian theologians* of the Renaissance saw these ancient gods as demons, and many of them frowned on magic as a demonic art. As a result, students of magic devoted considerable effort to explaining magic as a form of natural science. They likened magic to medicine, which often relied on the unexplained properties of natural objects such as herbs. Medical theories of the day could not explain why these herbs affected the body as they did, yet their properties were clearly natural and not demonic.

Theories of Magic. Several well-known Renaissance scholars devoted attention to the study of magic. Marsilio FICINO of Florence unearthed several texts on the subject by Neoplatonists, ancient thinkers who had studied and interpreted the works of the Greek philosopher PLATO. Ficino expanded on the Neoplatonists' ideas in a 1489 work called *Three Books on Life.* He noted that since ancient times, people had recorded many wonders that they could explain only in magical terms. Ficino developed a complex and influential theory of magic, which held that magical influence moved downward from mind to matter, entering into the natural objects that magicians used. He gave weight to his theory by tracing the roots of his ideas back through a long line of ancient thinkers.

The Italian philosopher Giovanni PICO DELLA MIRANDOLA also developed a theory of natural magic. In his 1486 *Oration on the Dignity of*

Renaissance astrology rested on the idea that movements in the heavens could influence events on earth. This star map from the 1500s by Francesco Ghisolfi charts the 12 astrological signs.

Man, he suggested that a life of study and discipline could raise humans to the level of angels and enable them to achieve a mystical union with God. However, he noted that in seeking to speak with angels, magicians ran the risk of calling up demons. To protect against this danger, Pico blended the Kabbalah into his theory of magic. He claimed that this ancient Jewish system had the power to ward off evil demons. Pico saw the letters of the Hebrew alphabet as holy shapes that held the power to tap divine energies safely.

Ficino and Pico both developed theories of natural magic designed to avoid the demons that they feared. Pietro POMPONAZZI, by contrast, dealt with this problem by simply eliminating demons from his theory of magic. He claimed that while the concept of demons had meaning in theology, they did not exist in the natural world. Pomponazzi viewed magic as a form of natural science that explored the links between the heavenly and earthly realms. He developed a world system based on astrology, in which the human world was a microcosm, or small universe, that mirrored events in the larger universe or cosmos.

Several other Renaissance scholars, including the Italian philosopher Giordano BRUNO and the German physician PARACELSUS, developed their own theories of magic. Others, however, criticized the practice. The

Nostradamus

One of the best-known astrologers of the Renaissance was the Frenchman Michel de Nostredame, known as Nostradamus (1503–1566). In his most famous work, known as the *Prophecies* or *Centuries,* Nostradamus claimed to have predicted events up through the year 3797. The work took the form of a series of verses, written in veiled language that could be interpreted in a variety of ways, making their accuracy impossible to prove or disprove. The *Prophecies* have appeared in many languages, often with commentary on how the verses might relate to historical events.

---

* **treatise**   long, detailed essay

* **Messiah**   heroic figure in Jewish lore whose promised arrival would free all Jews from bondage and signal the birth of a glorious kingdom; the earliest Christians were Jews who believed Jesus Christ to be the Messiah

See color plate 8, vol. 2

English philosopher Francis BACON, for example, disputed ancient theories of magic. He sought to reform the practice of magic along scientific lines. Other thinkers of the 1600s, such as the French theologian Marin Mersenne, rejected the idea of magic altogether. Their views eventually won out, and magic fell out of favor with learned Europeans.

Jewish Magic. Magic played a significant role in Jewish culture during the Renaissance, both as a subject of scholarly study among intellectuals and as a popular or folk belief among ordinary people. In Renaissance Italy, Jewish and Christian scholars involved in the study of magic often worked together. For example, Pico gained his knowledge of Kabbalah from Rabbi Yohanon Alemanno of Florence. Alemanno, in turn, had studied under Ficino. However, while Christian scholars developed their theories of magic under the watchful eye of a church that tended to be hostile toward the practice, the Jewish interest in magic extended all the way up to leading rabbis. Some Jewish scholars even interpreted the religious rituals of their faith in magical terms.

Astrology also flourished in Jewish communities, especially in Italy. Many Jewish astrologers worked at the courts of royal and noble families. One of the most famous, Calonymous ben David, served in the court of Naples. Ben David, also known as Maestro Calo, wrote treatises* in Hebrew predicting events in the 1490s, with chapters on the fates of various religions, nations, and professions. Other well-known astrologers included Abraham Zakkut of Portugal and Bonet (Jacob) de Lattes of Italy, who predicted that the Messiah* would come in 1505. In the late 1500s, a Jewish astrologer named Eliezer, about whom little is known, wrote a treatise called *A Valley of Vision.* This work contains a detailed theory of astrology as well as comments on the horoscopes of famous Renaissance figures.

While Jewish scholars developed complex theories of magic, common people followed folk magic practices that had been around for centuries. Jewish popular magic often focused on telling fortunes through such methods as palm reading and astrology. It also involved the idea that spirits or demons, known as dybbuks, could take control of human bodies. Rabbis developed techniques to rid people of dybbuks, combining elements of Kabbalah, magic, and even Roman Catholic ritual.

Christians of the Renaissance tended to regard Jews as expert magicians. This view mingled respect and fear. Because Jewish women were thought to be skilled in magic, some found employment as fortune-tellers or as makers of medicines and potions. However, their supposed powers also brought them under suspicion. In 1600 authorities in Mantua burned an elderly Jewish woman, Judith Franchetti, to death at the stake for the crime of sorcery. (*See also* **Alchemy; Jews; Religious Thought.**)

Man, Dignity of

The concept of the dignity of man (meaning humans in general) played a major role in Renaissance PHILOSOPHY and RELIGIOUS THOUGHT. Scholars contrasted the misery that people often experience in

their daily lives with the glory of their role in the universe. Some writers discussed the dignity of man in terms of human abilities and achievements. Others focused on religious concepts, such as the idea that man had been created in the image of God.

Humanist Writings. Humanists* began to write about the dignity of man in the mid-1300s. The Italian poet and scholar PETRARCH addressed the subject in *Remedies for Both Kinds of Fortune* (1366), in which he described the powers of the soul and the beauty and gifts of the body. Petrarch argued that the functions of the human mind, such as memory and speech, reflected the image of God. He also noted that the Christian belief in salvation offered man the promise of great glory.

Other humanist writers of the late 1300s and early 1400s discussed the condition of man in their works on other subjects, such as law and medicine. These writers explored both the theme of human misery and the idea of human majesty, joy, and power. Many of them drew ideas from theology* and referred to Bible verses on the creation of men and women.

In the mid-1400s, works on the dignity of man became a distinct genre* of humanist writing. Antonio da Barga, an Italian monk and friend of several prominent humanists, played a role in encouraging this trend. In the 1440s Giannozzo Manetti, a leading Florentine humanist and public official, dedicated a work on the dignity of man to Barga. Although this work has not survived, Barga wrote an outline of it, which he gave to another writer, Bartolomeo Facio, to complete. Facio's work emphasized man's creation in God's image and the fact that God had chosen man to rule over the animals and the natural world.

In the 1450s Manetti wrote *The Dignity and Excellence of Man* (first published in 1532). This four-part work drew on the writings of ancient and medieval* thinkers, such as CICERO, ARISTOTLE, and St. AUGUSTINE. The first three sections focused on the wonders of the human body, the human soul, and human beauty and cleverness. In the fourth book, Manetti attempted to counter the idea of human misery found in many ancient and Renaissance sources. Various other Italian humanists also explored the idea of human misery. Some argued that the world held no joy for mankind and that the only true happiness lay in religion. Others believed that men and women could combat misery and improve their lives through reason and intellectual ability.

Philosophical Works. The theme of human dignity found its fullest expression in the works of two Italian thinkers—Marsilio FICINO and Giovanni PICO DELLA MIRANDOLA. Trained in ancient and medieval philosophy, they were also familiar with humanist writings on the human experience. In his *Platonic Theology* (1474), Ficino expanded on the humanist idea of human dignity. This work discussed the powers of man over the natural world, including all living things. Ficino described the glory of human achievements in such areas as government, language, mathematics, the arts, and industry. He also stressed the freedom with which humans used their talents, noting that "men are the inventors of innumerable arts which they practice according to their own decision." Ficino's ideas strongly reflected the culture of Florence in the 1400s.

* **humanist** Renaissance expert in the humanities (the languages, literature, history, and speech and writing techniques of ancient Greece and Rome)

* **theology** study of the nature of God and of religion

* **genre** literary form

* **medieval** referring to the Middle Ages, a period that began around A.D. 400 and ended around 1400 in Italy and 1500 in the rest of Europe

Pico's writings combined concepts from the works of the Greek philosophers PLATO and Aristotle, as well as medieval Arabic and Jewish scholars. In 1486 he completed *Oration on the Dignity of Man,* which explored the theme of human dignity. Pico pointed out that, at creation, God had given humans the freedom to act according to their own will. In Pico's view, man's dignity sprang from his ability to choose his own destiny.

In another work, *Heptaplus* (1488–1489), Pico placed man at the center of the universe. Because man was created in the image of God, Pico argued, he symbolically contained everything in nature and united all parts of the world. Pico summed up his deep admiration for human nature by quoting the ancient writer Hermes Trismegistus, who had called man "a great miracle." (*See also* **Classical Scholarship; Humanism; Individualism.**)

Mannerism

See Art.

Mantegna, Andrea

ca. 1430–1506
Italian painter

* **apprentice** person bound by legal agreement to work for another for a specified period of time in return for instruction in a trade or craft

* **classical** in the tradition of ancient Greece and Rome

* **fresco** mural painted on a plaster wall

Andrea Mantegna was an influential painter in northern Italy during the second half of the 1400s. Like many Renaissance artists of the time, he drew inspiration from the sculpture of ancient Greece and Rome. This inspiration is reflected in Mantegna's painted figures, which have the strongly modeled, statuesque quality of sculpture on canvas.

Born in a village near Padua, Mantegna became an apprentice* in a painter's studio. There his training included instruction in the artistic ideals and practices of the Renaissance, such as copying models from the ancient world. His first major works, in which he used classical* themes as well as details from ancient Roman buildings, reflect this training. Mantegna's work also shows the influence of the Florentine sculptor DONATELLO, who worked in Padua for ten years. Both Donatello and ancient statuary played a role in the development of Mantegna's extremely sculptural treatment of the human figure.

In 1460 Mantegna became the court painter of the noble GONZAGA family of Mantua. One of his main surviving projects is the fresco* decoration of the Camera Picta, a room in the Gonzaga palace. This work included several scenes of the family, one in a landscape dotted with classical ruins and one in a realistic group portrait with rounded forms and rich colors. The group portrait seems to suggest that the family is physically present in the room.

In 1488 Mantegna went to Rome for two years to decorate a chapel for Pope Innocent VIII. Returning to work for the Gonzaga in Mantua, he completed a series of nine huge paintings known as *The Triumphs of Caesar.* They show a procession of the ancient Roman leader Julius Caesar in a setting filled with extremely accurate archaeological detail.

The final phase of Mantegna's career was spent working for Isabella d'ESTE, wife of one of the Gonzaga. In her apartments in the castle of Mantua she created a *studiolo,* a small room ornamented with artworks.

* **allegorical** referring to a literary or artistic device in which characters, events, and settings represent abstract qualities and in which the author intends a different meaning to be read beneath the surface

Mantegna produced several paintings of complex allegorical* subjects for this room. He also contributed two paintings that imitate bronze sculpture, evidence of the artist's skill in using paint to reproduce three-dimensional objects. However, Mantegna also worked directly in bronze. He created a bust of himself in the classical style that was placed, after his death, at the entrance to a memorial chapel in the church of San Andrea in Mantua. (*See also* **Art in Italy; Mantua.**)

Mantua

During the Renaissance, the fortunes of the northern Italian city of Mantua often reflected the history of one family, the House of GONZAGA. Members of this family ruled Mantua from 1328—when they first seized control of the government—to 1707. In the 1300s and 1400s, Mantua faced threats from the neighboring cities of Venice and Milan. The Gonzaga, especially Ludovico II (1412–1478), managed to steer Mantua through this difficult period and to maintain the city's independence with well-timed alliances and military assistance.

During the late 1400s and the 1500s, Mantua became involved in a struggle between competing European interests. Two powerful families, the HABSBURGS of Austria and Spain and the VALOIS of France, fought for control of northern Italy. In 1495 Francisco II Gonzaga (1466–1519) helped drive the French from Italy. Under another Gonzaga ruler, Frederico II (1500–1540), Mantua established close ties with the Habsburgs.

* **humanist** Renaissance expert in the humanities (the languages, literature, history, and speech and writing techniques of ancient Greece and Rome)

Mantua became an important cultural center during the Renaissance, and the Gonzaga invited many scholars and artists to the city. The humanist* VITTORINO DA FELTRE (1378–1446) established a school in Mantua that became a model for later humanist schools. Antonio PISANELLO and Andrea MANTEGNA were among the numerous artists who worked in the city. The Gonzaga also asked the Italian architect Leon Battista ALBERTI to design two churches, including San Sebastiano.

* **papal** referring to the office and authority of the pope

Mantua played a significant role in Renaissance religious history as well. Many members of the Gonzaga family served as bishops and cardinals in the Roman Catholic Church, and during their long involvement they had considerable influence on papal* policies. In 1562–1563 Cardinal Ercole Gonzaga acted as president and papal representative at an important meeting of Catholic leaders, the Council of TRENT. (*See also* **Italy.**)

Manuscripts

See *Books and Manuscripts.*

Margaret of Austria

1480–1530
Habsburg ruler

A member of the powerful HABSBURG DYNASTY, Margaret of Austria acted as regent* to her nephew, the future CHARLES V. The Habsburgs used Margaret as a political pawn, arranging marriages for her with various European rulers. However, she became a capable ruler

* **regent**   person who acts on behalf of a monarch who is too young or unable to rule

* **patron**   supporter or financial sponsor of an artist or writer

* **annul**   to declare legally invalid

* **Flanders**   region along the coasts of present-day Belgium, France, and the Netherlands

* **Holy Roman Emperor**   ruler of the Holy Roman Empire, a political body in central Europe composed of several states that existed until 1806

in the Netherlands, a patron* of the arts, and a major force in the northern Renaissance.

By age 24, Margaret had been married three times. Her first marriage, to the future French king Charles VIII, was annulled* in 1491 when her husband sought a partner with greater political advantage. Her second marriage, to the son of FERDINAND OF ARAGON and ISABELLA OF CASTILE, was meant to unite the Habsburgs with Spain. When her husband died in 1497, Margaret returned to Flanders* and became godmother to her brother's son, the future Holy Roman Emperor* Charles V. In 1501 Margaret became the unwilling wife of Philibert, the duke of Savoy. When Philibert died three years later, Margaret refused to marry again.

Following her brother's death in 1506, Margaret became regent for her nephew Charles in the Netherlands. She pursued the interests of the Habsburgs and sought peaceful solutions to crises. Her greatest political achievement was a treaty with the French in 1529, which temporarily ended hostilities between Charles and the French king FRANCIS I. Margaret also established a vibrant royal court. She employed artists and musicians, assembled a library and art collection, and was a patron to leading Renaissance intellectuals. (*See also* **Netherlands.**)

Margaret of Navarre

1492–1549
French writer

* **allegory**   literary or artistic device in which characters, events, and settings represent abstract qualities, and in which the author intends a different meaning to be read beneath the surface

* **theologian**   person who studies religion and the nature of God

French noblewoman Margaret of Navarre was an important political and literary figure of the 1500s. An accomplished author, she wrote a large body of work, most of which she did not publish during her lifetime. Critics rank her most famous piece, the *Heptameron,* as one of the greatest works of prose of the French Renaissance.

Margaret was the sister of the French king FRANCIS I. In 1527 she married the king of Navarre, a small kingdom in the Pyrenees (a mountain range on the border of France and Spain). As queen, Margaret set the cultural and intellectual tone of her court. She took an interest in a wide range of literature, ranging from the philosophy of PLATO to the Bible and the writings of the Italian poets Dante Alighieri and PETRARCH.

Margaret expressed her deeply religious spirit through her writing. She wrote poems and plays, most of which are allegories* of Christian life. Although she was a Roman Catholic, Margaret also supported reforms within the church. In 1531 she published *Mirror of the Sinful Soul,* a long poem that theologians* at the University of Paris condemned because it expressed certain views contrary to traditional Catholic doctrine. Many of Margaret's major works were not published until the 1800s and 1900s.

Margaret's best-known work was the *Heptameron,* a collection of stories modeled after the *Decameron* by the Italian author Giovanni BOCCACCIO. The plot centers on a group of male and female nobles, stranded by a flood, telling each other stories while waiting for someone to rescue them. Because it spoke openly about love and passion, the *Heptameron* disturbed many early readers. More recent critics, however, praise the work for its moral insights and its use of major female characters. (*See also* **French Language and Literature.**)

Marie de Médicis

1573–1642
French queen

* **regent** person who acts on behalf of a monarch who is too young or unable to rule

* **patron** supporter or financial sponsor of an artist or writer

Marie de Médicis was the second member of the powerful MEDICI family of Italy to become queen and regent* of France. A skillful politician, Marie shrewdly maneuvered for power at the highest level in France. She also exerted her influence as a patron* of the arts, commissioning works that expressed her belief in strong female rule.

Born in Florence in the Tuscan region of Italy, Marie was the daughter of Francesco de' Medici, grand duke of Tuscany. In 1600 she married the French king HENRY IV. By 1608 she had borne five children. One son later became king of France, and two daughters became queens of European countries.

Henry IV was assassinated in 1610. The day after his death, Marie boldly called an assembly of the French parliament to put her young son on the throne as Louis XIII and to recognize Marie as queen regent. Despite efforts to undermine her authority on the grounds that women could not rule, she exercised the office of regent publicly and carried out many of Henry IV's policies. Among her major concerns as regent were pursuing peace in Europe and arranging royal marriages for her children. For a while, Marie managed to hold out against rebellious nobles. However, in 1617 her son, influenced by her enemies, seized power and banished her from court. Marie led a revolt that ended with a peace treaty in 1620, after which she returned to Paris and served on the Royal Council. Her return to court lasted until 1631, when political differences forced her to flee again. She eventually settled in Cologne, Germany, where she died.

Marie de Médicis provided work for many French and European artists. She donated major artworks to numerous Paris churches and completed work on the Luxembourg palace. For the palace, she commissioned the *Life of Marie de Médicis,* a set of 24 large paintings by Peter Paul RUBENS that portrayed her as a heroic ruler, the embodiment of France and of justice. (*See also* **Art in France; Catherine de Médicis; France.**)

Marlowe, Christopher

1564–1593
English playwright and poet

* **classical** in the tradition of ancient Greece and Rome

Christopher Marlowe lived and worked in the late 1500s, a period when Renaissance drama was blossoming in England. His short life was packed with adventure, mystery, and violence. Although he died young, he had a lasting impact on the structure of English drama and left behind a collection of works that have earned the praise of generations of scholars.

Early Career. The son of a poor shoemaker, Marlowe received a scholarship at age 15 to study at the King's School in Canterbury, which offered places to "fifty poor boys." Marlowe learned classical* Latin at the King's School and later won another scholarship to Cambridge University. He began his studies in 1580 and received his bachelor's and master's degrees from Cambridge. Rumors that he had left the university to attend a school in France nearly cost him his master's degree, but royal officials spoke in his defense, claiming that he had been engaged

MARLOWE, CHRISTOPHER

Christopher Marlowe was one of the leading poets and playwrights in Renaissance England. His life was as dramatic as his work and included illegal counterfeiting schemes, spying, and death in a tavern brawl.

* **epic** long poem about the adventures of a hero

in the service of the queen, ELIZABETH I. Historians have suggested that Marlowe was acting as a spy for the English government.

Like most Renaissance scholars, Marlowe took an interest in the literature of ancient Greece and Rome. One of his earliest works was a translation of the *Amores,* a group of Latin love poems by the Roman poet Ovid. As the first translator of these pieces, Marlowe introduced Ovid's work to the English-speaking world, and it soon became a major influence on Renaissance poets. Another ancient work inspired one of Marlowe's first plays: *Dido, Queen of Carthage.* Based on the *Aeneid,* an epic* by the ancient Roman poet VIRGIL, it focuses on the passionate love affair between Dido and the hero Aeneas. Marlowe cowrote the play with another playwright, Thomas Nashe, and a company of child actors performed it around 1587.

* **blank verse** unrhymed verse, usually in iambic pentameter—lines of poetry consisting of ten syllables, or five metric feet, with emphasis placed on every other syllable

* **farce** light dramatic piece that features broad comedy, improbable situations, stereotyped characters, and exaggerated physical action

* **morality play** drama of the Middle Ages in which each character represented some human quality

* **Calvinist** refers to a Protestant church founded by John Calvin

Marlowe's first major dramatic work was *Tamburlaine the Great,* performed in 1588 by the acting group known as the Lord Admiral's Men. The play reveals Marlowe's interest in the fall of leaders, a theme he would return to later in his career. The hero of the piece, Tamburlaine, is a peasant who rises to the monarchy. Believing that his rule is the will of God, he argues that he has the right to destroy everyone who resists him. Unlike earlier plays about unjust rulers, Marlowe's work portrays violence at all levels of society. The mighty attack the weak, and vice versa.

Tamburlaine the Great was a huge success on the London stage and resulted in a sequel, *Tamburlaine, Part Two.* The entire drama became the most frequently quoted play of the English Renaissance. It also established blank verse* as the standard form for English drama. The leading English authors of the Renaissance, including William SHAKESPEARE, Ben JONSON, and John MILTON, all produced classic pieces in this style.

Dramatic Developments. In 1589 Marlowe became involved in a murderous feud between a fellow actor and another man. Marlowe spent two weeks in prison, where he became friendly with another prisoner, John Poole. Poole was a counterfeiter who shared some of his knowledge with Marlowe. He also had ties to a group of Roman Catholic rebels interested in overthrowing Elizabeth I. These connections eventually led Marlowe into danger.

Marlowe wrote several of his best-known plays in the early 1590s. *The Jew of Malta,* first performed in 1592, fell into a dramatic style known as the revenge play, in which a character commits bloody acts to take revenge on his enemies. Mixing tragedy and farce*, *The Jew of Malta* told the story of a Jewish merchant, Barabas, living in an immoral Christian society. Seeking revenge against the city's wealthy Christians for seizing his money, he commits a series of murders through trickery. At one point, he poisons an entire house of nuns. Eventually, one of his own schemes brings about his downfall. This play established the character type known as the "Machiavel," or scheming villain, a name taken from the political writer Niccolò MACHIAVELLI.

In *Doctor Faustus,* the title character sells his soul to the devil in exchange for 24 years of earthly pleasure. Marlowe based this work on the morality plays* of the Middle Ages, in which good and bad angels sought to direct the actions of the main character. The play mocked the Calvinist* belief in predestination, which held that only those chosen by God could enter heaven. Faustus turns this argument on its head to justify his evil actions: if he is already guilty in the eyes of God, his choices make no difference.

Marlowe's *Edward II* reflected the influence of Shakespeare's history plays. Like many of Shakespeare's works, it featured a weak king whose actions damage his country. Marlowe gave this theme a new twist by focusing on the king's homosexual affections for two of his favorite courtiers. By raising these lowborn men to power, Edward threatens the class structure. His actions provoke a rebellion, leading to a tragic cycle of violence and vengeance.

Final Acts. The last year of Marlowe's life saw him in trouble with the law on several occasions. He spent the winter of 1592 in the Netherlands, where he fell in with a gang of counterfeiters. When one of these men turned Marlowe in to the English governor, the playwright confessed his involvement but tried to shift the blame onto his attacker. The governor arrested Marlowe, but by spring he was back on the streets of London, where an officer arrested him again for disturbing the peace.

Later that year the plague* struck England, and officials closed all the playhouses in London. Along with other British playwrights, Marlowe turned his creative attention to other forms of writing, especially poetry. In his long narrative* poem *Hero and Leander,* Marlowe retold an ancient Greek myth about two young lovers. While the original story ended with Leander's tragic death, Marlowe chose to end his poem at the point when the lovers fulfill their passion for each other. *Hero and Leander* went through ten editions between 1598 and 1637, becoming the most widely read of Marlowe's works.

In 1593 Marlowe quarreled with another man about money. The other man stabbed Marlowe in the eye, killing him. The court found that the man had acted in self-defense, but some scholars believe the playwright was the victim of foul play. After Marlowe's death, his reputation rose and fell over the centuries. Many scholars attacked his plays as immoral, but others praised him for his skill with language and for his unique collection of unforgettable—if highly flawed—characters. (*See also* **Drama, English; English Language and Literature.**)

* **plague** highly contagious and often fatal disease that wiped out much of Europe's population in the mid-1300s and reappeared periodically over the next three centuries; also known as the Black Death

* **narrative** storytelling

Marriage

See *Love and Marriage.*

1516–1558
Queen of England

* **annul** to declare legally invalid

The life and reign of Mary I of England were shaped by the decision of her father, HENRY VIII, to break with the Roman Catholic Church. Henry wanted to divorce Mary's mother, CATHERINE OF ARAGON, who had failed to produce a male heir to succeed him on the throne. Because the Catholic Church did not permit divorce, Henry tried to convince the pope to annul* his marriage. Unsuccessful in that effort, the king persuaded Parliament that the pope had no authority in England.

In 1533 the English archbishop Thomas CRANMER declared Henry's marriage invalid. Mary, 17 years old, had suddenly become illegitimate. She was kept under virtual arrest in the household created for Elizabeth (ELIZABETH I), her infant half-sister by Henry's second wife. Outraged by her father's behavior, Mary suffered extreme stress and frequent ill health.

Upon Henry's death in 1547, the throne passed to EDWARD VI, Henry's son by his third wife. The teenage Edward died in 1553, and Mary claimed the crown, backed by a majority of the nation. She lost considerable support, however, when she made it clear that her main goal was to restore Roman Catholicism to England. She was heavily influenced

* **Holy Roman Emperor** ruler of the Holy Roman Empire, a political body composed of several states in central Europe that existed until 1806

by her cousin, the Holy Roman Emperor* CHARLES V, and she married his son, Philip, prince of Spain (later PHILIP II). The marriage was controversial and unpopular in England.

The following year, 1554, proved to be the most successful of Mary's reign. Philip helped negotiate a return to good relations with the pope, and in the fall Mary was declared pregnant. However, by the summer of 1555, the queen's pregnancy had failed—and there is some doubt whether she had ever been pregnant. Most people realized that the 39-year-old queen was unlikely to have an heir and that her half-sister Elizabeth, whom Mary disliked and distrusted, would probably succeed her on the throne.

Philip left England and turned his attention to taking over his father's many responsibilities as Charles V gradually withdrew from public life. The quality of government in England declined as experienced advisers died and Mary appointed less able men to take their place. Her chief adviser was her cousin Reginald Pole, a Roman Catholic cardinal. Together they focused on making sure that people became good Catholics and on persecuting Protestants. In 1556 Thomas Cranmer, who had played a key role in Protestantism in England, was burned to death at the stake.

The second half of Mary's short reign was grim. Poor harvests and an 18-month-long influenza epidemic weakened the nation. Relations with the Roman Catholic Church worsened after Philip went to war with Pope Paul IV in Italy, and England was drawn into the war on Philip's side. The French seized the port of Calais, England's last possession on the European continent.

The queen's health, never strong, began to fail. Finally, with great reluctance, she named her half-sister Elizabeth as heir to the throne. Mary had been devoted to England, and despite her pride and stubbornness she had done her duty as queen to the best of her abilities. Elizabeth, however, hated her, and when she came to the throne she did nothing to glorify the memory of Mary I. (*See also* **England; Protestant Reformation.**)

Mary Stuart

1542–1587
Queen of Scots

The turbulent life and tragic death of Mary, queen of Scots, remains one of the most colorful tales in the history of Britain's royal families. The daughter and heir of James V, king of Scotland, Mary also had a strong claim to the English throne. Her grandmother, Margaret Tudor, was the elder sister of HENRY VIII of England.

James V died soon after Mary's birth, and she became queen of Scotland in 1543. Mary spent her childhood in France, where she was educated with the French royal children. In 1558 she married Francis of VALOIS, the heir to the French throne. That same year ELIZABETH I, daughter of Henry VIII, became queen of England. Some disputed her claim to the throne, including the French king Henry II, who declared his daughter-in-law Mary the rightful ruler of England.

When Francis died prematurely in 1560, Mary returned to Scotland. There she established a brilliant court that encouraged literary efforts in

MASACCIO

* **patron** supporter or financial
sponsor of an artist or writer

* **coat of arms** set of symbols used to
represent a noble family

numerous languages. An important patron* and book collector, Mary
had a special fondness for poetry. However, trouble, arose on several
fronts. The Protestantism of John KNOX dominated religious life in
Scotland, but Mary was a Catholic and tried to convert the nobility to
her faith. She also had ambitions for the English crown and refused to
sign a treaty with Elizabeth or to stop using the English royal coat of
arms*. In 1565 Mary married Henry Stewart, Lord Darnley, who also had
a claim to the throne of England.

Mary and Darnley disagreed about his power as king of Scotland.
With the support of some lords, Darnley led an attack on David Riccio,
Mary's secretary and rumored lover. Riccio was stabbed to death. In the
midst of a deteriorating political situation, Mary gave birth to a son,
James, and some months later Darnley was murdered. One of the men
accused of conspiring to kill Darnley was James Hepburn, earl of
Bothwell. Mary not only protected Bothwell but married him after he
divorced his wife. Widespread outrage led to a Scottish revolt against
Mary and her new husband. Bothwell fled, but Mary was captured and
imprisoned for a year before escaping to England. She left the Scottish
crown to her young son.

Arriving in England in 1568, Mary became the prisoner of her cousin,
Elizabeth I, whom she never met. English Catholics rallied to Mary's
cause, and Elizabeth's supporters produced letters, apparently written by
Mary, that encouraged plots against the crown. In 1587 Elizabeth's royal
secretary came into possession of a letter in which Mary approved of a
plot to assassinate Elizabeth. Mary stood trial for treason. The court convicted her, and the following year she was beheaded. Mary's lifelong
ambition for the English throne was realized by her son. In 1603 he succeeded Elizabeth to become King JAMES I of England. (*See also* **England;
Scotland.**)

Masaccio

**1401–ca. 1428
Italian painter**

* **perspective** artistic technique for
creating the illusion of three-
dimensional space on a flat surface

* **guild** association of craft and trade
owners and workers that set standards
for and represented the interests of its
members

The Italian painter Masaccio is considered the founder of Italian
painting of the 1400s. Many Renaissance artists studied and copied
his work. LEONARDO DA VINCI admired Masaccio for his faithfulness to
nature; others praised Masaccio's use of perspective* and his technical
mastery.

Born Tommaso di Giovanni de Simone Cassai in the village of San
Giovanni Valdarno, Masaccio spent most of his brief career in FLORENCE.
The first record of him as an artist dates from 1418. In January 1422 he
joined the Florentine painter's guild*, and two years later he became a
member of the Company of San Luca, a professional organization of
painters.

Masaccio's work features solid, muscular figures. The light illuminat-
ing his paintings gives them a feeling of depth and makes figures and
objects appear three-dimensional. The artist's use of perspective also
clearly defines the spaces within his paintings.

One of Masaccio's earliest surviving works is the *San Giovenale
Triptych*, painted in 1422. The three-panel painting shows the Virgin
Mary and the Christ child surrounded by angels and saints. Another

THE RENAISSANCE

well-known work by the artist, the *Pisa Altarpiece,* was commissioned for a chapel in the city of PISA. This piece also focuses on the Virgin and Child.

* **fresco**   mural painted on a plaster wall

Masaccio's most celebrated work is a series of frescoes* for a chapel in the Church of Santa Maria del Carmine in Florence, which he worked on with Masolino da Panicale. Begun in the 1420s but left unfinished, the series was completed by the painter Filippino Lippi in the early 1480s. The frescoes focus on the life and ministry of St. Peter but also feature biblical scenes of Adam and Eve. In a scene entitled *Expulsion from Paradise,* Masaccio uses body language and facial expression to show the profound sadness and anguish of Adam and Eve as they leave the Garden of Eden. This scene, along with others by Masaccio, reveals great psychological complexity.

Masaccio's career ended early, and few of his works survived. However, he served as an inspiration for Italian artists of his day. One admirer, the architect Leon Battista ALBERTI, regarded Masaccio as the equal of the great masters of ancient Greece and Rome. (*See also* **Art in Italy.**)

Mathematics

The field of mathematics made great strides during the Renaissance. Social and economic changes, along with the recovery of ancient Greek texts, helped promote new discoveries in mathematics. These advances, in turn, affected fields such as accounting, art, navigation, and astronomy. The boom in mathematical awareness set the stage for the scientific revolution of the 1600s.

Roots of Renaissance Mathematics.   Like many other areas of culture, mathematics benefited from the renewed interest in classical* knowledge during the Renaissance. For example, humanists* of the period explored the ideas of the Greek philosopher PLATO and his followers. Their writings promoted the view that mathematics was the key to understanding nature. Other cultural traditions also influenced mathematics during the Renaissance. The modern numbering system, for example, had originated in the Hindu-Arabic world.

* **classical**   in the tradition of ancient Greece and Rome

* **humanist**   Renaissance expert in the humanities (the languages, literature, history, and speech and writing techniques of ancient Greece and Rome)

The Rise of Algebra.   In the early 1300s, mathematicians in Italy wrote a series of practical texts on the Islamic technique known as algebra. These books, intended for use by merchants and accountants, taught the Hindu-Arabic system of numerals. They also introduced new symbols and abbreviations for use in algebra. The texts used algebra to solve problems related to commerce, banking, and weights and measures. These works stimulated an interest in algebra in other countries, including France, England, and Germany. The first German algebra text appeared in 1525, and the royal physician Robert Recorde published the first English algebra in 1557. This book, The *Whetstone of Witte,* introduced the equal sign. Other now-familiar symbols that first appeared during the Renaissance included +, -, ÷, <, and >.

MATHEMATICS

Advances in geometry helped expand the fields of navigation, mapmaking, and art. This painting by Jacopo de' Barbari shows mathematics teacher Luca Pacioli giving a lesson in geometry.

* **treatise**   long, detailed essay

The most famous Renaissance algebra was Girolamo Cardano's *Great Art,* published in 1545. It was the first European text to make major advances beyond earlier Islamic works. Cardano provided solutions to several problems that had frustrated European mathematicians for years. Perhaps more importantly, he inspired a wide range of new problems and topics for exploration. In addition to *Great Art,* Cardano also published the first treatise* on applying mathematics to games of chance.

In 1591, François Viète of France began to use letters to represent entire classes of numbers in algebraic equations. This change enabled mathematicians to solve equations in general terms. For example, instead of solving the equation "$x^2 + 5x + 6 = 0$," they could write out the general equation "$ax^2 + bx + c = 0$" and solve it for x in terms of a, b, and c. This meant that mathematicians could use the general solution to solve all problems of the same type. Viète's invention made algebra both more abstract and more powerful. Viète also introduced the "let *x* = the unknown" approach to solving word problems, which is now standard in algebra.

Trigonometry and Geometry. Advances in geometry and trigonometry (a branch of mathematics dealing with the properties of triangles) paved the way for new methods in navigation, mapmaking, and art. In the early 1500s, maps of the seas showed meridians—imaginary circles on the Earth's surface that pass through the North and South Poles—as straight lines an equal distance apart. However, the flat maps of the time did not account for the fact that the Earth is round. A sailor who used a meridian on such a map as a guideline for plotting a

56

THE RENAISSANCE

Flemish relating to Flanders, a region along the coasts of present-day Belgium, France, and the Netherlands

straight course would travel in a spiral that ended up at the North or South Pole.

Gerard Mercator, a maker of mathematical instruments in the Flemish* city of Louvain, created a map that solved this problem. Mercator's map projected the Earth's surface onto the surface of a cylinder. This kind of projection involves, in effect, wrapping a flat sheet of paper around a sphere, then tracing a straight line out from every point on the sphere's surface to a matching point on the paper. The unrolled sheet then becomes a flat map.

Mercator's map successfully represented a constant course as a straight line. The map worked well if one stayed on the same latitude—that is, the same distance north or south of the equator. However, it did not account for the fact that the distances between meridians grow shorter as one moves farther from the equator. In 1599, the English sailor and mathematician Edward Wright solved the problem by working out the trigonometric theory behind Mercator's projection. His work enabled navigators to use Mecator's map to calculate distances between points anywhere on Earth.

Renaissance artists used geometry to create perspective—the illusion of three-dimensional space on the flat surface of a drawing or painting. The rediscovery of a work on optics by the ancient Greek mathematician Euclid led several artists, including the Italian PIERO DELLA FRANCESCA, to do original work in geometry. In his treatise *On Perspective in Painting*, Piero explained how to show objects in three dimensions from any point on the plane of the picture. Albrecht DÜRER, one of the best-known artists in Europe, wrote the first geometric text in German.

The field of astronomy also benefited from work in mathematics. Johann Müller of Königsberg, better known as Regiomontanus, wrote the first complete European work on trigonometry in 1464. His book, *On Triangles of All Kinds,* influenced Georg Joachim Rheticus, a student of the Polish astronomer Nicolaus COPERNICUS. Copernicus drew on Rheticus's knowledge of this subject to work out the details of his new idea that the Earth revolved around the Sun, rather than the other way around.

As astronomy and navigation became more complex, so did the calculations needed to chart the stars and plot courses at sea. In the early 1600s, Scotland's John Napier developed the system of logarithms to make calculations in trigonometry easier. A logarithm is the power to which a base, such as 10, must be raised to produce a given number. It is possible to find the product of any two numbers by adding their logarithms. The slide rule, a simple computer for adding logarithms, put fast calculation within the reach of everyone who worked with numbers.

Mathematics and the Future of Europe. Mathematicians in the Middle Ages had begun to work on problems whose answers did not have definite limits. A number of Renaissance scholars continued and refined this work, resulting in major advances in mathematics and science.

For example, the German astronomer Johannes KEPLER became curious about how wine merchants estimated the volumes of the barrels

Top Secret Equations

Italian mathematicians sometimes took part in public contests to win money, honor, and teaching positions. In 1535, two mathematicians competed to solve a series of problems called cubics. Girolamo Cardano later persuaded the winner of this contest to tell him his method, which he promised not to reveal. However, Cardano then published the solution in his book *Great Art.* The outraged scholar responded by publishing the text of the oath Cardano had broken. This story reveals how Renaissance society often encouraged scholars to keep their findings secret—an idea quite foreign to modern mathematicians.

they used to store wine. He invented a system that involved thinking of the area of a curved surface as the sum of an infinite number of straight lines. This technique gave rise to the field of analytic geometry, created by French mathematicians Pierre de Fermat and René Descartes in the early 1600s. In time, these new methods led to the development of calculus, which revolutionized science and mathematics in Europe.

Along with its practical benefits, mathematics had a broader cultural meaning. It taught European thinkers the ideas of symbolic reasoning and the power of abstract ideas. It also showed that mathematical analysis could solve many types of real-world problems. The advances in mathematics during the Renaissance reflected a general sense of intellectual power and progress. (*See also* **Astronomy; Classical Scholarship; Geography and Cartography; Science; Sciences, Physical.**)

1459–1519
Holy Roman Emperor

* **Holy Roman Emperor** ruler of the Holy Roman Empire, a political body in central Europe composed of several states that existed until 1806

Maximilian I, one of the most remarkable rulers of the Renaissance, served as the Holy Roman Emperor* from 1493 until 1519. Under his leadership, the HABSBURG family came to dominate in Europe in the 1500s. Maximilian added vast lands to the family holdings and used diplomacy, warfare, and marriage to make the empire more secure.

The son of the Holy Roman Emperor Frederick III, Maximilian grew up in southern Austria. He was a well-educated man who spoke seven languages and enjoyed hunting. In 1477 he married Mary of Burgundy, one of the wealthiest women in Europe and heir to the duke of BURGUNDY. When her father died two years later, the French tried to seize Burgundy. Maximilian defeated the French at the Battle of Guinegate and added Burgundy to the Habsburg possessions.

King and Emperor. The ruler of the Holy Roman Empire also held the title "king of the Romans." In 1486 Maximilian was chosen king of the Romans and joined his father in managing the empire. Maximilian soon gained control of the Tyrol, a mountainous area in western Austria with rich copper and silver mines. The mines helped him finance many of his wars. Not all of these wars were successful. His attempt in 1490 to take the throne of Hungary failed, although he did succeed in driving the Hungarians out of other areas of central Europe.

In 1493, after the death of his father, Maximilian I became head of the house of Habsburg and ruler of the Holy Roman Empire. Unable to pass through Italy for coronation as Holy Roman Emperor by the pope, Maximilian assumed the title "Elected Roman Emperor."

War and Peace. Throughout his reign, Maximilian fought frequently with France over control of Italy. In 1495 he joined forces with Spain, the Italian city-states of Milan and Venice, and the pope to drive the French from Italy. Maximilian failed to force the French out of Milan or to make the citizens of Venice give up territory to him.

The emperor waged war on other fronts as well. The Ottoman Turks* constantly threatened the empire's eastern frontier. Maximilian also

* **Ottoman Turks** Turkish followers of Islam who founded the Ottoman Empire in the 1300s; the empire eventually included large areas of eastern Europe, the Middle East, and northern Africa

went to war against the Swiss, who refused to pay royal taxes to support his war efforts. However, during his reign Maximilian proclaimed eternal peace and banned private warfare. He also established a supreme court of law.

Money was a constant problem for Maximilian. He financed many of his wars with money borrowed from bankers, such as the FUGGER FAMILY of Germany. He also arranged marriages for his children and grandchildren with many of Europe's powerful and wealthy families, adding much new territory to the Habsburg realm. The marriage of Maximilian's son Philip to a daughter of the Spanish monarchs FERDINAND and ISABELLA eventually brought the throne of Spain to the Habsburgs.

* **patron** supporter or financial sponsor of an artist or writer

Maximilian I was an important patron* of the arts as well. In the empire's capital city of Innsbruck, he remodeled the imperial palace and built a new arsenal. In addition, he supported both church and court music and commissioned many beautifully illustrated works to honor the achievements of the Habsburgs. Maximilian also wrote about hunting and completed large sections of his three-part autobiography. (*See also* **Holy Roman Empire.**)

1527–1576
Holy Roman Emperor

* **Holy Roman Emperor** ruler of the Holy Roman Empire, a political body in central Europe composed of several states that existed until 1806

* **patron** supporter or financial sponsor of an artist or writer

* **papal** referring to the office and authority of the pope

Maximilian II held multiple thrones. He served as Holy Roman Emperor* (1564–1576), king of Bohemia (1549/1562–1576), and king of Hungary (1563–1576). Maximilian failed to achieve many of his political goals, but he had a lasting influence as a patron* of the arts.

Maximilian was a member of the HABSBURGS, one of Europe's most powerful families. His father, FERDINAND I, ruled the Holy Roman Empire from 1558 to 1564. Maximilian spent his early years in the Austrian city of Innsbruck, the imperial residence of the Habsburgs. Although raised as a Catholic, Maximilian probably became familiar with Protestant ideas through one of his tutors.

In 1544 Maximilian went to live at the court of his uncle, CHARLES V, the king of Spain and Holy Roman Emperor (ruled 1519–1556). In 1548 he married the emperor's daughter Maria. Maximilian was generally expected to succeed his father as emperor, but he faced opposition from papal* circles because of his tolerant attitude toward Protestants. He considered himself a Christian and wanted to be neither Catholic nor Protestant. For a time, Maximilian's Spanish relatives also tried to block his rise to power.

Nevertheless, after the death of Ferdinand in 1564, Maximilian II became Holy Roman Emperor. He did not enjoy much success as a statesman during his reign. Despite his tolerant policies, he failed to restore unity between Catholics and Protestants. In addition, constant lack of money curbed many of his political goals.

Although Maximilian II faced many problems, he was a popular emperor who spoke German, Spanish, Czech, Italian, French, and Latin. Maximilian wanted to make Vienna a center of European intellectual life. At his court in Vienna, he created an academy of famous European scholars and scientists. The palace he built southeast of Vienna held a rare collection of non-European plants and animals. It became an important center for the study of natural science in central Europe.

A supporter of the arts, Maximilian hired many talented painters, sculptors, and architects. Some of his paintings still hang in collections in Vienna. The emperor was also a great music lover, who arranged to have musical activities of the highest order at his court. (*See also* **Bohemia; Holy Roman Empire; Hungary.**)

Medici, House of

The Medici family dominated the Italian city of FLORENCE throughout the Renaissance and beyond, from 1434 to 1737. The Medici headed Europe's largest bank, became Florence's richest family, and controlled Florentine politics. Three Medici men became popes, and many Medici children married into the Catholic royal houses of Europe. In 1569, Cosimo I de' Medici won from the pope the hereditary title of grand duke of Tuscany, the region around Florence.

The house of Medici rose to prominence around 1291, when a Medici served in the *signoria,* Florence's city council. The family's fortunes swelled with the success of their bank starting in the 1390s, when Giovanni di Bicci de' Medici moved some of the family's banking operations from Rome to Florence. His son, Cosimo the Elder (1389–1464), turned the bank into a fast-growing business that operated throughout Europe. The bank handled financial affairs for the papacy*, which gave the Medici great power. They could sometimes arrange for their supporters to receive positions within the church.

* **papacy**   office and authority of the pope

Medici Rulers. During the 1430s the Medici, headed by Cosimo the Elder, took over the leadership of Florence. Although Cosimo rarely held important political posts, he placed power in the hands of special councils packed with Medici supporters. Another of Cosimo's tactics was to pay some of the city's military captains from his own pocket, making them loyal to him personally. In addition to building up a core of followers through the use of wealth and favors, Cosimo and the leaders of the other Medici households gained support from the general public by spending large sums on charity and public works, such as the repair of churches.

In 1469 Cosimo's grandson Lorenzo the Magnificent (1449–1492) became head of the family and, for all practical purposes, ruler of Florence. He managed to hold onto power despite a rebellion by prominent Florentines and a war with the pope. A few years after his death, however, the French invaded Italy. When Lorenzo's son Piero gave in to French demands, the Florentines rebelled and exiled the most prominent members of the Medici family. This led to the collapse of the Medici bank in 1494.

Cardinal Giovanni de' Medici (1475–1521, later Pope LEO X) arranged for his exiled relatives to return to Florence in 1512, and the family set about regaining power. Another rebellion against the Medici in 1527 led to a second period of exile from Florence, but in the 1530s the leading

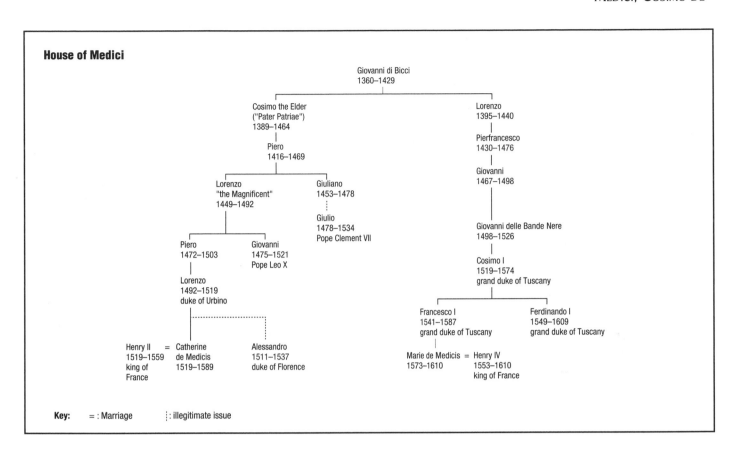

House of Medici

Giovanni di Bicci
1360–1429

Cosimo the Elder
("Pater Patriae")
1389–1464

Piero
1416–1469

Lorenzo
"the Magnificent"
1449–1492

Giuliano
1453–1478

Giulio
1478–1534
Pope Clement VII

Piero
1472–1503

Giovanni
1475–1521
Pope Leo X

Lorenzo
1492–1519
duke of Urbino

Henry II
1519–1559
king of
France
= Catherine
de Medicis
1519–1589

Alessandro
1511–1537
duke of Florence

Lorenzo
1395–1440

Pierfrancesco
1430–1476

Giovanni
1467–1498

Giovanni delle Bande Nere
1498–1526

Cosimo I
1519–1574
grand duke of Tuscany

Francesco I
1541–1587
grand duke of Tuscany

Ferdinando I
1549–1609
grand duke of Tuscany

Marie de Medicis
1573–1610
= Henry IV
1553–1610
king of France

Key: = : Marriage   ┆ : illegitimate issue

See color
plate 4,
vol. 3

* **Holy Roman Empire** political body
in central Europe composed of several
states; existed until 1806

* **Protestant Reformation** religious
movement that began in the 1500s as a
protest against certain practices of the
Roman Catholic Church and eventually
led to the establishment of a variety of
Protestant churches

citizens of Florence, weary of decades of civil strife, coups, and exile, accepted Medici rule in return for stability. Cosimo I de' Medici (1519–1574), descendant of a secondary branch of the family, rose to power in 1537. He proved to be one of the strongest and most independent rulers in Florence's history. He acquired new territories—including the city of SIENA—and the title of grand duke of Tuscany, which his descendants held until 1737. The reign of Cosimo I placed the Medici on a level with many of the other ruling families of Europe.

Medici Influence. Several strategies helped the Medici gain and hold power. One was the shrewd use of marriage. At first, members of the family arranged marriages for their children to seal economic and political alliances with other Florentine families. Lorenzo widened the family's horizons, marrying into the Roman nobility, and from then on the Medici gained status through marriages with noble families throughout Europe. Medici sons and daughters married into royal houses in the Holy Roman Empire*, France, and Spain.

The Medici also used the Roman Catholic Church to further their ambitions. Lorenzo maneuvered for years to have his son Giovanni appointed a cardinal. As Pope Leo X, Giovanni labored to make the Medici the rulers of Florence. So did his cousin Giulio (1478–1534), who became Pope Clement VII. Their pursuit of policies that advanced the Medici drew their attention from vital matters such as the Protestant Reformation*. Pope Leo XI also a Medici, was less influential.

* **patron** supporter or financial sponsor of an artist or writer

* **humanist** referring to a Renaissance cultural movement promoting the study of the humanities (the languages, literature, and history of ancient Greece and Rome) as a guide to living

Medici, Cosimo de'

1389–1464
Florentine banker and statesman

* **patron** supporter or financial sponsor of an artist or writer

* **papal** referring to the office and authority of the pope

* **diplomatic** having to do with formal relations between nations

The Medici were major patrons* of Renaissance intellectuals and artists. Cosimo I did much to make Florence a center of art and culture, providing financial support for painters and encouraging scholarship. Several later Medici, including Cosimo II, showed strong interest in mathematics, literature, and science. The Medici collected books, founded libraries, and supported the studies of humanist* scholars and philosophers. The Medici's greatest cultural contribution, however, was commissioning works by many of the major artistic figures of the Renaissance, including Filippo BRUNELLESCHI, MICHELANGELO, Benvenuto CELLINI, and Sandro BOTTICELLI. Through the exercise of their wealth and their taste, the Medici helped shape the art and cultural life of an era. (*See also* **Catherine de Médicis; Marie de Médicis; Medici, Cosimo de'; Medici, Lorenzo de'; Popes and Papacy.**)

Born into the powerful Medici family of FLORENCE, in the Tuscan region of Italy, Cosimo de' Medici became a leading citizen and patron* of the arts. He also served as head of the bank that was the foundation of Medici wealth and influence.

Political Influence. The Medici were part of Florence's ruling class from at least 1291. But the family's fortunes rose after Giovanni di Bicci, Cosimo's father, founded the Florentine branch of the bank in the 1390s. By the time Cosimo and his brother took over in 1420, the Medici bank handled much of the business of the papal* court. Cosimo had great ability as a banker, and the family bank expanded and prospered under his direction. It reached the height of its influence by the 1450s, when it had branches or partners throughout western Europe.

As the elder son, Cosimo de' Medici inherited his father's political influence. Cosimo advised the city council and was often a leader in diplomatic* missions to other states. He also engaged in local politics and power struggles in Florence. By the late 1420s the Medici family had grown to 27 households in Florence. They used their increasing wealth and reputation to win followers and promote the appointment of their friends to public office.

The Medici and their followers, led by Cosimo and his cousin Averardo, became Florence's leading political party. As they gained power, they began to face opposition. In 1433 political opponents managed to have Cosimo and other Medici leaders exiled from Florence. However, the city soon recognized that it needed Cosimo to finance its wars and conduct relations with foreign royalty. A pro-Medici government recalled Cosimo to Florence in 1434 and openly acknowledged him as its leading citizen. In the 1450s Cosimo turned over direction of the bank to his sons, but he remained involved in both business and politics. In 1454 he negotiated the Peace of Lodi, which ended half a century of warfare among several Italian states, including Florence.

Artistic Patronage. Throughout his life, Cosimo devoted attention to the arts. Like other prominent Renaissance citizens, the Medici purchased artwork for public display and private use. They often hired artists such as Lorenzo GHIBERTI, DONATELLO, and Fra ANGELICO to produce important pieces.

In 1419 Cosimo and his father commissioned a statue of St. Matthew by Ghiberti to decorate one of Florence's civic buildings. A few years later they oversaw the construction of a papal tomb, which featured work by Donatello. Cosimo also paid for and supervised the rebuilding of the church of San Lorenzo in Florence. Under Medici leadership, the restoration of this church symbolized the rise of the family's power.

* **classical** in the tradition of ancient Greece and Rome

In the late 1450s, Cosimo completed a magnificent new residence, the Palazzo Medici, which combined classical* elements with traditional Florentine features. It was filled with fine artwork, including Donatello's *David,* a bronze statue. As a patron of literature, Cosimo sponsored the work of the philosopher Marsilio FICINO as well as scholars who discovered lost classical manuscripts. He also assembled a large library and donated books to the collections of religious houses.

* **republican** refers to a form of Renaissance government dominated by leading merchants with limited participation by others

Although some critics feared that Cosimo de' Medici's power was a threat to Florence's republican* government, most Florentines saw him as a statesman who had protected the city's independence and brought peace. Not long after Cosimo's death, the government of Florence declared him *Pater patriae,* the "father of his country." (*See also* **Medici, House of.**)

Medici, Lorenzo de'

1449–1492
Florentine statesman
and author

* **republic** form of Renaissance government dominated by leading merchants with limited participation by others

Lorenzo de' Medici, also known as Lorenzo the Magnificent, was a member of the wealthy and powerful Medici family of FLORENCE, Italy. From 1469 until his death he managed the affairs of the Florentine republic* while strengthening the position of his family. He also took a keen interest in the intellectual and artistic activities of Renaissance Florence.

Political Career. Lorenzo was the grandson of Cosimo de' Medici (1389–1464), who had been Florence's leading citizen two generations earlier. As international bankers and statesmen, the Medici possessed both money and connections with many noble and royal houses. From an early age Lorenzo was groomed for political leadership. Florence had a republican government, but Lorenzo was treated as a prince. After his father's death in 1469, members of the Medici political party asked Lorenzo to take on the leadership of the city-state. Although Lorenzo never served on the city council, he belonged to many important committees and governing bodies and wielded enormous influence. He controlled the city more by arranging for his supporters to fill government positions than by holding public office himself.

Lorenzo de' Medici, shown here in a painting by Giorgio Vasari, ruled Florence for 23 years. In addition to his political life, Lorenzo was a patron of the arts and the author of songs, poetry, and a play.

* **papacy**   office and authority of the pope

* **vernacular**   native language or dialect of a region or country

* **patron**   supporter or financial sponsor of an artist or writer

* **villa**   luxurious country home and the land surrounding it

Lorenzo's growing personal power, however, distressed other local leaders, including some within the Medici party. The Pazzi family, longtime Medici supporters, formed a plot against Lorenzo. In 1478 they managed to kill his brother Guiliano but only wounded Lorenzo slightly before he escaped. Pope Sixtus IV (reigned 1471–1484) also opposed Lorenzo, but on a larger scale. He sent an invading army into Tuscany, the region around Florence. Lorenzo was forced to turn to French allies for help, but he survived the crisis, made peace with the pope, and maintained control of Florence. He tried to ensure future good relations with the papacy* by marrying one of his daughters to the nephew of Pope Innocent VIII (reigned 1484–1492). Lorenzo's only shortcoming in promoting his family's interests was his management of the Medici bank. It suffered large losses in the 1480s and early 1490s.

Writer and Patron of the Arts.   As an author, Lorenzo produced songs, a play, and poems. His poetry ranged from youthful verses in praise of country amusements to mature sonnets, a philosophical debate, and mythological poems. Lorenzo wrote his poetry in the Tuscan dialect, and he had strong ideas about the use of language. In the introduction to a collection of his sonnets, he declared that poets should write in their vernacular* languages. Lorenzo also encouraged the work of other writers, and was a friend and supporter of scholars such as Giovanni PICO DELLA MIRANDOLA and Angelo POLIZIANO.

Lorenzo was a patron* of the arts as well. He commissioned works for public projects, such as Florentine churches, and for private ones, such as the decoration of his villas*. For one villa he purchased murals by Sandro BOTTICELLI, PERUGINO, Filippo Lippi, and Domenico Ghirlandaio. For another he obtained two bronze statues by Andrea del VERROCCHIO. Lorenzo also sent major works as gifts to the kings of Naples and Hungary. Through his leadership of the city of Florence, as well as his writing and his support of the arts, Lorenzo the Magnificent earned a prominent place in Renaissance history. (*See also* **Medici, House of; Medici, Cosimo de'.**)

Medicine

Renaissance medicine was not the same as modern medicine. Physicians based their understanding of how the body functioned in health and in illness on a set of theories that were very different from today's theories. Although they understood diseases well enough, Renaissance doctors usually could not do very much to cure a sick person.

Medical Practice.   A variety of people provided medical services during the Renaissance. The most highly trained were physicians, who treated disease. Surgeons, a separate group, tended to wounds and bro-

MEDICINE

* **apothecary**   pharmacist

ken bones. Apothecaries* mixed medicines, and midwives assisted at births. Most villages had "wise women" and "cunning men" believed to have a talent for magic or a divine gift for healing. Specialists such as bonesetters and tooth-pullers performed many of the tasks now associated with medical doctors. Quacks and sellers of fake cures were common. Traveling healers known as charlatans performed cures in public squares and used showmanship to sell medicines.

Many patients treated themselves or received treatment from family members. Housewives often made their own drugs and tried to cure even the most serious diseases. Patients did not tend to give physicians the final say on medical matters. They often questioned the doctor's judgment or called in someone else if they disagreed with his advice.

Most people received treatment at home, but hospitals provided care for some of the poor and ill. The level of care in hospitals varied greatly. Their mission included not only caring for the sick but also providing aid to the poor and housing disorderly people. They often excluded people with incurable or infectious diseases, such as plague* or smallpox.

* **plague**   highly contagious and often fatal disease that wiped out much of Europe's population in the mid-1300s and reappeared periodically over the next three centuries; also known as the Black Death

Governments paid attention to health measures only during times of plague. After an epidemic in the mid-1300s, some Italian cities set up systems to isolate plague victims and those who lived with them. Other European cities developed ways to spread news of plague outbreaks, restricted travel, and inspected goods. By 1500, Italian towns and cities, especially those that could not attract private doctors, had begun hiring official town physicians. They provided free medical care to the poor, advised local governments on matters of hygiene, and offered their services to the wealthy for pay. Cities in Northern Europe, such as Berlin and Amsterdam, also employed their own doctors.

The Care of Women. In the area of women's health—especially childbearing—physicians played only a minor role. Although male doctors treated some disorders, midwives usually examined patients prior to treatment. Except among the highest classes, midwives also managed most births. Women called in surgeons only in extreme cases.

Many texts on obstetrics (delivering children) and gynecology (caring for the female reproductive system) came from ancient Greece and Rome. These works often focused on philosophical topics such as the differences between the sexes and how human life arises. However, Renaissance physicians wrote a number of works on women's health, many of them aimed at female readers. By the late 1500s, works on obstetrics written by and for male surgeons began to appear. As a result, men eventually came to dominate this area of medicine.

* **classical**   in the tradition of ancient Greece and Rome

* **humanist**   Renaissance expert in the humanities (the languages, literature, history, and speech and writing techniques of ancient Greece and Rome)

Ancient Theories. The Renaissance passion for classical* knowledge extended to the field of medicine. By the early 1500s, humanists* had translated a variety of Greek and Latin medical texts. Important ancient texts included Greek works by the physicians GALEN and HIPPOCRATES. Hundreds of new editions of Galen's works appeared during the 1500s.

The basis of Renaissance medicine was the theory of humors, first developed by Hippocrates and refined by Galen. According to this theo-

During the Renaissance, doctors treated diseases and surgeons, a separate group, tended wounds and broken bones. In this 1443 painting of an Italian hospital by Domenico di Bartolo, a surgeon treats a man with a large wound on his leg.

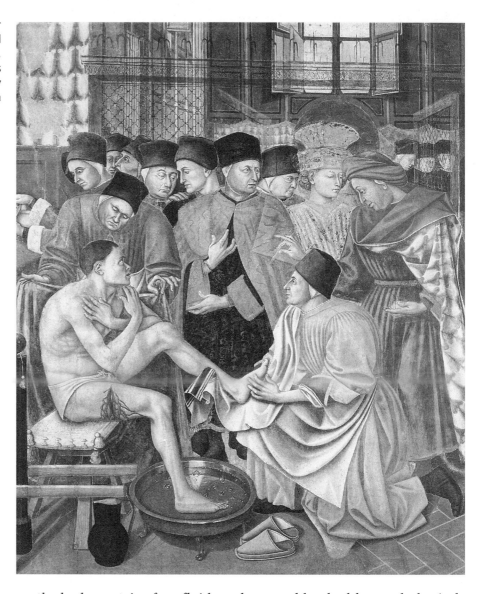

ry, the body contains four fluids, or humors: blood, phlegm, choler (yellow bile), and melancholy (black bile). Renaissance doctors saw the humors as representing different combinations of the four basic qualities—hot, cold, wet, and dry—that the Greek philosopher ARISTOTLE claimed made up the world. They also viewed the human body as a microcosm, or little world, that reflected events in the world at large, such as the changing seasons. For example, because they believed blood to be most abundant during spring, physicians routinely bled people at that time of year.

A basic principle of medicine was that opposites cured opposites. Thus, for example, doctors used "hot" remedies to treat "cold" illnesses. In applying this principle, doctors tried to account for each patient's individual temperament. They believed that each person contained a unique mix of humors that shaped his or her physical and mental characteristics. They tried to balance the patient's natural blend of humors

The Struggle to Live

Poor sanitation, malnutrition, and disease made life during the Renaissance much more uncertain than it is today. About 25 percent of infants who survived birth died within a year. Half of all people died by age 15, and few could expect to live more than 35 to 45 years. People survived longer in rural areas than in overcrowded poor areas of towns, where diseases such as smallpox, measles, and influenza spread quickly. Plague, which broke out every 20 to 30 years, took many lives. Medicine made little impact on disease until diet and living conditions improved in the mid-1800s.

See color plate 9, vol. 4

* **alchemist** person who practiced alchemy, an early science that sought to explain the nature of matter and to transform base metals, such as lead, into gold

* **mystical** based on a belief in the idea of a direct, personal union with the divine

with medicine or food. For example, since they saw phlegm as a cold and wet substance, they advised "phlegmatic" individuals to avoid watery foods and to eat dry and hot items. However, few guidelines existed for determining a patient's balance of hot, dry, cold, and wet.

According to medical theory, the body was porous, or spongy. Humors could clog up the body and cause disease, which could then travel from one part of the body to another. Doctors sought to release bad humors from the body by means such as bleeding, sweating, vomiting, purging (use of laxatives), and blistering (burning the skin to raise blisters). Both physicians and surgeons relied on these theories and procedures. Besides treating illness, physicians gave advice on how to lead a healthy lifestyle, tailoring their suggestions to the individual. Many books on health became available to the public during the 1500s.

Sources of Drugs. All medical caregivers used medicines made from plants, animals, and minerals. Healers had used these items to cure disease since ancient times. A *simple* was a medicine that contained a single ingredient, while a *compound* might include many different items. Towns and universities built botanical gardens to raise medicinal plants, and medical professors sometimes took students on field trips to the countryside.

Many of the plants mentioned in ancient texts were unfamiliar to European physicians, so they conducted extensive searches to locate "lost" plants. Physicians also used plants and remedies found in new lands such as Africa, Asia, India, and the Americas. They adopted spices from Asia and American plants such as tobacco, sassafras, and guaiac wood. They had no trouble fitting these new cures into the ancient system of humors.

New and Old Diseases. European explorers unknowingly brought Old World diseases to America. Illnesses such as smallpox, measles, tuberculosis, and scarlet fever devastated the native people of the New World, who had never been exposed to them before. One illness, according to many scholars, made its way from the New World back to Europe: syphilis, a dangerous sexually transmitted disease. Doctors at first treated syphilis with mercury, which caused a host of horrible side effects. Later, guaiac wood became a popular remedy for the disease. Spaniards had seen American Indians using the wood for this purpose and made large profits importing it into Europe. Many people regarded new diseases such as syphilis and the "English sweat" (perhaps influenza) as God's punishment for human sinfulness.

Medical Change. The German physician and alchemist* PARACELSUS (1493–1541) and his followers criticized the theory of humors. They saw bodily functions as chemical processes and argued that doctors should use chemical remedies to treat diseases. While outwardly modern, the theories of Paracelsus were highly mystical*. He believed that heavenly influences could spread disease and that a physician's ability came from God, not from study. He advised physicians to learn medicine by observing nature rather than attending colleges or reading books. Paracelsus

also claimed that like cures like. For example, he suggested the use of walnuts to treat disorders of the brain, because the walnut looks like a brain.

Despite these odd features, the medical ideas of Paracelsus slowly gained favor after his death. By the late 1600s, Galen's ideas were in decline, and doctors increasingly accepted new chemical theories of medicine. Still, much of medical practice stayed the same until the 1700s, when the idea of the body as a machine replaced older theories. (*See also* **Alchemy; Anatomy; Hospitals and Asylums; Plague.**)

Mediterranean Sea

* **maritime**   relating to the sea or shipping

From ancient times the Mediterranean Sea served as a great highway, linking the lands around its shores. It played an important role in the Roman Empire, in the rise of Italy's maritime* cities, and in the expansion of the Islamic world across northern Africa to Spain. In the centuries before the Renaissance, VENICE and GENOA regarded the Mediterranean as their own special province to use and to fight over.

Economic Role of the Mediterranean. The economic importance of the Mediterranean Sea in the late Middle Ages was reflected in the prosperity of the northern Italian cities that controlled the sea. Venice served as the hub of European commerce throughout the 1400s. The most profitable part of its trade was in spices obtained from ports in Egypt and along the eastern Mediterranean coast. Venice also imported Egyptian cotton, Greek wine, North African grain, and other goods from around the Mediterranean in exchange for cash or cloth, usually from Germany.

Venice's maritime and commercial rival, Genoa, dealt in spices as well. However, Genoa was better known for its trade in silks, which came from China by way of ports on the Black Sea. Genoa also controlled the trade in alum, a mineral salt from the eastern Mediterranean that was used in the manufacture of cloth. The city exported alum to England and Flanders* in exchange for wool. From the mid-1400s Genoa's trade in the eastern Mediterranean was threatened by the rising power of the Ottoman Turks*. As a result, Genoa focused its commercial activity on the western part of the sea.

Ottoman Rise. The Ottoman Turks emerged as a major force in the Mediterranean during the 1400s. In 1453 they conquered the Byzantine* capital of Constantinople (present-day Istanbul). With control over Constantinople's harbor and shipbuilding industry, the Turks had the means to become a major naval power. Against them stood Christian Europe. Their main rivals in the eastern Mediterranean Sea were the Venetians, who had established a string of coastal and island forts to contain the Ottoman threat. The Turks broke this chain in 1480, landing an invasion force in Italy. Although they abandoned the invasion on the death of their leader, MEHMED II, they maintained the pressure on the Venetian bases in the eastern Mediterranean.

* **Flanders**   region along the coasts of present-day Belgium, France, and the Netherlands

* **Ottoman Turks**   Turkish followers of Islam who founded the Ottoman Empire in the 1300s; the empire eventually included large areas of eastern Europe, the Middle East, and northern Africa

* **Byzantine**   referring to the Eastern Christian Empire based in Constantinople (A.D. 476–1453)

By the mid-1500s the Turkish fleet greatly outnumbered that of Venice and its allies. However, the Ottomans knew that the key to maritime domination was the possession of bases in key locations. They captured Egypt in 1517, the Greek island of Rhodes in 1522, and the North African port of Tripoli in 1551, extending their control of Mediterranean lands from Dalmatia to Morocco.

In 1570 an Ottoman attack on Cyprus, an island controlled by Venice, led to a naval alliance between Spain, Genoa, Venice, and the papacy*. The following year, the Christian fleet soundly defeated the Turks at the Battle of Lepanto. Although the Turks built a new fleet and occupied Cyprus, they no longer presented a major threat to Europeans. However, for the next century the Mediterranean saw constant piracy, raiding, and naval skirmishes between Europeans and Turks.

By the end of the 1500s, Europe's economy had shifted away from the Mediterranean to the manufacturing and banking centers of England and central and northern Europe. However, for the two centuries of the Renaissance the Mediterranean Sea had served as the major route between the Western and Eastern worlds, the place where Christians and Muslims met in trade and in war. (*See also* **Constantinople, Fall of; Economy and Trade; Ottoman Empire.**)

* **papacy**   office and authority of the pope

Mehmed II

1432–1481
Ottoman sultan

* **Ottoman Turks**   Turkish followers of Islam who founded the Ottoman Empire in the 1300s; the empire eventually included large areas of eastern Europe, the Middle East, and northern Africa

* **Byzantine Empire**   Eastern Christian Empire based in Constantinople (A.D. 476–1453)

Known as "the Conqueror," Mehmed II led the Ottoman Turks* in their victory over the Byzantine Empire* and in their expansion westward. In 1453 Mehmed's forces captured the Byzantine capital of Constantinople, then went on to conquer Serbia, Bosnia, Herzegovina, and Greece. This great triumph of Ottoman power came against weak opponents, however, and Mehmed did not succeed in attempts to take over Albania, Montenegro, Crete, or Cyprus. In 1480 he alarmed Christian Europe by landing troops in Italy, but this action did not lead anywhere. Mehmed also seized large areas of land in what are now southern Ukraine and northeastern Turkey.

The significance of Mehmed II rests as much on his internal policies as on his military achievements. He laid the foundation for a stable structure of the Ottoman Empire by reorganizing the existing legal system. He conquered many Christian lands, but he allowed Christians in the empire to practice their faith and to have a fair degree of independence. (*See also* **Ottoman Empire.**)

Melanchthon, Philipp

1497–1560
Scholar and Lutheran reformer

Philipp Melanchthon was an important figure in the world of education and humanism* in Germany. He founded schools throughout Germany and wrote several works on scholarly subjects. In addition, he played a key role in the Protestant Reformation*, first as a supporter of Martin LUTHER and later as a Protestant leader.

In 1509 Melanchthon studied at a Latin school, where he quickly mastered both Latin and Greek. At the age of 14, he received a bachelor of arts degree from the University of Heidelberg. Three years later

MEMLING, HANS

* **humanism** Renaissance cultural movement promoting the study of the humanities (the languages, literature, and history of ancient Greece and Rome) as a guide to living

* **Protestant Reformation** religious movement that began in the 1500s as a protest against certain practices of the Roman Catholic Church and eventually led to the establishment of a variety of Protestant churches

* **classical** in the tradition of ancient Greece and Rome

* **rhetoric** art of speaking or writing effectively

* **theologian** person who studies religion and the nature of God

Melanchthon received a master's degree at the University of Tübingen. While at Tübingen, Melanchthon produced his first scholarly work, an edition of plays by the ancient Roman author Terence.

In 1518 Melanchthon became the first professor of Greek at the University of Wittenberg, where he taught for the rest of his life. Melanchthon was determined to reform the university's course of studies along humanist lines. He wanted to alter the school's curriculum to include courses in the classical* languages of Greek, ancient Latin, and Hebrew. He also emphasized the need for courses in humanistic disciplines such as rhetoric* and history. Melanchthon's efforts changed education throughout Germany. In 1525 he helped found a new Latin school in Nürnberg, and he established similar schools in several other cities.

Melanchthon produced widely used grammar books in both Greek and Latin. He also published many texts by Latin and Greek authors for his students. His introductions and notes for these texts reveal his interest in such classical authors as the poets Homer and VIRGIL and the ancient Greek philosopher ARISTOTLE. Melanchthon also produced his own poetry, and copies of his letters appeared in print throughout the 1500s. In addition, he wrote one of the most important contributions to the humanities, *Principles of Rhetoric.*

Melanchthon won respect as a theologian* as well. Luther's writings greatly influenced Melanchthon. He blended his study of classical literatures with Luther's teachings, encouraging the study of the humanities as an introduction to religious studies. Melanchthon also produced the first religious textbook of the Protestant Reformation, *Basic Topics in Theology.* This work influenced generations of Protestants. (*See also* **Education; Protestant Reformation.**)

Memling, Hans

ca. 1430/1440–1494
Flemish painter

* **Flemish** relating to Flanders, a region along the coasts of present-day Belgium, France, and the Netherlands

Hans Memling (also Memlinc) was the first Flemish* painter to set portraits of individuals against landscape backgrounds. His skill in reproducing the real world made him a much-sought-after portraitist. Many of Memling's works have religious themes, and the Virgin and Child was one of his favorite subjects.

Born near Frankfurt, Germany, Memling went to Flanders for instruction in painting, and he may have completed his artistic training at the workshop of Rogier van der WEYDEN in Brussels. In 1465 Memling became a citizen of the Flemish city of Bruges, where he remained for the rest of his life. The artist worked mainly for wealthy merchants, foreigners, and the local clergy of Bruges.

Among Memling's better-known works is the *St. John Altarpiece* (1479), painted for a hospital chapel in Bruges. This three-paneled work contains scenes of the Virgin Mary, the infant Christ, and various saints. The warm-toned colors that Memling used in the altarpiece show the influence of Flemish artist Jan van EYCK. However, the slender figures were inspired by van der Weyden. Memling's paintings reveal great technical skill, but some critics have said that the artist lacks the expressiveness and insight of van der Weyden. (*See also* **Art in the Netherlands.**)

Mercantilism

See color
plate 2,
vol. 2

Mercantilism, an economic theory promoting government regulation of a nation's economy, was designed to increase state power and wealth at the expense of rival nations. German historians first used the word *mercantilism* in the 1800s, but many of its goals date back to the early Renaissance.

Between the 1500s and the 1700s, many European states wanted to expand business at home, increase foreign trade, and export more goods than they imported. For this reason, they established new colonies around the world. They also developed, supported, and protected their own industries.

The Renaissance marked the first stage in the gradual use of mercantilist policies. Three factors influenced the growth of mercantilism: economic problems, increased trade competition, and military ambition. Officials in major cities established policies that would bring in cheap food supplies and raw materials. They also set up regional market monopolies* to favor their own merchants and craftsworkers.

* **monopoly** exclusive right to engage in a particular type of business

Countries often used mercantilism to control and to protect their industries. England, for example, wanted to protect the sale of woolens, its main industry. As a result, in the 1400s, England barred all foreign wool and silk from entering the country. During the late 1500s, England used money and market restrictions to attract foreign artisans* to start new businesses.

* **artisan** skilled worker or craftsperson

In France, King Louis XI offered financial aid to his country's mining efforts and production of cheap woolen goods for export. He also supported silk manufacturing in France by stopping luxury imports from foreign countries. In the 1500s, the Holy Roman Emperor* CHARLES V tried to aid Spain's production of goods by forbidding the export of raw materials.

* **Holy Roman Emperor** ruler of the Holy Roman Empire, a political body in central Europe composed of several states that existed until 1806

Because many political leaders in the Renaissance also wanted to safeguard their gold and silver reserves, they stockpiled precious metals. Some even tried to stop the export of any gold or silver.

The effects of mercantilism in the Renaissance were limited. Few governments had the money to finance new industries, and those industries that depended on government funding often failed. Still, many of these attempts pointed toward future efforts by governments to increase national wealth and power. (*See also* **Economy and Trade; Taxation and Public Finance.**)

Mercenaries

A mercenary is a soldier hired to fight for pay for a foreign country. Mercenaries may be employed because of their special skills or their willingness to take part in activities that the state's citizens avoid. Sometimes mercenaries fight alongside a country's own forces. The use of mercenaries began in the ancient world, and by the Renaissance, mercenaries formed the basis of most armies.

Renaissance Mercenaries. The mercenary units of the Renaissance stood out because of their large size—several hundred to several thou-

sand troops. Estimates of the total number of mercenaries in Europe in the 1500s and 1600s range from 100,000 to 1 million. Sometimes mercenaries came from within the state that hired them, but more often they came from foreign countries. During the Middle Ages, a mercenary unit might include people from various lands. However, Renaissance states usually recruited mercenaries as a group from certain regions, such as Germany, Switzerland, or Italy. As warfare became more common and more destructive, the number of mercenaries employed in Europe increased.

The most popular mercenaries were soldiers armed with pikes or primitive guns called arquebuses. Units of artillery filled out the ranks. Heavy cavalry, or mounted knights, and gunners formed the core of Italian armies during the Renaissance.

The Mercenary Life. Men joined mercenary companies for a variety of reasons. Pay was the most obvious reason, although the wages that mercenaries received barely enabled them to make a living. However, other financial opportunities were available to mercenaries. Armies often sacked the towns that they conquered, seizing control over the city and its residents. Troops reportedly looted more than 20 million ducats after the sack of Antwerp in 1576. Taking prisoners and holding them for ransom was another way to earn money.

Mercenary life held other attractions, too. It offered adventure and a sense of freedom from the boredom of everyday life. Some men used mercenary service as an opportunity to indulge in violence and sexual excesses outlawed by civilized society. Although it paid little, mercenary service did offer steady work in an age plagued by underemployment and unemployment.

Mercenaries had a reputation for being undisciplined and difficult to control. In fact, they were usually reliable unless their pay was late or missing. In such cases their behavior could be unpredictable, from taking out their anger on the local population to forcing commanders to attack against their wishes. Even when they received their pay, mercenaries might disobey orders for their own reasons. For example, the leader of the Holy League army at the battle of Fornovo in northern Italy in 1495 ordered his troops to take no prisoners. However, many soldiers ignored this order to profit from ransoming captives.

The Italian political writer Niccolò MACHIAVELLI popularized the image of the undisciplined mercenary who avoided combat and fought only to collect pay. He also accused mercenaries of refusing to engage in real combat when facing foes that came from the same region. Like Machiavelli, many people questioned the loyalty of mercenaries. Critics accused them of changing sides at will and encouraging citizens to avoid military careers. Modern historians have shown that this picture is largely inaccurate. They find mercenaries in general to be loyal and skilled at the art of war.

Contract Fighters. The most effective Renaissance mercenaries were the Italian condottieri, named for their employment contract, or *con-*

dotta. The condottieri arose from the commercial success of Italian states that could afford to pay others to fight for them. They were also a product of the reluctance of most rulers to arm civilians. Condottieri leaders usually came from the noble classes, and the profits of war often generated much-needed revenue for their principalities.

At first, contracts called for a firm period of employment (the *ferma*) and an option period, during which the employer could renew the contract. The normal *ferma* lasted for three months. This system suited the needs of the employer and the seasonal nature of warfare in the Middle Ages, when armies went home during the winter. But as standing armies emerged, states faced a continuous need for soldiers. The terms of the contracts changed to meet this need, and some mercenaries served for extended periods of time. This often led to changes in the relationship between mercenary units and the state that employed them. Venice, for example, offered many benefits, such as property, pensions, and even eligibility for public office, to ensure the loyalty of its condottieri. (*See also* **Arms and Armor; Warfare.**)

Michelangelo Buonarroti

1475–1564
Italian artist

* **patron** supporter or financial sponsor of an artist or writer

* **apprentice** person bound by a legal agreement to work for another for a specified period of time in return for instruction in a trade or craft

* **classical** in the tradition of ancient Greece and Rome

* **humanist** referring to a Renaissance cultural movement promoting the study of the humanities (the languages, literature, and history of ancient Greece and Rome) as a guide to living

Michelangelo Buonarroti, a leading Renaissance sculptor, painter, and architect, is universally recognized as one of the greatest artists of all time. During his long career, Michelangelo worked for many wealthy and powerful patrons*, including nine popes and members of the MEDICI family. Some of his creations, such as the marble statue called the *Pietà* and the gloriously painted ceiling of Rome's Sistine Chapel, are famous examples of artistic genius. Although better known as a visual artist, Michelangelo was also a poet who produced a large body of verses based on his own experiences.

Early Career. Michelangelo was born in Caprese, a small town in Tuscany, but he grew up on the outskirts of the city of FLORENCE. He believed that he was descended from a noble family, the counts of Canossa, and this belief drove him to improve his family's social and economic status.

Michelangelo left school when he was about 13 years old to begin training as a painter. His father opposed his choice of career because painting and sculpture were considered lowly, manual occupations. Nevertheless, Michelangelo became an apprentice* to Domenico Ghirlandaio, Florence's most fashionable painter. From Ghirlandaio he learned drawing and design, skills that became the foundations of his art. However, Michelangelo left before completing his apprenticeship. In about 1490 he found a position in the large household of Lorenzo de' MEDICI, which contained many fine pieces of classical* and Renaissance art. During the next two years the young artist met many of the important literary and intellectual figures of the day. He also received the beginnings of a humanist* education, alongside two young members of the Medici family—Giovanni and Giulio—who later became popes.

After the death of Lorenzo de' Medici in 1492, Michelangelo spent several years working for various patrons and producing some sculpture.

Michelangelo produced many large and ambitious works of sculpture during the 1490s. His *Pietà,* carved from a single block of marble, remains one of the best-loved religious images of all time.

See color plate 8, vol. 1

Then, in 1496, he moved to Rome. Inspired by the ancient monuments there, he began to create larger, more ambitious works. One of them, the *Pietà* (1497–1499), consists of two figures—Jesus and Mary—carved from a single block of marble. The only work Michelangelo ever signed, it is one of the best-loved religious images of all time. Another marble figure, *David,* combined classical and Christian traditions by depicting the young biblical hero in ancient style. The success of these two sculptures brought Michelangelo public recognition and guaranteed him patrons for life.

In 1505 Michelangelo began work on a tomb for Pope JULIUS II—a project that dragged on for four decades, through six designs, and four contracts. Meanwhile, Michelangelo accepted many other commissions. In 1508 he took on a task of a different type: painting the ceiling of the Sistine Chapel in the Vatican, the headquarters of the popes in Rome. For four years he devoted immense energy and creative power to this challenging assignment, filling the ceiling with biblical and classical figures and scenes.

Between 1516 and 1534 Michelangelo worked in Florence on a variety of projects at San Lorenzo, the Medici family church. His boyhood friend Giovanni de' Medici had recently become Pope LEO X. Leo hired the artist to build and decorate a chapel at San Lorenzo to house the tombs of several members of the Medici family. In 1523 Giulio de' Medici, now Pope Clement VII, commissioned Michelangelo to design the Laurentian Library, an elegant reading room also at San Lorenzo. But in 1532 the Medici abolished Florence's republican* constitution. Distressed at the loss of liberty in the city, Michelangelo moved to Rome, where he spent the rest of his life.

Later Career. In Rome the new pope, Paul III, lost no time in employing Michelangelo's talents. He asked the artist to paint the *Last Judgment* (1534–1541) on the altar wall of the Sistine Chapel. Michelangelo also completed two large frescoes*, the *Conversion of Saul* and the *Crucifixion of Peter,* in the nearby Pauline Chapel. All three paintings depict scenes of deep religious significance.

In 1546 Paul III appointed Michelangelo to direct the building of St. Peter's Church in Rome. Although the building underwent many changes during its 150-year construction, it is largely Michelangelo's creation. The chief activity of Michelangelo's final years, St. Peter's is the largest Christian church in the world, an impressive symbol of the pope's authority, and the crowning achievement of Renaissance architecture.

During his later years, Michelangelo completed a series of major architectural projects that changed the face of Rome. He redesigned an entire district, the Capitoline Hill, turned the ancient Roman baths of Diocletian into a Christian church, and designed several other public buildings. Busy with other endeavors, he produced only three sculptures in the final 30 years of his life.

Personal Life and Poetry. Michelangelo had a large circle of friends and acquaintances. His surviving letters provide a view of a cross-section of Renaissance society in the first half of the 1500s. Always sharply aware of his own claim to nobility, Michelangelo was especially attracted to persons of high social status, as well as those of keen intelligence or sensitivity.

For many years, one of the artist's closest friends was Vittoria Colonna, a poet from an old Roman family. Michelangelo also had a significant relationship with a young aristocrat named Tommaso de' Cavalieri. His love for Cavalieri inspired the first large collection of love poems by one man to another in modern Western literature. Michelangelo also presented Cavalieri with highly finished drawings. Widely circulated and published, the drawings gained instant fame.

As a poet, Michelangelo took his role seriously, consulting literary advisers and revising his work many times. Above all, he considered poetry a vehicle for self-expression. Although he was less gifted in literature than in sculpture and painting, he produced more than 300 poems. In some he complained of the difficulties of everyday life, such as the discomfort of painting the Sistine ceiling or the pains of growing

* **republican**   refers to a form of Renaissance government dominated by leading merchants with limited participation by others

* **fresco**   mural painted on a plaster wall

The Role of the Artist

Michelangelo's legacy included more than his artworks. He also changed the way society viewed artists. Firmly convinced of his family's noble origins, Michelangelo managed to turn himself from a humble stone carver into an aristocrat of art. His way of life was that of a courtier as well as an artist, and he mingled business and friendship in his relations with his patrons. More than any other individual of his time, Michelangelo helped raise the status of the artist.

old. In others he explored issues of love and art. In his late years Michelangelo wrote on Christian themes and produced religious drawings, including a series of images of the Crucifixion. (*See also* **Art; Art in Italy.**)

Middle Ages

* **antiquity** era of the ancient Mediterranean cultures of Greece and Rome, ending around A.D. 400

* **humanist** referring to a Renaissance cultural movement promoting the study of the humanities (the languages, literature, and history of ancient Greece and Rome) as a guide to living

* **medieval** referring to the Middle Ages, a period that began around A.D. 400 and ended around 1400 in Italy and 1500 in the rest of Europe

* **epic** long poem about the adventures of a hero

The term *Middle Ages* refers to the period between the decline of the Roman Empire, which began around 400 A.D., and the beginning of the Renaissance in Italy about 1400. Renaissance scholars, who sought to restore the glory of the ancient world, generally dismissed this period as insignificant. They developed the term "middle age" to reflect their view that true culture had disappeared with the fall of Rome and that the years between Roman civilization and their own was little more than a gap in the history of European culture. Yet though the scholars had little respect for the culture of the Middle Ages, it continued to have a great influence on their thinking.

The Italian writer PETRARCH was one of the first authors to look back with longing toward the ancient world. He wrote of his desire to mix with the great men of antiquity* rather than the "thievish company" of his own day. Other humanist* writers echoed his call for a culture based on ancient literary and artistic models. The artist and writer Giorgio Vasari outlined three stages in the history of art: perfection in antiquity, decay after the 300s, and renewal in the late 1200s led by the Italian artist GIOTTO DI BONDONE.

Nonetheless, Renaissance thinkers drew much inspiration from the Middle Ages. Historians and legal scholars showed a keen interest in studying the medieval* period. Poets and writers also borrowed medieval tales and developed them into new stories. The epic* *Orlando Furioso,* by Italian author Ludovico ARIOSTO, was based on a medieval French poem called the *Song of Roland.* English playwright William SHAKESPEARE based his famous tragedy *Hamlet* on a story from the 1100s. In the field of religious studies, Catholic scholars continued to follow the traditions of the Middle Ages, combining them with new critical techniques from the Renaissance. Most artists, by contrast, broke cleanly away from the methods of the Middle Ages. Negative views of medieval art persisted until the 1700s. (*See also* **Art; Humanism; Renaissance: Influence and Interpretations.**)

Milan

An important Italian city since Roman times, Milan emerged in the early Renaissance as one of the five major powers in Italy. During this time the political and economic influence of the Milanese city-state could be felt throughout Europe. But the power and prestige of Milan faded in the 1500s, when it became part of the HABSBURG empire.

Society and Economy. Located in the fertile Po Valley, Milan occupied a strategic position between Italy and northern Europe. Agriculture played an important role in the city's economy, but commerce brought it prosperity. Milan gained fame for the arms and armor it produced, as well as for luxury goods such as silk, satin, and velvet.

Throughout the 1300s, members of the Visconti family shared control of the region. Giangaleazzo Visconti came to power in 1378 and soon turned Milan into a city of great wealth and power. As lord and duke, he enlarged the Milanese state considerably. However, he died of the plague* in 1402, and the years after his death were marked by conflict.

Francesco Sforza returned Milan to its greatness when he became duke in 1450. He was a skilled statesman who formed profitable alliances with the MEDICI family of Florence, the king of Naples, and the kings of France. These unions enabled Sforza to rebuild the administrative and military power of the state.

Culture and the Arts. Although other cities enjoyed greater renown in the arts, Milan was identified with some of the leading literary and artistic figures of the Renaissance. The poet and scholar PETRARCH spent time at Milan's court when the Visconti family began assembling a great library in the 1300s. Milan was also a major musical center during this time. The dukes supported a famous choir, which attracted important composers and singers from across Europe.

Milan became an attractive place for artists as well. The cathedral of Milan, begun in 1386, was Milan's largest and most important center of artistic activity. Because city officials wanted the cathedral to be the finest in Europe, they hired many famous sculptors and architects to work on its statues and stained-glass windows.

The Italian painter LEONARDO DA VINCI spent most of the 1480s and 1490s in Milan. He painted *The Last Supper,* one of the world's great frescoes*, on the walls of a Milanese convent. He also entered a competition to design the dome for the cathedral of Milan but withdrew before the judges reached a decision.

In the late 1500s, Milan emerged as a center of the Catholic Reformation in Italy. The bishop of Milan, St. Charles Borromeo, emphasized preaching, religious instruction, and education for the people of Milan. (*See also* **Art in Italy; Catholic Reformation and Counter-Reformation; Italy.**)

* **plague** highly contagious and often fatal disease that wiped out much of Europe's population in the mid-1300s and reappeared periodically over the next three centuries; also known as the Black Death

* **fresco** mural painted on a plaster wall

Milton, John

1608–1674
English poet

John Milton stands alongside playwright William SHAKESPEARE as one of the most celebrated English poets of all time. Milton wrote of his desire to use all his skill to enrich the English language. He viewed poetic talent as a "gift of God" with the power to plant "seeds of virtue" in the English people. He also promoted political and religious reforms and sought to advance the cause of liberty. For Milton, there was no separation between his political, religious, and poetic callings.

A Scholarly Life. Born to a Protestant family in London in 1608, Milton earned a reputation as a scholar in childhood. He began his studies at home and then attended St. Paul's School for five years. In 1625

he entered Christ's College at Cambridge University, and he received his master's degree in 1632. That same year Milton published his first poem, "On Shakespeare," which appeared in a collection of Shakespeare's works.

Milton soon became an accomplished poet in three languages: English, Latin, and Italian. In 1638 he left London for a two-year tour of Europe, including visits to Paris and Italy. During his travels he met with many noted scholars, including the Italian scientist Galileo GALILEI. While in Catholic Rome, Milton defended his Protestant faith whenever he heard it attacked. He returned to England upon receiving the news that a civil war had broken out there. He became a teacher and began writing works in support of political and religious reforms in England.

Early Poems. In 1645 Milton published a collection of his English, Italian, and Latin poetry. The volume contained odes*, hymns, sonnets* in both English and Italian, and masques (a form of court entertainment that combined drama, dance, and music). Some of the best-known pieces in the volume are the ode "On the Morning of Christ's Nativity [birth]" and the two companion poems, "L'Allegro" and "Il Penseroso," which discuss, in turn, the life of activity and the life of quiet reflection.

Another famous poem in this book was "Lycidas," a lament for the early death of Milton's college classmate Edward King. This piece fell into the pastoral* tradition in two ways, presenting King both as a shepherd-poet and as a talented pastor (who tended his flock) in the English church. "Lycidas" poses troubling questions about the ways of God, wondering what point there is in sacrificing pleasure to pursue a high calling if the virtuous person's life can be cut short so suddenly.

Milton wrote two masques (also spelled "masks") for the noble Egerton family, whose members acted out several of the parts in the entertainment. In *A Mask Presented at Ludlow Castle* (sometimes called *Comus*, after one of its characters), three of the Egerton children played roles, as did Henry Lawes, the composer of the masque's music. In this play the virtuous Lady—played by 15-year-old Alice Egerton—tries to defend her honor from Comus, who seeks to tempt her with wasteful luxury.

Major Prose Works. Most of Milton's prose works deal with issues of freedom in the home, church, and state. Several of them, such as *Of Reformation Touching Church-Discipline in England,* call for religious reforms. Milton's most famous argument for liberty—and one that may have inspired the founders of the United States—appeared in his essay *Areopagitica* (1644). The title refers to the Areopagus, the location of the law court in the ancient Greek city of Athens. Milton wrote *Areopagitica* in response to the English Parliament's decision to require books to be licensed before publication. Although Milton did not oppose all forms of government control, he argued that suppressing a book before it had appeared in print was a form of murder. He claimed that laws could not remove sin and that in trying to drive out sin, the law would also block virtuous works.

* **ode**   poem with a lofty style and complex structure

* **sonnet**   poem of 14 lines with a fixed pattern of meter and rhyme

* **pastoral**   relating to the countryside; often used to draw a contrast between the innocence and serenity of rural life and the corruption and extravagance of court life

Milton also wrote on the importance of learning in *Of Education* (1644). This essay claimed that the purpose of education was to "repair the ruins of our first parents" (a reference to Adam and Eve) by regaining a true knowledge of God. Milton urged teachers to introduce their students to "easy and delightful" books that would inspire a love of classical* learning. He also recommended a broad program of study, including ancient and modern languages, literature, mathematics, science, law, music, and a variety of other subjects. Milton also wrote important prose works defending divorce and attacking absolutist* monarchs.

Epic Works. Milton's most famous literary achievement is his epic* *Paradise Lost* (1667). This work retells the biblical story of Adam and Eve and their fall from paradise. Milton declared that his purpose in writing this work was to prove the justice of God's ways to human beings. The epic explores the nature of sin and human freedom. Unlike early church leaders who taught that Eve had sinned out of pride and vanity, Milton made his Eve a responsible woman capable of making her own choices.

Milton also breathed life into the character of Satan, creating a fascinating figure who has attracted readers for centuries. Scholars have viewed Milton's Satan in conflicting ways, either as an evil destroyer or as a hero who refuses to submit to another's will. In either case, Satan combines incredible energy with such human traits as pride, courage, ambition, suffering, and confusion. Although he opposes what he considers the unjust power of heaven, he does not offer anything better to take its place. Satan's rebel government illustrates the damage that earthly rulers can cause when they seek only to serve their own interests.

In 1671 Milton published *Paradise Regained,* a retelling of the biblical story of Satan's temptation of Christ. Like his Satan, Milton's Christ combines human and superhuman qualities. Satan tempts him by presenting him with moral dilemmas, arguing that he should use his powers to feed the hungry and to overthrow cruel and unjust rulers. *Paradise Regained* appeared in print along with another poem, *Samson Agonistes,* a dramatic version of the biblical story of Samson and Delilah. Like Milton's other characters, Samson is complex and morally unclear. Scholars disagree as to whether Milton intended this work—which is structured not as an epic but in a form similar to a Greek tragedy—as a companion piece to *Paradise Regained.* (*See also* **Censorship; English Language and Literature; Poetry; Poetry, English.**)

* **classical** in the tradition of ancient Greece and Rome

* **absolutist** refers to complete control by a single ruler

* **epic** long poem about the adventures of a hero

Mining and Metallurgy

Although the mining of metals has been practiced since ancient times, developments during the Renaissance significantly changed the nature of mining. Among these developments were an increase in the number and size of mining districts in Europe, economic growth that led to greater mechanization of mining, and greater specialization in the organization and administration of mining.

Economic and Technological Change. An increase in the pace and mechanization of warfare during the Renaissance led to greater con-

As technology advanced, new positions emerged in the fields of mining and metalworking, such as mine manager, digger, and smelter. This print shows a smelter wearing a safety mask while loading copper into a furnace.

* **Low Countries** region bordering on the North Sea, made up of present-day Netherlands and Belgium

sumption of iron. This, in turn, drove up the price of metal. Other economic activities, such as housing and construction, also enlarged the demand for metals and alloys (mixtures of two or more metals) such as lead, brass, copper, and tin. At the same time, the expansion of mining and metalworking led to concerns about a shortage of wood, the main fuel used for these activities. As a result, the Low Countries* began to develop their coal resources, and coal mining also grew remarkably during the 1500s.

The increasing demand for metal produced new mining techniques, particularly a more extensive use of machines. Miners needed devices such as blast furnaces, pumps to remove water from mines, and mechanical ventilators to supply fresh air. These machines often resembled those used in the Middle Ages, but during the Renaissance the

machines became the focal point of the production process. The use of machines significantly increased the productivity and complexity of mining and metalworking after 1450.

One result of the new sophistication of mining was the growth of a large body of technical and scientific knowledge associated with the field. The amount of specialized knowledge was too great to be mastered by a few individuals. This led to a division of labor in mining and metalworking. The leading work in the field, *On Metals* by Georgius Agricola, listed at least 25 different mining jobs, such as mine director, mine manager, digger, and smelter. The importance of mining to local economies also produced a large body of laws related to mining at this time.

Scientific Treatises. One of the earliest specialized works on metallurgy—the science and technology of metals—was Vannoccio Biringuccio's *On Pyrotechnics,* published in 1540. It described in detail the main techniques and equipment used in metalworking, as well as how to make glass and prepare gunpowder. Agricola's *On Metals,* published 16 years later, was the most thorough treatise on metalworking ever written. It described all aspects of the mining and metalworking processes in the tiniest detail and featured nearly 300 woodcut illustrations.

One of Agricola's most significant achievements was the introduction of standardized terms for mining and metalworking processes. By developing a single accepted terminology, Agricola made technical information about the field available and understandable to all readers. The success of *On Metals* led to the publication of other works on mining and metallurgy. The amount of published knowledge about the field eventually led to the founding of the first mining school in Stockholm, Sweden, in 1631. (*See also* **Economy and Trade.**)

Missions, Christian

During the Renaissance, explorers from Christian Europe made contact with distant lands and sought to spread their faith among the native populations there. The Spanish brought Catholicism to the Americas and the Philippines; the Portuguese worked to convert inhabitants of Africa, Asia, and Brazil; and French missionaries introduced Catholicism to Canada. Their efforts met with varying degrees of success.

Missions in Africa. The Portuguese undertook the first missions to western Africa. Pope NICHOLAS V granted Portugal the right to occupy this region in 1454, and a later pope put the Order of Christ in charge of missionary work in all Portuguese territories in Africa. By the early 1500s, Portugal had built missions in Senegal, Ghana, Benin, Angola, and Kongo. The people of Kongo readily accepted the new faith, and king Nzinga Nkuwu converted in 1491. So did his successor, Alphonso I, whose son Dom Henrique became a priest and then, in 1518, a bishop. However, the mission fell into decline by the mid-1500s because the Portuguese were involved in slave trading and were interfering in African politics.

Jesuit priests from Portugal traveled to Asia in the 1540s under the leadership of Francis Xavier, who worked with local people to help spread Christianity. This Japanese screen, dating from the late 1500s, shows Jesuit missionaries in Japan.

* **Jesuit** refers to a Roman Catholic religious order founded by St. Ignatius Loyola and approved in 1540

In 1561 Jesuit* priests baptized the king of Monomotapa in present-day Mozambique. However, he soon abandoned Christianity and executed the leader of the mission as a spy. Missionaries enjoyed more success in Ethiopia, which Portugal had aided in its struggle with Muslim neighbors. Many Ethiopians, including the leader Susenyos, converted to Catholicism in the 1600s. At first, the converts practiced a blend of African religion and Catholicism, but church leaders later tried to force a stricter form of Catholicism on the people. This attempt led to a civil war and the destruction of the mission there.

* **papacy** office and authority of the pope

Missions in the Americas. The papacy* granted the kings of Spain and Portugal the right to colonize the Americas, with the understanding that they would convert the native peoples to Catholicism. The

kings taxed their subjects to pay for the missionaries' travel and living expenses, as well as the cost of building churches and missions overseas.

Missionary work in the Americas began on the islands of Hispaniola (present-day Haiti and the Dominican Republic), Puerto Rico, and Cuba. It later expanded to Mexico and Peru. The first missionaries in Mexico arrived in 1524—a group of Franciscans known as the "Twelve Apostles of Mexico." Three years later Juan de Zumárraga became the first bishop of Mexico. He also brought the printing press to the region. The most active religious orders in Mexico and South America were the Franciscans and the Dominicans*. By contrast, the Jesuits led missionary efforts in Portuguese Brazil as well as in French Canada.

* **Dominican** religious order of brothers and priests founded by St. Dominic

The first missionaries in the Americas eagerly learned local languages with the help of native children. They also used pictures and music to spread Christianity. One missionary, Peter of Ghent, wrote a famous catechism* based on Aztec artwork. Missionaries built churches, hospitals, and schools and colleges to educate native youth. Scholars at these schools translated catechisms into the local languages. One of these became the first book printed in the southern hemisphere.

* **catechism** handbook of religious teachings

One obstacle to missionary work was the harsh treatment of native people under the *encomienda* system. This system placed the land and those who lived there under the control of Spaniards. In return for this power, the Spaniards had to instruct the people in the Catholic faith. In the early 1500s the missionary Bartolomé de LAS CASAS sought to defend the rights of native people. He helped to replace the *encomienda* with the *repartimiento,* which replaced outright slavery with short periods of forced labor at low wages.

In an effort to convert more native people, missionaries helped to found stable settlements called reductions. These settlements used European farming practices and tools. Many of them departed from the forced labor and other harsh measures of the *encomienda* and *repartimiento.* However, they usually sought to keep the local people separate from colonists.

Art and Faith

Christian missionaries often used European paintings and images to help teach their faith. In many areas, themes from European art blended with local styles. Artists in India copied religious images in wall paintings, miniatures, and portraits. The Spanish taught painting and sculpture to Native Americans, finding them excellent students. In China, the Jesuit painter Giuseppe Castiglione adapted Western styles to Chinese art forms. However, most missionaries looked down on local art as pagan in contrast to the Christian art of Europeans.

Missions in Asia. In the late 1490s Portuguese explorers brought missionaries to India. There they found a community of 100,000 people who called themselves "Thomas Christians," supposedly founded by the apostle Thomas. At first the Indians welcomed the Portuguese as allies against hostile Muslims. However, troubles arose later when the Portuguese tried to take control of the community from the local religious leaders. By 1533 the port city of Goa, which had its own Catholic bishop, had become the center of mission efforts throughout East Asia.

The Portuguese clergy members who accompanied early Asian explorers made little effort to convert native people. Their lack of desire to learn the local language hampered missionary efforts. The poor morals of Portuguese colonists also hurt the spread of Christianity. In the 1540s the newly founded Jesuit order began missionary work in Asia under the leadership of Francis Xavier. He traveled throughout southern India in the 1540s, learning and using local languages. In 1549 Xavier went to Japan, where he worked with local leaders to spread the Christian faith. He died three years later on a mission to China.

Xavier and other Jesuits accepted local cultures and customs, adapting them to Christian beliefs. The Jesuit Matteo RICCI founded the first missions in China. He obtained permission from the Chinese emperor to preach the Gospel and he converted many nobles and scholars. Another Jesuit missionary, Roberto di Nobili, worked in India. He adopted the dress and lifestyle of a local holy man and studied major Hindu religious works. Both Ricci and Nobili respected local practices. They viewed native customs as cultural expressions, not religious ones that presented a barrier to conversion. Alessandro Valignano of Italy followed many of these same practices as part of his work in Japan. Unfortunately, later disputes led several Asian rulers to persecute missionaries.

Protestant Missions. The Protestant countries of Europe did not establish overseas colonies during the Renaissance. However, Protestant leaders and scholars did express views on the conversion of native people. Unlike Xavier and his followers, Martin LUTHER rejected pagan* beliefs and practices. He saw no common ground between native religions and Christianity. John CALVIN, another Protestant leader, agreed with most of Luther's ideas about the missions. However, he also believed that Protestants had a duty to spread their faith. As a result, he supported a short-lived Protestant mission to Brazil in the late 1550s.

* **pagan**   referring to ancient religions that worshiped many gods, or more generally, to any non-Christian religion

Critical Views. Some Europeans criticized missions. The Catholic scholar Desiderius ERASMUS supported the concept of missionary work but condemned the harsh practices of many Catholic missionaries. He argued that they should befriend native people and should not try to profit from their spiritual work. He claimed that conversion should have nothing to do with colonization, slavery, or material gain. (*See also* **Africa; Americas; Asia, East; Christianity; Religious Orders.**)

Monarchy

* **Bohemia**   kingdom in an area of central Europe now occupied by the Czech Republic

* **Holy Roman Empire**   political body in central Europe composed of several states; existed until 1806

The monarchy was the most common form of government in Europe during the Renaissance, though monarchies varied greatly in size and type. In some—Scotland, England, and France—hereditary rulers held power. In others—including Poland, Hungary, Bohemia*, and the Holy Roman Empire*—rulers were elected. The variation in Renaissance monarchies involved social as well as political differences. While a few monarchies were made up mostly of people of the same language or ethnic group, the majority included a diversity of languages, dialects, ethnic groups, and regions. Sometimes, kingdoms united under a joint monarch. Poland and Lithuania formed such a union of crowns, as did Denmark, Sweden, and Norway.

Claims and Images of Monarchy. Many Renaissance monarchies made grand claims to power and independence. For example, the advisers of CHARLES V, the Holy Roman Emperor, assured him that he had the power of God behind him. Charles believed it was his duty to lead Christian Europe against the enemies of God, such as Muslims and

Lutherans. Many advisers at European royal courts helped advance the grand ideas of their rulers by supplying them with ancient Roman or Greek texts that supported such notions.

Renaissance kings and queens spent vast sums of money enhancing the image of the monarchy. Their patronage* of artists, writers, architects, and others served to glorify the reputation of the monarch and his rule. Monarchs wore magnificent clothes and finery to remind subjects of their power and majesty. They held elaborate pageants at coronations, weddings, and other occasions. Such displays of power and wealth occurred throughout Europe except in SCANDINAVIAN KINGDOMS, where monarchs adopted a policy of plain dress and behavior.

* **patronage**   support or financial sponsorship

Powers of Monarchy.   Some scholars have noted the development of a new type of state in Renaissance monarchy, one distinct from kingdoms of the Middle Ages. This new state tended to centralize power, end feudal* privileges, and increase the power of a bureaucracy* staffed by men of the educated middle class. Scholars believe that kings and queens either ignored or overpowered REPRESENTATIVE INSTITUTIONS of the time, such as the English Parliament.

* **feudal**   relating to an economic and political system in which individuals gave services to a lord in return for protection and use of the land

Many Renaissance monarchs no doubt had dreams of ruling without interference from nobles and assemblies. However, no Renaissance king or queen ever achieved absolute power. All had to deal on a daily basis with the complex workings of government and with political obligations similar to those faced by rulers of the Middle Ages.

* **bureaucracy**   administrative organization and its officials

Some Renaissance rulers took steps to control the church and the clergy in their lands. In the 1530s, King HENRY VIII of England attempted to divorce his wife, Catherine of Aragon. When the pope would not consent to the divorce, Henry broke away from the Roman Catholic Church and created the Church of England with himself at its head. Outside England, other Protestant monarchs also ruled the Protestant churches in their lands. In Catholic countries, rulers introduced policies that gave them great authority over church activities within their borders. In the late 1400s, the Spanish monarchs FERDINAND OF ARAGON and ISABELLA OF CASTILE appointed church officials and controlled the INQUISITION, the country's most important court. The French kings had the power to name bishops and to keep papal* messages out of the kingdom. These measures increased the loyalty of priests and nobles because the crown was the source of church careers and income for their family and supporters.

* **papal**   referring to the office and authority of the pope

Finding enough money to support their activities posed an ongoing problem for Renaissance monarchs. In the Middle Ages, rulers had depended on crown-owned lands to finance government. This was no longer possible in the Renaissance because of the huge expense of government. The cost of warfare and the construction of splendid buildings had soared, and patronage of artists and writers also drained royal treasuries.

Kings and queens met these financial challenges in various ways. Some raised funds by selling lands owned by the crown. In England and other Protestant countries, the ruler sold lands taken from the Catholic Church. Monarchs could also revive long-forgotten feudal dues or sell

state or church offices. In fact, many rulers invented new offices strictly for that purpose. Such sales opened careers to members of the middle class and reinforced the view of royalty as the source of authority. In addition, monarchs could raise funds by taking loans from banking houses. But at some point every monarch had to consider raising taxes.

Kings and queens seeking new taxes often had to obtain the consent of representative assemblies. Although rarely eager to raise taxes, such assemblies recognized the needs of government. As governments grew in size, rulers had to pay closer attention to the opinions of their subjects. They also had to acknowledge the powerful loyalties that people felt toward old noble families. At the same time, monarchs looked beyond noble families for skilled managers. Although this practice often created tension between the established ruling class and new civil servants, both played a vital part in Renaissance government. The old noble families, in particular, played key roles in governing provinces and leading military forces.

Monarchs, royal councils, courts, and assemblies all gained power during the Renaissance. No kingdom could function without cooperation among these various groups. Nobles dominated the military and politics, middle-class professionals contributed legal and administrative skill, and the king served as the patron and ruling authority of the state. Such developments marked a dramatic change from medieval feudalism. However, absolute monarchy was still a thing of the future. (*See also* **Government, Forms of; Nation-state; Protestant Reformation; Taxation and Public Finance.**)

Money and Banking

Money in the form of metal coins circulated freely in Europe during the Renaissance, and many of the techniques and institutions of modern banking emerged at that time. Italian merchants led the way in these advances. However, by the 1500s Italian banks had declined, and the center of banking activity shifted to northern Europe.

TYPES OF BANKS

Renaissance banks can be divided into three basic categories: pawnbrokers, merchant banks, and deposit banks. Each type performed distinct activities and served different customers, but their activities overlapped to some extent. For example, merchant banks sometimes offered savings accounts, while deposit banks at times made small loans or engaged in long-distance commerce.

Pawnbrokers. The smallest Renaissance banks were pawn banks, which lent money to individuals who pledged some form of personal property as security for the loan. Pawnbrokers charged interest on these loans, even though doing so violated the church ban on usury—the practice of charging interest for the use of loaned money. In many places the interest rate reached 60 percent. Early pawnbrokers were

Although most Renaissance moneylenders charged about 5 percent interest on loans, some charged as much as 60 percent. Artist Quentin Massys's *The Moneylender and his Wife* shows a couple counting money at their shop.

* **plague**   highly contagious and often fatal disease that wiped out much of Europe's population in the mid-1300s and reappeared periodically over the next three centuries; also known as the Black Death

mostly Christians, but Jews became more active in this line of work in the 1300s and 1400s. Italian cities, hit hard by plague*, famine, and war during this time, sought out Jewish moneylenders. Christian opposition to Jewish moneylenders led to the establishment of nonprofit Christian pawn banks that charged a very low interest rate. These banks later developed into public banks run by powerful local political figures.

Merchant Banks. Also known as international banks, merchant banks lent large sums of money and extended credit across borders to promote trade abroad. Northern Italian cities took an early lead in this form of banking, establishing branches in several European countries. A board of directors owned the company and hired employees to manage the branches.

The three major Italian merchant banks collapsed by 1345. The reasons for their failure included changing markets; unwise business practices, such as loaning money to monarchs; and poor organization. For example, the board of directors of the Peruzzi bank of Florence owned all the bank's branches. When one branch failed, the rest followed soon afterward.

A new generation of bankers arose in Florence to replace the failed banks. The best known of these was the Medici bank, with five branches in Italy and four in northern Europe. The Medici bank derived much

MONEY AND BANKING

* papacy   office and authority of the pope

* maritime   relating to the sea or shipping

* Low Countries   region bordering on the North Sea, made up of present-day Netherlands and Belgium

of its profit from providing services to the papacy*, and it had a more stable structure than the earlier banks. Each branch was run by a separate partnership with its own funds and its own set of books. The branch managers shared in the profits, while the senior partners in Florence owned about half of the capital at each branch. This meant that one branch could fail without causing the collapse of the others.

Merchant banks engaged in activities such as trade and commerce, foreign exchange, and maritime* insurance. Profit in foreign exchange came through the bill of exchange, one of the great banking developments of the time. The bill of exchange involved four parties: a deliverer and taker in one place, and a payer and a payee in another place. The deliverer lent money to the taker, who gave a bill of exchange in return. The bill was then payable in another location in another currency after a certain period of time. The bill specified a certain exchange rate between the two currencies. Profits came from hiding interest rates in the exchange rates, which enabled the banks to avoid the church ban on usury. Bills of exchange made it much easier to transfer funds over long distances without the risk and cost of transporting coins.

Renaissance merchants and bankers also made important advances in ACCOUNTING. New practices, such as the double-entry method of bookkeeping, made it easier to keep track of profits and losses, as well as increased trade activity. Italian merchants introduced this new system sometime around 1300. By 1500 it had become widespread throughout Europe.

Deposit Banks. Local deposit banks accepted deposits, exchanged coins, and made payments by transferring funds between accounts. The two main types of deposits were non–interest-bearing accounts, used by merchants to settle short-term business debts, and longer-term time deposits that paid interest to the depositor. Deposit banks rarely settled accounts by transferring coins. Rather, they adjusted the book balances of their depositors' accounts, enabling the banks to invest much of the deposits in commercial enterprises or to lend them at interest. This created the phenomenon of "bank money," in which a bank holds only a small portion of its total deposits in cash. Bank money is one of the foundations of the modern banking system.

While these practices increased the amount of money in circulation and promoted trade and commerce, they were risky. Investments did not always yield profits, and many banks failed because of bad investments. Deposit banks all but disappeared from the Low Countries* during the 1400s, and a financial panic in 1498–1499 caused most of the banks in Venice to fail. These failures led to the establishment of public banks, created by the government and run by public officials. Public banks could not make loans to private individuals or hold the accounts of private banks.

A shift in the centers of European banking accompanied the rise of public banks. Italian banks such as the Medici bank declined, while banks in southern Germany prospered. Financial problems in Rome and the failure of Italian banks to recognize profitable new markets con-

88

THE RENAISSANCE

tributed to the change. Jacob FUGGER, a merchant from Augsburg, ran the greatest of the new banks. German banks adopted an organization similar to the Italian banks and followed many of the same practices. Public banks, particularly those in England and the Netherlands, dominated banking after the 1500s.

MONEY

During the Renaissance people used three types of coins for money: gold, silver, and billon (silver mixed with a base metal such as copper). Most small transactions in the marketplace involved billon, while people paid rents and made large purchases in silver. Merchants and businessmen used gold coins for large international transactions.

A coin's value depended on its weight and the purity of the metal from which it was made. The popular and widely imitated florin, minted in Florence, consisted of 3.5 grams of 24-karat gold. Silver coins varied from the 2-gram Italian *grossi* to the Tyrolese *guldiner* at 31.6 grams. The amount of silver in circulation increased after the discovery of rich deposits in southern Germany in the 1400s. In the following century the Spanish conquest of America introduced large amounts of silver into Europe's economy. Silver pennies were the common unit of exchange for many people. Most pennies contained little silver, so they were frequently debased, or reduced to billon. Because debased pennies grew dark with use, people referred to them as "black money." Mints made little profit from producing pennies, which led to a shortage of them throughout Europe. (*See also* **Coins and Medals; Economy and Trade; Medici, House of.**)

Ghost Money

Renaissance merchants and accountants used moneys of account, or "ghost money," to balance books and keep accounts. These represented a measure of value rather than a store of wealth. For example, merchants' books in Italy listed account balances in lira, *soldi,* and *denaro,* but only the *denari* was an actual coin. The others represented imaginary units of money: 12 *denari* equaled one *soldo,* while 20 *soldi* equaled one lira. An exchange rate, which varied over time, existed between real coins and moneys of account. The introduction of new coins complicated the system. By the 1500s Europe used dozens of different moneys of account.

Montaigne, Michel de

1533–1592
French essay writer

* **genre** literary form

Writer and philosopher Michel de Montaigne played a large role in the development of the essay as a literary genre* in the Renaissance. His unique writing style and his ideas on the "art of living" influenced thinkers and writers through the 1900s.

Montaigne was born near the city of Bordeaux in southwestern France. He attended school there and later studied law. At the age of 21 Montaigne began his legal career, eventually taking a position at the Court of Justice in Bordeaux. However, he became bored with the law, and in 1570 he resigned to devote his life to reading, thinking, and writing.

Perfecting the Essay. Scholars before Montaigne had used the term *essay* to refer to a formal philosophical work. Montaigne was the first to apply the word to short, informal discussions in the style of everyday speech. He used this new form to test his judgment and to explore his views on life and on himself. The first collection of Montaigne's *Essays,* in two volumes, was published in 1580. A new three-volume edition appeared in 1588.

Through his essays, Montaigne tried to relate the experiences of his life. He combined personal elements with humor, a graceful style, and

* **classical**   in the tradition of ancient Greece and Rome

new and unusual themes. Neither stiff nor artificial, Montaigne's essays are full of witty sayings and stories—many of them drawn from his reading of classical* literature. The pieces show the influence of such ancient Roman authors as CICERO, Seneca, and Plutarch. Montaigne cleverly blended his personal ideas and concerns with the teachings of the Greeks and Romans.

The titles of Montaigne's essays reveal their wide range of topics: "Of Liars," "Of the Power of the Imagination," "Of the Education of Children," and "Of the Art of Conversation." In many of his essays Montaigne attempted to answer a basic question of existence that haunted him: "What do I know?"

Self-Knowledge. Montaigne's essays also captured the spirit of INDIVIDUALISM that arose during the Renaissance. He often discussed the art of living well. To Montaigne, happiness and knowledge exist within the self, in a person's everyday life and experience. He argued that to be fulfilled, people had to learn to know themselves. In "Of Experience," Montaigne explained his theory of self-awareness, claiming that "we ... go out of ourselves because we do not know what is within us."

Montaigne once stated: "I am myself the subject matter of my book." However, his individualism was not a form of selfishness. Montaigne saw himself as an example of all humanity, and he wanted to show the "universal being" of his individual self. He claimed that "Every man contains within himself the form of the human condition."

Montaigne's essays influenced many thinkers and writers who followed him, including the French philosopher René Descartes. A number of English authors also found inspiration in Montaigne's work. The English writer Francis BACON, for example, borrowed Montaigne's title, *Essays,* for his own collection of essays. In his play *The Tempest,* William SHAKESPEARE quoted directly from Montaigne's essays. (*See also* **Classical Scholarship; French Language and Literature.**)

Montefeltro Family

* **duchy**   territory ruled by a duke or duchess

* **humanist**   Renaissance expert in the humanities (the languages, literature, history, and speech and writing techniques of ancient Greece and Rome)

The Montefeltro family ruled the duchy* of Urbino in eastern Italy from the mid-1100s to the early 1500s. In 1369 the pope's representative forced the family into exile. However, church authorities misgoverned the state, and in 1375 the people asked Count Antonio da Montefeltro (1348–1404) to return as their signore (lord). Antonio added new towns to the territory and formed alliances with the rival Malatesta family through marriage. He maintained contacts with humanists* in Florence and educated his children in the humanist tradition.

Antonio's son Guidantonio (1378–1443), a successful general, took over the duchy after his father's death. As a reward for services to Pope Martin V, he received the duchy of Spoleto (south of Urbino) in 1419. Guidantonio married the pope's niece, and his son, Oddantonio, succeeded him as Urbino's ruler at the age of 16.

Oddantonio (1427–1444) proved to be an irresponsible and cruel leader. He took part in atrocities against some of Urbino's citizens and drained the city's treasury. Meanwhile, Sigismondo Malatesta—ruler of the neighboring towns of Rimini and Fano—encouraged the young man's bad conduct, hoping it would lead the people of Urbino to revolt. Indeed, after only a year in power, Oddantonio was murdered by a group of angry citizens.

* **illegitimate** refers to a child born outside of marriage

After Oddantonio's death, his illegitimate* half-brother, Federico da Montefeltro (1422–1482), took over. Federico ruled in the style of his father, Guidantonio, and gained a reputation as an outstanding leader. However, when he died, his ten-year-old son Guidobaldo was too young to rule. Even after he came of age, he suffered from ill health. Guidobaldo failed to produce an heir and the Montefeltro line ended with his death in 1508. (*See also* **City-States; Dynastic Rivalry; Italy; Princes and Princedoms; Urbino.**)

See color plate 6, vol. 3

Monteverdi, Claudio

1567–1643
Italian composer

* **Baroque** artistic style of the 1600s characterized by movement, drama, and grandness of scale

Claudio Monteverdi was a leading Italian composer of the late Renaissance. His music marks a transition from Renaissance styles to the new forms of the Baroque* movement. Some music historians have labeled him the first modern composer.

Monteverdi was born in Cremona, Italy. As a young man he studied composition with a well-known musical director. From about 1590 to 1612 Monteverdi worked in the court of Mantua, first as a member of the instrumental group and later as *maestro di cappella* (chorus master). In 1613 he became chorus master at St. Mark's church in Venice, a position he held for the rest of his life.

Monteverdi's career spanned 61 years, and musical styles changed profoundly during this period. Throughout the 1500s, Renaissance music focused on melodic lines, blending several independent melodies together in a technique called polyphony. Around the end of the century, however, a new, grander, and more complex style of music emerged. This new Baroque style featured instrumental support beneath solo vocal lines of one or more parts. It also focused more on emotional expression and less on "correct" technique.

* **madrigal** piece of nonreligious vocal music involving complex harmonies, usually for several voices without instrumental accompaniment

Monteverdi's music reflected these changes. Before 1605, most of his works were madrigals* for five equal voices. After that point, he experimented with new combinations of voices and instruments, as well as with new forms such as OPERA. Monteverdi raised this form to new heights, creating two of the earliest operas that are still performed—*Orfeo* (1607) and *The Coronation of Poppea* (1642). However, Monteverdi never fully abandoned the principles of Renaissance music. He produced some of the finest madrigals of the Renaissance, and toward the end of his career he also wrote motets (religious vocal pieces without instruments) and other sacred music. (*See also* **Baroque; Music; Music, Vocal.**)

Montmorency Family

The Montmorency family was one of the three families that struggled for control of the French crown during the Wars of Religion between 1562 and 1598. In time, the Montmorency became allied with the BOURBON family against the Guise, the third of the competing groups. The Bourbon sided with the Protestant cause, while the Guise remained unbendingly Catholic. Members of the Montmorency joined both the Catholic and Protestant sides in an effort to promote religious tolerance.

The power of the family suffered a long decline during the MIDDLE AGES but revived under Guillaume Montmorency (died 1531), who served King Louis XI in the 1460s. Guillaume's son Anne (1493–1567) became first duke of Montmorency in 1551 and expanded the family's domain. Under his leadership, the family gained control of land in central, western, and southern France, as well as its holdings in northern France and Paris.

Anne advanced the family's influence by securing powerful offices such as constable, governor, admiral, and cardinal for his relatives. He also sought to marry his children into leading families. His eldest son François married the daughter of King Henry II. Despite these ties to the Montmorency, the French monarchy sought to balance the family's power against that of their main rivals. Upon the death of Henry II, the Guise gained considerable power as uncles to the new king, Francis II.

When King Charles IX took power in 1560, his mother CATHERINE DE MÉDICIS turned to the Bourbon and Montmorency families to promote religious toleration in France. But the Guise resisted these efforts, leading to the nation's Wars of Religion. Although Anne remained on the Catholic side, other family members joined forces with Protestants opposed to the Guise. His sons François and Henri supported the Catholic side but called for tolerance toward Huguenots, French Protestant followers of John CALVIN.

* **heresy** belief that is contrary to the doctrine of an established church

In 1576 the Guise formed the Catholic League to fight heresy* in France and to oppose the claim of Henry of Navarre, a Protestant, to the French throne. Henri de Montmorency-Damville and his brothers urged Catholic opponents of the Guise to join the Protestant forces. In 1585 he allied himself with Henry of Navarre. This support helped Henry take the throne of France as HENRY IV in 1589 and end the religious wars in 1598. Henry IV's victory also increased the power of the crown at the expense of local nobles. Ironically, this growth of royal authority limited the influence of the Montmorency family. (*See also* **France; Guise-Lorraine Family; Wars of Religion.**)

More, Thomas

ca. 1478–1535
English statesman and writer

* **martyr** someone who suffers or dies for the sake of a religion, cause, or principle

Thomas More was one of England's leading thinkers and writers during the Renaissance. He held several high government offices and wrote many works on political and religious subjects. A devout Catholic, More became a martyr* for refusing to support the English king in his efforts to break away from the Roman Catholic Church.

Education. More was born into a well-to-do middle-class family in London. His father, a successful lawyer, provided his son the best possi-

ble education. More's father also had important connections: when Thomas was about 12 years old, his father sent him to live in the house of John Morton, a cardinal in the Catholic Church and a key adviser to the king, HENRY VII.

As a young man More attended Oxford University, where he considered becoming a priest or a monk. However, he chose instead to enter the London law school known as the INNS OF COURT. There More became familiar with the new humanist* methods of reading ancient Greek and Roman texts. Around 1501 he gave a lecture on *City of God,* a book by the early Christian writer AUGUSTINE OF HIPPO.

In 1499 More met the Dutch humanist Desidirius ERASMUS, who was impressed by the young More's learning and wit. Together the two men translated some works by Lucian of Samosata, an ancient Greek author known for his satires*. From Lucian's writings, More and Erasmus learned the art of using humorous ridicule to make serious points. More adopted this approach in his own writing, particularly his poetry, using wit and sarcasm to teach readers about the virtuous and sensible life.

Personal and Professional Growth. Around 1504, More married Jane Colt, a young woman from rural England. The couple had four children before she died in 1511. Within a month, More took a second wife, a widow named Alice Middleton. More made sure that his children received a proper education, and reports indicate that he also made efforts to educate both of his wives.

When Henry VII died in 1509, More wrote several poems that lavishly praised the new king, HENRY VIII, with whom More had been friendly in his youth. A collection of these poems was published in 1518. Twelve of the poems in this volume attacked tyranny*, and one expressed a preference for republican* government over monarchy. More argued that in a republic people could choose their leaders on the basis of reason, while monarchs rose to power through blind chance.

More also wrote a history of Richard III, an English king who had ruled briefly during More's childhood. More presented Richard as a ruthless monarch who murdered his two young nephews in order to keep his throne. More wrote one version of his *History* in English and a shorter one in Latin. In the English version, More mixed fiction and fact, even inventing conversations based on second- and third-hand sources. However, More was less interested in strict accuracy than in teaching a lesson. He aimed to show that people are never safe under tyrants, who will always bend the law to protect their own power.

Searching for Utopia. The discovery of the AMERICAS in 1492 inspired More to write *Utopia,* a story about an imaginary and ideal country. The first part of the book features a conversation between More and a Portuguese sailor named Raphael Hythloday, who has been to the New World. As Hythloday tells More of his journeys abroad, he expresses great scorn for Europe, with all its social problems. He especially criticizes the economic system that places wealth in the hands of a few people while many suffer in poverty, begging or stealing to survive. More suggests that Hythloday should become a counselor to a European

* **humanist** referring to a Renaissance cultural movement promoting the study of the humanities (the languages, literature, and history of ancient Greece and Rome) as a guide to living

* **satire** literary or artistic work ridiculing human wickedness and foolishness

* **tyranny** form of government in which an absolute ruler uses power unjustly or cruelly

* **republican** refers to a form of Renaissance government dominated by leading merchants with limited participation by others

MORE, THOMAS

In *Utopia,* a novel set on an imaginary island off the coast of Brazil, Thomas More described his concept of an ideal society. Ambrosius Holbein created this engraving of the fictional island in 1518 to appear in the front of More's work.

monarch, but Hythloday disagrees, claiming that most kings refuse to listen to good advice.

In the second part of *Utopia,* Hythloday describes a country called Utopia, located on an island off the coast of Brazil. In Utopia, private property does not exist and all people share the society's wealth. Every Utopian male must work six hours each day at a craft, and everyone must spend two years working on a farm. The nation has no king or central ruler, but an assembly elects mayors for each city. Elected coun-

94

THE RENAISSANCE

cils handle the business of government; one branch deals with day-to-day business and another with important matters of policy.

To modern readers, this perfect society has many disturbing features. Husbands and wives are rarely alone, because Utopians eat, work, travel, and spend all their free time in groups. Laws prevent people from having any private life or individuality. Private political discussions are crimes punishable by death, as is adultery*. The society also allows slavery, and brutally murders slaves who revolt. The state also controls religion. All Utopians must believe that God exists and that in a future life he will reward the good and punish the evil.

* **adultery** sexual relationship outside of marriage

Politics, Religion, and Conflict. More rose steadily in his professional career, holding a series of positions in government. He served as a member of the royal council, as speaker of Parliament, and as lord chancellor, the highest office in the English government.

More was a strict Catholic who, according to his son-in-law, beat himself with whips as a religious exercise. During the Protestant Reformation*, More became a strong defender of the Catholic faith. In a series of books, More engaged in bitter religious debates with the German Protestant leader Martin LUTHER. He also attacked English Protestant reformers and supported burning heretics* at the stake.

More's strong religious beliefs limited his political influence when England became a Protestant nation in the early 1530s. When Henry VIII made himself head of the newly formed Church of England, More resigned from his office as lord chancellor. He continued to publish anti-Protestant writings, even as the king sought to reach out to Protestants in England and elsewhere. In 1533 the royal council ordered More to stop publishing.

The following year More was arrested for refusing to sign an oath supporting all of the king's actions against the Catholic Church. He spent more than a year imprisoned in the Tower of London, steadfastly refusing to sign the oath. In 1535 he was tried, convicted of treason, and beheaded. Five hundred years later, the Catholic Church made More a saint. (*See also* **Humanism; Protestant Reformation.**)

* **Protestant Reformation** religious movement that began in the 1500s as a protest against certain practices of the Roman Catholic Church and eventually led to the establishment of a variety of Protestant churches

* **heretic** person who rejects the doctrine of an established church

Moriscos

In the 1500s the Spanish began using the unflattering term *Moriscos* to refer to Muslims who had converted to Christianity. Two royal decrees, one in 1502 and one in 1525, ordered all Muslims living in Spain to become Christians or leave the country. Almost 400,000 Muslims chose to stay in Spain as Christians.

Moriscos were fairly rare in most regions of Spain. However, they made up some 20 percent of the population in Aragon and one-third of the residents of the city of Valencia. Most of them were peasants skilled in irrigation or in raising cereals and tree fruits, such as olives and oranges, on dry lands. The Moriscos of Granada, in southern Spain, also worked in the silk, construction, and leather industries. Culturally they were diverse: many had lived alongside Christians for years, while oth-

ers had only recently come under Christian rule. Some spoke only Arabic, while others spoke no Arabic at all.

In the early 1500s, Spanish authorities tried to do away with many aspects of Muslim culture. They banned the wearing of traditional dress and regulated birth, marriage, and burial customs. After 1526 Spanish leaders used gentler means to persuade Moriscos to adopt the Christian way of life. Preaching by RELIGIOUS ORDERS such as the Jesuits* and Franciscans met with little success, however. In 1566 Spain began to enforce the anti-Muslim laws it had ignored for many years. This decision led to a Morisco revolt in the southern region of Granada, which lasted two years and resulted in the exile of 80,000 Moriscos.

Some Spaniards still felt that the Moriscos could be convinced to abandon their Muslim culture. Others called for more severe actions, such as deporting the Moriscos to the New World or even wiping them out completely. One proposed solution was to force all Moriscos out of Spain, but Spanish priests opposed this plan because they did not want Moriscos to settle in other Islamic lands. Noble landowners, who had come to depend heavily on the labor of Morisco peasants, also fought against the idea. Such resistance managed to block an attempt to expel the Moriscos from Valencia in 1582. However, anti-Morisco feelings still ran high in Spain. Some Spaniards accused the Moriscos of conspiring with Muslim and Protestant enemies of Spain. In 1609 King Philip III expelled the kingdom's Moriscos. About 350,000 people left Spain, most of them moving to North Africa. The expulsion severely damaged the economies of those regions that had once had the most Moriscos. (*See also* **Islam; Spain.**)

* **Jesuit** refers to a Roman Catholic religious order founded by St. Ignatius Loyola and approved in 1540

R enaissance Europeans did not generally idealize motherhood or give special praise to the role of mothers. The one exception, the widespread love and respect for the Virgin Mary as mother of Christ, did not carry over to mothers in everyday life. Fathers acted as heads of the family, supervising children's upbringing and making decisions about their futures. Death or desertion took fathers from many households, however, leaving women alone with children to raise.

Pregnancy. Society expected married women to be mothers. Most women became pregnant within a year of marriage, and a large number of brides were pregnant when they married. A steady stream of pregnancies usually followed, spaced two or three years apart, for the rest of the woman's childbearing years. Most women breast-fed their babies for at least a year or two. Breast-feeding reduced their chances of becoming pregnant during this period, as did social customs that discouraged sexual activity for nursing mothers. Women of the upper classes, however, often did not breast-feed their infants themselves but instead turned them over to wet nurses—usually peasant women whose own infants had died. For this reason, wealthy wives might have babies as often as once a year.

Infertility, a woman's failure to become pregnant, was a source of distress to married couples. Doctors assumed that the source of this prob-

lem lay with the woman, labeling childless married women as "barren." Some barren women sought help by praying to the Virgin Mary. Folklore also offered methods for improving fertility, such as eating crabs or wearing amulets*.

Most people did not try to avoid pregnancy through planning or the use of birth control. Prostitutes and courtesans* were believed to have secret methods for preventing unwanted pregnancies, but respectable society frowned on the idea. Abortion also had shady associations, yet it may have been fairly common. There was little concern about ending a pregnancy in its very early stages, before the mother had "felt life" (movement within the womb).

Birth. Renaissance women gave birth in the company of many other women. Female relatives and neighbors gathered at a birth to offer help, comfort, and social contact. Men, even doctors, had no place at the scene of a birth. The most important attendant was a midwife, an older woman who had borne children and received training in the skills needed to assist at childbirth. However, if serious complications threatened the life of the mother or the child, a male surgeon might be called.

Childbirth posed medical risks for both mothers and infants. The main cause of death for mothers was probably infection, usually caused by a hand or instrument inserted into the birth canal. Newborns also faced many dangers. Between 20 and 40 percent of all babies died during their first year. Half of those who reached their first birthday died before the age of 10. People at all levels of society, aware of the high rate of infant and childhood deaths, wanted their babies baptized as soon as possible, to protect their souls in case of premature death.

Bringing Up Children. Little information is available about the relationships between mothers and their young children in the Renaissance. In general, poor mothers had more and closer contact with their children than wealthy women, whose children often spent their first years under the care of wet nurses in the nurses' own homes.

Wet-nursing aroused mixed feelings. Both medicine and religion strongly urged women to nurse their own babies, and images of the Virgin Mary nursing the infant Jesus became very common in Renaissance art. In addition, many people believed that children absorbed character traits along with breast milk, which led to fears that upper-class children might acquire undesirable qualities from the peasant women who nursed them. Despite these concerns, however, many parents who could afford to employ wet nurses did so, either so that they could remain sexually active or for other reasons. Wet-nursing was a thriving and highly organized business throughout Europe.

Mothers tended to keep small children out of trouble by restricting their movement. They usually kept infants wrapped in "swaddling clothes," which kept them warm and prevented them from moving around. Most babies stayed in cradles near the fire, with a mother, a servant, or an older child keeping an eye on them while going about other tasks. Even once they came out of swaddling clothes, babies were not allowed to crawl or walk around freely. Children in poor households,

* **amulet**   small object or ornament worn as a magic charm to ward off evil

* **courtesan**   prostitute associated with wealthy men or men in attendance at a royal court

who were less strictly controlled, sometimes seriously injured themselves.

Mothers in Society. Mothers affected their children's lives through their family connections. Children, whether they lived in the village society of peasants or in the great world of nobles, benefited from whatever wealth and status their mother's family possessed. Maternal grandparents and other relatives could also make up an important part of a child's emotional life.

Mothers played a role in the inheritance of money and property, usually by passing property from their husbands to their children. The law viewed mothers not as the owners of property but as temporary caretakers, safeguarding it for their children. When a man died, his children commonly inherited his possessions, with a certain amount set aside for their widowed mother to use during her lifetime. Some men, however, made their wives their heirs, especially if their children were quite young.

Conflicts sometimes arose when a widow with children remarried, especially if she had children by her second marriage. Children of the "first bed" and the "second bed" frequently battled over their mother's property in court. In 1560 the French crown protected children of first marriages by setting limits on the amount a widowed mother could carry into a new marriage. (*See also* **Family and Kinship; Love and Marriage; Medicine; Women.**)

Museums

* **humanism** Renaissance cultural movement promoting the study of the humanities (the languages, literature, and history of ancient Greece and Rome) as a guide to living

* **antiquity** era of the ancient Mediterranean cultures of Greece and Rome, ending around A.D. 400

* **artifact** ornament, tool, or other object made by humans

Although interest in collecting artworks and historical objects began long before the Renaissance, the collection and display of cultural items took on new meaning in the Renaissance. In the Middle Ages, rulers often displayed gems and other precious objects to show their power and authority. They did not view collecting as a cultural activity. The idea of the museum as a place to house culture and knowledge emerged only in the Renaissance, promoted by the attitudes and values of humanism*.

With their passion for antiquity*, humanists encouraged collectors to seek out coins, statues, manuscripts, and other artifacts* from ancient Greece and Rome. Many early collectors, such as Cosimo de' MEDICI in Florence and Isabella d'ESTE in Mantua, kept their treasures in their libraries. By the mid-1500s the material considered worth collecting had expanded from ancient artifacts to items related to many fields of knowledge. For example, the European discovery of the Americas spurred interest in collecting natural and cultural objects from the New World. The use of the word *museum* for these Renaissance collections was inspired by the great Museum of Alexandria, which supposedly held all of the knowledge of the ancient world. The word also referred to the nine Muses, mythological guardians of the arts and sciences.

Renaissance collectors saw themselves as inheriting the role of ancient encyclopedists (collectors of knowledge) such as the Greek philosopher ARISTOTLE and the Roman scholar Pliny. Collecting allowed

* **classical**   in the tradition of ancient
Greece and Rome

them to see the changes in knowledge that had taken place since ancient times and gave them a more complete view of classical* culture. Eventually these private collections took on a more public and social role. By the 1600s, visiting the most famous museums, known as "cabinets of curiosity," became part of the travels of Europe's educated upper classes.

Despite the popularity of these private collections, few of them survived the death of their creators. Usually, the collector's family sold the pieces and divided the profits. As a result, people began to leave their collections to cities to preserve them. This reflected a growing understanding that museums should be public institutions run by the state.

However, the early state-controlled museums were not necessarily open to the public. For example, in the late 1500s Florence's Uffizi galleries were a set of state office buildings taken over by the grand duke Francesco I as a space for his favorite collectibles. The privilege of viewing the collection was usually limited to family members and diplomats. Only over time did royal collectors and governments see museums as valuable public institutions and open them to all visitors. (*See also* **Art; Art in Italy.**)

Music

During the Renaissance, widespread support for the arts led to a surge of interest in music. European composers and performers developed a rich and varied body of music that reflected the major cultural influences of the time. New musical forms emerged in France and the Netherlands in the 1400s and gradually spread to Italy and the rest of Europe. Musicians adopted these new forms and combined them with their local traditions to create distinctive regional styles.

MUSIC IN RENAISSANCE SOCIETY

* **patron**   supporter or financial
sponsor of an artist or writer

Three factors contributed to the growth of music during the Renaissance. First, wealthy patrons* supported the musical arts, especially at the powerful courts of Europe's major cities. Second, advances in printing allowed composers and publishers to distribute copies of new works to a wide audience. Third, Catholic and Protestant churches hired some of Europe's finest musicians to create pieces for religious worship.

Patronage. Certain European cities became major centers of musical activity during the Renaissance. In northern Europe, many cathedrals and religious societies supported groups of singers and musicians. The cities of Ghent, Bruges, and Nürnberg became famous for their musicians, and Antwerp attracted many instrument makers and music publishers. Musicians from these cities, such as singers trained at the cathedral choir schools, worked all over Europe. Wealthy patrons sought out talented performers, often competing for the most skilled musicians.

The courts of Renaissance rulers promoted music by bringing composers and performers together. The rulers of France, England, and the

During the Renaissance, singing and playing music became a fashionable hobby for upper-class men and women. Some scholars saw musical training as an important part of the education of all members of the nobility.

* **Holy Roman Empire**   political body in central Europe composed of several states; existed until 1806

Holy Roman Empire* employed musicians to accompany services in their royal chapels. Wealthy nobles such as the dukes of Burgundy spent large sums of money to hire composers, singers, and instrumentalists, and to purchase books of music.

In Italy, music developed differently from the other arts. The painters, sculptors, and writers active in the region were mostly Italians. Many of Italy's professional musicians, by contrast, had been trained in other parts of Europe. Music flourished at princely courts in Naples, Mantua, and Milan. In Florence, the House of MEDICI—the city's most powerful family—supported musicians along with other artists.

Music Publishing. During the 1500s, musical knowledge spread quickly throughout Europe, thanks in part to developments in printing. In 1501, Ottaviano dei Petrucci of Venice developed the first method for printing music. He published songs by some of the leading composers of the day. Around 1520 Pierre Attaignant of PARIS began using a more efficient printing process that drastically cut costs. Nevertheless, most composers had to find wealthy patrons to pay the costs of printing their works. As a result, many Renaissance editions of music are dedicated to a patron.

Music publishing developed into a successful industry, with major centers in Venice, Nürnberg, Rome, Antwerp, and Paris. Gradually, printed music replaced hand-copied manuscripts, enabling new music to reach customers more quickly. For example, by the 1590s, merchants in Gdansk, Poland, could receive copies of new pieces from Italy within months.

Role of the Church. The religious institutions of Renaissance Europe strongly influenced the development of music. Music played a central role in the religious life of most communities. In Catholic regions, religious leaders and organizations were major patrons of the musical arts. The best musicians in Europe played at the two papal* chapels in Rome, and Catholic monarchs hired musicians to perform sacred music at their courts. Composers also wrote religious pieces for special occasions, such as royal processions and weddings.

* **papal** referring to the office and authority of the pope

Music served a variety of purposes in Protestant communities. Martin LUTHER admired music, and his followers established a set of German hymns to be sung in church. In the Netherlands, Anabaptists who were imprisoned for their beliefs used hymns and sacred songs to support each other and to strengthen their faith. In England, composers such as William BYRD created an impressive body of music for the royal chapel of the Protestant queen ELIZABETH I.

Influence of Humanism. Various Renaissance scholars wrote about music, and they often turned to ancient philosophy for inspiration. For example, the Italian humanist* Marsilio FICINO drew on the ideas of the ancient Greek philosopher PLATO to discuss the role of music in human experience. Plato had described the human soul in musical terms. He believed that ideally, the body and the soul should exist in harmony. In *Three Books on Life* (1489), Ficino developed this idea, claiming that sweet music could create harmony in the human soul—and could even affect the planets and the stars. Many Renaissance scholars believed that musical harmony reflected the order of the universe. In their view, music could lead a soul to the divine source of harmony—that is, to God.

* **humanist** Renaissance expert in the humanities (the languages, literature, history, and speech and writing techniques of ancient Greece and Rome)

The thoughts of the ancient Greek philosopher ARISTOTLE also influenced Renaissance scholars of music. Many of them, for example, accepted Aristotle's view of music and all other arts as forms of imitation. They also agreed with Aristotle's claim that music had the power to inspire passions and to cleanse people of unwanted emotions.

Women and Music. Many European women contributed to the development of Renaissance music, although not always in obvious ways. Catholic nuns contributed to the growing musical output in many Italian cities. Female printers—such as Catherina Gerlach of Nürnberg— helped the spread of music. Women also served as patrons of the musical arts. Isabella d'Este of Mantua, a member of Italy's powerful House of ESTE, was a keen musician and musical patron. She played a role in the development of the *frottola,* a type of Italian song for four voices.

Some Renaissance scholars, such as the Italian writer and diplomat Baldassare CASTIGLIONE, believed that music was especially suited to

women. Castiglione claimed that music should form part of a noble education for both men and women. However, he also noted in his *Book of the Courtier* (1528) that the sweetness of music made it fitting for women. In Antwerp, the musical presses produced editions of works intended for women and girls to perform.

MUSICAL FORMS AND COMPOSERS

The rich musical environment in Renaissance Europe created many opportunities for musicians to practice their art. In cities and towns across the continent, composers produced new music for singers and instrumentalists. Their work built on the musical traditions of the past and, at the same time, developed new forms and styles.

Musical Forms. Several new musical forms emerged during the Renaissance. Vocal music was the most common type, both in the form of popular songs and in sacred settings such as the Catholic Mass. Renaissance Masses often involved the use of counterpoint, a form of harmony that weaves together several distinct lines of melody. This style of music, also known as polyphony, became increasingly common during the 1400s. By the 1500s, parts of the Mass were sung in four-part harmony.

Another major form of music was the motet, a Latin text set to music. The texts ranged from verses in honor of the Virgin Mary to lines marking a political occasion or honoring a prominent patron. Composers often wrote motets for religious services, such as memorial Masses. Many also wrote songs in the vernacular*, often for performances at princely courts. The madrigal—a complex piece for several voices—developed around 1530 and became the most popular form of nonreligious music for voices. Around 1600, composers began to produce operas, full-length dramas performed in song.

Composers. Many of the important musicians of the early Renaissance came from France and Flanders*. Guillaume Dufay (ca. 1397–1474), born near Brussels, spent many years working in Italy and for the duke of Savoy. He combined features of French, English, and Italian music to help create a new international style. The French composer JOSQUIN DES PREZ (1450–1521) worked for the dukes of Anjou and Ferrara, among others. In his many Masses, motets, and songs he developed new techniques that allowed the music to express the meaning of the text.

A leading composer of the late Renaissance was Orlando di LASSO of Flanders (1532–1594). Lasso held various posts in Italy and Bavaria and wrote hundreds of pieces of vocal music. During his lifetime he was the most widely performed composer in Europe, with groups as different as Italian nuns and German townspeople singing his songs. The Italian singer and composer Giovanni Pierluigi da PALESTRINA (ca. 1525–1594) focused on religious music. He worked in Rome, where he produced many Masses and other sacred works for the Roman Catholic Church.

Becoming a Musician

Most musical learning during the Renaissance probably took place on an individual basis, with a master passing the art down to a student. Cathedral schools in France, Flanders, and Italy offered some organized instruction. In the late 1500s, printers produced musical primers, textbooks to teach the basics of music. Trained musicians could find work at major churches or in the household of a wealthy patron. However, they could easily lose their jobs if their patrons died or fell from power, or if the church ran short of funds.

---

* **vernacular** native language or dialect of a region or country

* **Flanders** a region along the coasts of present-day Belgium, France, and the Netherlands

The last great composer of the Renaissance was Claudio MONTEVERDI (1567–1643), also from Italy. Monteverdi wrote a wide variety of music, from madrigals and motets to Masses and operas. He was one of the first composers of Baroque* music, which moved away from the strict rules of counterpoint to create a new, highly expressive style. (*See also* **Baroque; Dance; Humanism; Music, Instrumental; Music, Vocal; Musical Instruments; Opera; Patronage; Printing and Publishing.**)

* **Baroque** artistic style of the 1600s characterized by movement, drama, and grandness of scale

During the Renaissance, more music was composed for voices than for instruments. In fact, almost no written instrumental music exists from before 1500. However, there is ample evidence that highly skilled musicians played a wide variety of instruments throughout the period. Music historians have used surviving pieces of sheet music, as well as other sources, to learn about the different forms and styles of instrumental music played during the Renaissance.

INSTRUMENTAL PERFORMANCE

See color plate 15, vol. 4

Written music from the Renaissance suggests that the instrumental repertory—that is, the types of music performed on instruments—remained much the same throughout the period. Improvisation and embellishment seem to have played a large role in the art of playing an instrument. Improvisation means making up tunes or parts of tunes on the spur of the moment. Embellishment involves adding musical flourishes to an existing melody. Some written music appears to be for instruments alone. Other pieces were probably composed for voices with instrumental accompaniment.

Repertory. Throughout the Renaissance, instrumentalists performed several types of dance music. The earliest known sources of written music for instruments include dances called *estampies*. These pieces have several sections of irregular length, with each section repeated. Most written dance pieces from the 1400s were also irregular in form. This fact suggests that if simple, regular dance music existed at this time, no one bothered to write it down. Collections from the 1500s include various types of elaborately composed dances, arranged in groups of three. In the late 1500s, English composer William BYRD wrote several complex instrumental pieces based on earlier forms of dance music.

Perhaps the most common type of instrumental music during the Renaissance was the intabulation. This was an instrumental version of a piece of music originally composed for several voices. Composers often altered the original works, making the lower "voices" simpler and the upper ones more complex. Around 1530 abstract pieces called fantasias became common. These were often very similar in form to the vocal pieces known as motets*, making them hard to distinguish from intabulations. By the end of the 1500s, however, the fantasias had taken on

* **motet** sacred musical work for several voices, usually performed without instruments

MUSIC, INSTRUMENTAL

Musicians played a variety of instruments during the Renaissance. Popular instruments of the time included the flute and the guitar-like lute, both shown in this painting from the early 1500s.

* **lute** guitarlike stringed instrument with a rounded back

a distinct style of their own. Composers wrote fantasias for lute*, for keyboard, and for groups of melody instruments (such as flutes).

Composers also adapted chants—early pieces of religious vocal music with a single melody line—for groups of instruments. They generally placed the melody, with its relatively long notes, in the lower range. Above this ran a high harmony line, known as a descant. The descant was usually fast and complex and often had little relation to the melody. Playing this type of piece was one of the main functions of the organ in Renaissance churches.

Fantastic Forms

The word *fantasia* is a general term referring to a type of abstract instrumental piece, similar in form to the motet. Composers used several more specific words for different types of fantasias. The *canzona*, for example, was similar in style to the French *chanson*, or song. The *ricercar*, from an Italian word meaning "to seek again," repeated a theme in a systematic manner. The *tiento*, by contrast, was more relaxed in design than a formal fantasia. Keyboard fantasias were often called *toccatas*, from the Italian word for "touched."

To illustrate the different ways of adding a descant to a given melody line, composers produced pieces called *fundamenta*. The earliest *fundamenta* were for organ, but several printed books from the late 1500s showed how solo wind or string players could improvise on a melodic line. The *fundamenta* became the basis for a new musical form, the set of variations. In this form, a composer took a basic theme and altered or embellished it to create several different versions. First found in Spanish music, variations remained relatively rare until the late 1500s, when the form became popular among keyboard composers in England.

In the early 1500s a type of music called the prelude began to appear in keyboard and lute books. These pieces were usually very short and often served merely to set the key, or pitch, of a longer instrumental piece that followed.

Improvisation and Embellishment. Few records exist of the improvisations done by musicians of the 1400s. The available sources suggest that instrumental groups of the time mostly performed dance pieces called *bassadanzas*, which featured long notes in the tenor range. During the process of learning and rehearsing one of these pieces, some of the musicians probably developed separate melody lines that they played against the main tune. At the time, musicians relied largely on memory in performing, so playing without written music would not have posed too great a challenge for them.

The earliest written sources on the art of improvisation are manuals dating from the later 1500s. They explained how performers could ornament melodic lines. Lute and keyboard sources from the late 1500s also contain a large number of notes instructing the player to add ornamentation.

Instruments and Voices. It is not clear how often instruments were used to accompany vocal music. No pieces of polyphonic music (that is, music that combines several different melody lines) from the 1400s and earlier mention any instrument. However, most songbooks of the 1300s and 1400s supply text only for the highest line of music in each piece. This fact suggests that the lower lines may have been for instruments rather than voices. On the other hand, a number of descriptions of music from the 1400s state clearly that singers performed all the lines, while no descriptions exist of voices and instruments working together until about 1475. Also, the history of MUSICAL INSTRUMENTS seems to suggest that most instruments of the time were not suitable for taking part in polyphonic music.

These facts led musical scholars of the 1980s to conclude the polyphonic songs of the early Renaissance had involved only voices and not instruments. However, that idea is probably not accurate. Some instruments of the time—including the harp, the lute, and certain woodwinds—were capable of playing complex melodic lines. Also, in many songs, the lines that have text match the notes to the words, while the lower voices follow a completely different structure. If instruments played these lower lines, it would explain why they did not need to match the text.

Musical Terms

DESCANT—high harmony line

EMBELLISHMENT—adding flourishes to a melody

FANTASIA—abstract instrumental piece

IMPROVISATION—making up tunes on the spur of the moment

INTABULATION—instrumental version of a vocal piece

POLYPHONIC—combining several different melody lines

REPERTORY—types of music performed

TABLATURE—musical notation

VARIATIONS—different versions of a basic theme

WRITTEN SOURCES

Musical historians have gained most of their knowledge about Renaissance instrumental music from written sources. Sheet music of the period appears in several different types of notation, or tablature. The system of tablature in a piece of written music often indicates what instruments were used to play it.

Keyboard Tablature. The earliest known musical manuscripts that are clearly for instruments are all in a form called keyboard tablature. They show several different melody lines on a single page, with no accompanying text. Many of these manuscripts contain some type of letter notation in addition to the musical notes. The only surviving musical document from before 1400 is a fragment of a score that has the upper line in a musical staff with notes, with the rest of the score written in letters to represent the note names. Although no other pieces like it have survived, the notation within the text is fairly consistent, suggesting that the document—known as the Robertsbridge Fragment—was not the only one of its kind, and that instrumental music was already a well-established tradition.

The Robertsbridge Fragment contains three pieces that appear to be dances and three intabulations. Similar types of music appear in sources from the 1400s. The first substantial Renaissance manuscript in keyboard tablature dates from northern Italy in the early 1400s. Known as the Faenza Codex, it contains nearly 50 pieces, mostly versions of French and Italian songs, with some dances and pieces of church music. Another large source, the Buxheim Organbook, dates from the mid-1400s in southern Germany. This book contains over 250 pieces, as well as a long series of examples of musical embellishments.

Although these documents all appear in a form commonly known as "keyboard" tablature, it is not clear that they were actually written for the keyboard. The Faenza Codex, for example, contains several passages of overlapping "voices" that would be almost impossible to perform on a single keyboard instrument. The only specific information about instruments in any of these early sources is a statement above one of the pieces in the Buxheim Organbook, which describes it as "for stringed instruments or also for organ." Overall, it seems likely that many types of instruments could have used these early "keyboard" sources.

The first music that is clearly for keyboard instruments dates from the early 1500s in England. Composers such as William Byrd produced a body of music for the virginal, a type of small harpsichord. These pieces are musically ambitious and technically challenging, and they seem to reflect a style that is unique to the keyboard.

Lute Tablature. Unlike early keyboard pieces, early lute tablature leaves no doubt about its purpose. It includes instructions for the player on where to finger the strings, making the pieces unusable for any instrument other than the lute. Although lutes are known to have existed in western Europe as early as the 1200s, lute tablature did not appear until the late 1400s.

The earliest substantial body of European lute music appears in a series of lutebooks printed in Venice from 1507 onward. Over the course of the 1500s, more than 200 lutebooks were published—much more than any other form of instrumental music. Much of this early lute music requires great technical skill on the part of the musician. All the early collections of lute music focus on the same few genres. They include simple dance music, intabulations, preludes, fantasias, and accompaniments for vocal songs.

By the 1530s, the lute had become the leading instrument of the Renaissance. Famous lute players earned high praise for their skill. A number of these musicians left large collections of their works for lute. Around 1523, a series of popular printed lutebooks in Germany started a tradition of music that was much easier to play. These works appear to have reached a large audience.

Ensemble Sources. Many pieces of Renaissance music appear in ordinary staff notation, making it unclear whether they were written for voices or instruments. However, some musical manuscripts have little or no text added to the music, suggesting that these pieces were for groups of instruments rather than for voices. Documents of this type became much more common around 1480. For example, a set of three songbooks published in Venice in the early 1500s contains almost 300 pieces, nearly all without text beyond a few opening words.

Many of the songs from these three books survive in other versions with text, suggesting that they were originally written for voices. Others, however, seem designed specifically for instrumental groups. Unlike earlier works for instruments, these pieces weave melody lines together in a clear, structured pattern. This suggests that the instrumental style of the 1400s, which relied heavily on improvisation, was giving way to more established forms.

This more formal style, however, does not appear to have taken root. After about 1510, most published works for instrumental groups are either very simple dance pieces or fantasias. Partbooks—sets of books that contain the music for only one instrument in each—were also common at this time. The most striking partbooks from the Renaissance are two manuscript sets from the 1550s and 1560s, which seem to have belonged to wind players at the royal court of Denmark. These two sets of manuscript contain over 300 pieces, including church music, motets, and various types of nonreligious songs. (*See also* **Dance; Music; Music, Vocal.**)

Music, Vocal

Singing played a vital role in Renaissance culture, both as a form of religious worship and as a form of entertainment. Between 1400 and 1600, singers and composers flocked to the great courts and cathedrals of Europe. At the same time, music publishers produced many editions of new songs and choral pieces. Vocal works became increasingly complex as composers wrote more elaborate harmonies and strove to express a wide range of ideas through music.

SACRED VOCAL MUSIC

The Roman Catholic Church had a long tradition of vocal music. In many cathedrals and royal chapels, choirs sang during regular services as well as on special occasions. Some religious institutions commissioned composers to create music for their choirs. When Protestant churches formed in the late Renaissance, many of them also adopted singing as a form of worship.

Gregorian Chant. During the Middle Ages, the main form of music sung in the Roman Catholic Church was Gregorian chant, a type of song with a single melody line, no harmony, and a relatively free rhythm. By the mid-1300s, an enormous body of chants existed. Choirboys began their training by learning to sing chants, eventually memorizing all the melodies used by the church during the year. Because most Renaissance composers made their living as singers in religious institutions, they also became extremely familiar with Gregorian chant. For this reason, much of the music produced during the Renaissance was heavily influenced by chant melodies.

In the late 1500s, Catholic Church officials tried to revise the melodies of many Gregorian chants, claiming that the form had decayed over time. A commission appointed by Pope Gregory XIII (reigned 1572–1585) produced a new edition of all the chants, removing certain features—such as extra notes sung over short syllables—that were viewed as incorrect. However, the church never really enforced the use of the revised melodies.

The Motet. During the Renaissance, more composers began producing polyphonic music, which contained more than one melody line. One of the major forms of polyphonic religious music was the motet, a musical setting of a given text. The earliest motets featured two voices singing fast-paced melodies over a slow-moving tenor.

During the 1400s, composers began to write motets for four voices singing at the same speed. One of the great composers of the four-part motet was JOSQUIN DES PREZ (ca. 1450–1521) of France, who wrote more than 50 motets. He developed the technique of introducing each line of the text with a short musical segment, sung by all the voices in sequence.

By the middle of the 1500s, the motet had become the most popular form of sacred vocal music in Europe. Some composers produced 200 or more motets, either taking their texts directly from the liturgy (the text of the religious service) or creating new lyrics. Music publishers produced volumes of motets to meet the demand for new pieces.

The Mass. In the Catholic Church, vocal music centered around the Mass, particularly the Ordinary, the parts of the service that do not change from day to day. During the 1400s, musical settings of the Ordinary of the Mass developed from short, isolated pieces into full-length works covering all five parts of the service.

Vocal music grew more complex during the Renaissance, often involving several voices or even several choirs. This sculpture by Luca Della Robbia is part of a larger piece called *Cantoria* or "singing gallery," which was originally displayed at the cathedral of Florence in the 1430s.

* **motif** theme or subject

* **Flemish** relating to Flanders, a region along the coasts of present-day Belgium, France, and the Netherlands

Composers found different methods of connecting five parts of the Mass (Kyrie, Gloria, Credo, Sanctus, and Agnus Dei). Some introduced each section with the same musical motif*. Others used a given melody, known as the cantus firmus, in all five sections, varying the rest of the composition around it. The cantus firmus was usually sung by the tenor voice in the choir. In England, where the five-movement Mass first emerged, the composer often borrowed a melody from Gregorian chant to use throughout the work. Later, Flemish* composer Guillaume Dufay (ca. 1397–1474) and others adapted tunes from nonreligious works as the basis for Masses. The use of the cantus firmus varied, with some

composers moving this melody from the tenor voice to other sections of the choir.

Other Sacred Forms. Renaissance composers created several other types of music for use in religious settings. Hymns, songs of praise containing many verses, appeared throughout the year. They often followed an alternating pattern, with half the verses sung in polyphony and half in Gregorian chant. The Magnificat (a song of praise to the Virgin Mary) and the Psalms also inspired many polyphonic pieces.

In the 1500s, composers began creating works for two or more choirs to sing in an alternating pattern. By 1600, this style, known as polychoral music, had spread throughout Europe. The performances could involve as many as four choirs accompanied by instruments, creating a monumental effect.

When the Protestant Reformation* spread across northern Europe it influenced the use of sacred music in many countries. Some Protestant leaders allowed polyphonic music in their churches. The German reformer Martin LUTHER (1483–1546) created a new type of vocal work called the chorale—usually a song of praise in the vernacular*. He wrote a number of chorales (such as "A Mighty Fortress Is Our God") and encouraged composers to create polyphonic settings for them. The chorale became the basis of the music used in Lutheran churches.

By contrast, the French reformer John CALVIN (1509–1564) rejected most religious music, permitting only simple vocal settings of the Psalms. He published several books of psalms set to music, which had a tremendous impact on church music. Many of the pieces were later sung in Protestant churches in Germany, Holland, England, Scotland, and America.

SECULAR VOCAL MUSIC

Styles of secular (nonreligious) vocal music changed greatly in the 1400s and 1500s. The rigid structures developed in the Middle Ages gave way to more expressive and personal forms. The two most popular types of secular songs—the French chanson and the Italian madrigal—were based on lyric poetry*.

Chansons. The chanson, defined simply as a song with French words, rose to popularity in the 1400s. Composers all over Europe took poems with several stanzas* and set them to music, usually writing parts for three solo voices. The highest voice sang the main melody line, and the two lower voices sang supporting melodies. Instrumentalists sometimes played along with one or more of the voices or even replaced them.

Many of the great chanson composers, such as Guillaume Dufay, came from Flanders. Dufay wrote more than 70 chansons, mostly based on love poems. Although some of the Flemish musicians remained in northern Europe, many took positions in Italy at princely courts or at the papal* chapel. As a result, Italy developed a brilliant musical culture superior in many ways to that of Spain, France, England, and Germany in the early Renaissance.

* **Protestant Reformation** religious movement that began in the 1500s as a protest against certain practices of the Roman Catholic Church and eventually led to the establishment of a variety of Protestant churches

* **vernacular** native language or dialect of a region or country

* **lyric poetry** verse that expresses feelings and thoughts rather than telling a story

* **stanza** section of a poem; specifically, a grouping of lines into a recurring pattern determined by meter or rhyme scheme

* **papal** referring to the office and authority of the pope

* **classical** in the tradition of ancient Greece and Rome

After 1520, a simpler and more elegant type of chanson developed in Paris. The French chanson had a graceful melody that harmonized with chords sung by the three lower voices. The music closely followed the rhythm of the poetic text, with one note for each syllable. French composers such as Clément Janequin, Claudin de Sermisy, and Pierre Certon produced songs of this type.

Some French chansons were linked to a particular scene or event. One song by Janequin vividly described a battle, complete with trumpet fanfares, battle cries, and cannon fire. In the late 1500s, Claude Le Jeune composed chansons to texts by members of the Pléiade, a group of seven French poets who sought to imitate classical* poetry. Le Jeune's songs closely followed the rhythm patterns of the poems, using long notes for long syllables and short notes for short syllables. This approach, which resulted in an irregular rhythm, influenced French composers for the rest of the 1500s.

Madrigals. The madrigal first appeared in Italy in the 1500s, and it soon took the place of the French chanson as the most important Renaissance musical form. The madrigal grew out of another Italian form, the *frottola*. Popular in northern Italy from about 1480 to 1520, the *frottola* was usually based on a light, entertaining poem. It had four vocal parts, with the highest and lowest voices singing the more important melodies and the two middle voices filling in the harmony. During the early 1500s, serious poetry became increasingly popular at court. As a result, madrigals based on literary texts gradually replaced the *frottola*.

In the madrigal the four vocal parts were equally important, and each voice sang the entire text. Composers used the music to express the meaning and changing moods of the poem. Musically, the madrigal resembled the motet, which also involved four equal vocal parts. However, unlike the motet, the madrigal did not have a religious theme. Some madrigals—especially in Italy—maintained the lighter tone of the *frottola*. In time, however, composers in France and the Netherlands developed more serious, complex madrigals.

* **imagery** pictorial quality of a literary work, achieved through words

In the mid-1500s, composers added a fifth voice to the madrigal, and the music began to reflect the imagery* of the words more clearly. For example, high and low musical tones in the melody represented the ideas of "highness" and "lowness." The melody might also mirror actions—falling, climbing, or rising—mentioned in the text. As the poetry became more dramatic, composers used complex harmonies to reflect powerful emotions.

The madrigal reached its peak in the late 1500s and early 1600s. Musicians continued to look for the best ways of expressing the meaning and mood of the text through music. In Italy, composers such as Carlo Gesualdo and Claudio MONTEVERDI added new features to the form, such as rich and varied harmonies, solos, and instrumental accompaniment. However, some of these features conflicted with the basic idea of the madrigal as a balanced work for four or five voices.

At about the same time, audiences at the Italian courts (especially Ferrara, Mantua, and Florence) developed a preference for music that

Music in Many Languages

Most Renaissance religious music was sung in Latin. However, composers also produced sacred songs in their local languages. Examples include the carol (a song of praise or joy) in England and the *noël* (a Christmas song) in France. In Italy, singers performed the *lauda,* a song of praise, in Italian. Most *laude* were religious poems set to music for two or more voices. They became popular in cities such as Florence, Venice, and Rome, where religious organizations encouraged the development of sacred vocal music.

featured outstanding solo singers. This trend helped bring about the decline of the madrigal in Italy. It also paved the way for the growth of other vocal music forms—such as OPERA—that placed more emphasis on soloists.

Meanwhile, the madrigal remained popular in other parts of Europe, particularly England, Germany, Denmark, Poland, and the Netherlands. In England, interest in the form surged in 1588, with the publication of a collection of Italian madrigals with English texts. English composers such as Thomas Morley, Thomas Weelkes, and John Wilbye began writing madrigals modeled on the lighter Italian version of the form. Morley published five collections of madrigals. Weelkes, by contrast, produced bold, dramatic works in the style of Gesualdo and Monteverdi.

Other Vocal Forms. Another popular form of vocal music in England was the *ayre,* or air. Written for a solo voice usually accompanied by the lute (a stringed instrument), airs began to appear in print in the 1590s. John Dowland, an accomplished lute player and composer, published *First Booke of Songes or Ayres* in 1597. Often more literary than the texts of madrigals, the English airs include poetry by writers such as Philip SIDNEY, John DONNE, and Ben JONSON.

An important song literature developed in Spain, where the *villancico* (similar to the Italian *frottola*) became widespread in the late 1500s. In Germany, the most popular form of vocal music was the lied, a four-part song with the melody in the tenor voice. Early lied composers created a distinctly German musical style. From about 1565 to the end of the century, the finest composers of this form were Orlando di LASSO of Italy, who worked in Munich for many years, and Hans Leo Hassler. Their works pushed aside the distinctive German elements and brought in influences from other regions, especially Italy. (*See also* **Music; Music, Instrumental; Musical Instruments; Poetry.**)

Musical Instruments

* **medieval** referring to the Middle Ages, a period that began around A.D. 400 and ended around 1400 in Italy and 1500 in the rest of Europe

* **lute** guitarlike stringed instrument with a rounded back

Many musical instruments of the Renaissance were inherited from the Middle Ages. However, some of these medieval* instruments changed in shape and size in response to changing musical needs and tastes. The growing popularity of polyphonic music, which had several interwoven melody lines, created a demand for new types of instruments. At the same time, some popular medieval instruments, such as the bagpipe, fell out of favor as performance instruments, although they remained common in folk music.

Meanwhile, amateurs took a greater interest in musical performance. They favored instruments that could play chords and several musical lines at once, such as keyboards and the lute*. Musicians used them for solo performances, to accompany singers, and to provide a background for amateur music-making in people's homes. Another factor that changed instruments during the Renaissance was the growth of theatrical productions and spectacles in the 1500s. To fill large performance halls with sound, composers began producing music for large groups of different instruments. The demands of the theater also gave rise to new instruments.

Stringed Instruments. Some Renaissance stringed instruments were played with bows, others by plucking the strings with the fingers. Various bowed instruments had survived from the Middle Ages, but only one of these—the viol—was adapted to meet the new musical demands of the Renaissance. In fact, the viol evolved into an entire family of instruments, each of a different size and capable of playing in a different musical range. The members of the viol family became very popular for amateur performance.

A new type of bowed instrument, the violin, appeared in the late 1400s. A shoulder-held instrument with four strings, it combined features of several earlier medieval instruments. Originally used only to perform dance music, the violin became the instrument of choice for a wide variety of musical styles. Like the viol, the violin was joined by related instruments that could play in different ranges. The violin and its relatives, the viola and cello, have remained essentially unchanged since the Renaissance.

Many plucked instruments of the Middle Ages lost favor during the Renaissance and were used only for folk music after that period. Only the harp and lute evolved to meet the needs of the new musical styles. The Renaissance harp had new strings added to expand its range and to enable it to play all the notes of the scale. These changes made it more suitable for use in the theater. The lute also went through a series of changes that enabled it to play more than one melody line at the same time. During the 1500s new types of lutes emerged with larger numbers of strings. Versatile and portable, the members of the lute family remained in constant demand to accompany solo and group performances. Another type of plucked instrument, the guitar, first appeared during the Renaissance. In England and France, four-string guitars served for both solos and accompaniment. In Spain, a six-string version became very popular in the 1500s.

Wind Instruments. During the Middle Ages, most woodwind instruments, such as flutes and recorders, had played in the alto range. Larger and smaller versions of these instruments emerged during the Renaissance to cover higher and lower ranges. Recorders had traditionally been popular for making music in the home, while flutes had played a role in the military. In the late 1400s, however, both these instruments came into common use for performances—sometimes in groups of the same instrument and sometimes mixed with other instruments or with voices.

Another popular woodwind was the shawm, a double-reed instrument that had often played alongside the bagpipe in the late Middle Ages. In the Renaissance, the shawm commonly appeared with a larger version of itself, known as the bombard because it resembled a small cannon. Ensembles of two or three shawms—often joined by a trombone—became the chief type of instrumental group employed by town governments and royal courts.

Renaissance trumpets and other types of horns all featured a cup-shaped mouthpiece. They could be made of a variety of materials—brass, silver, and even wood. Trumpets commonly served as signal

instruments and to "announce" people or events. Ceremonial trumpets were usually made of silver and hung with pennants bearing the symbols of a government or a noble family. Renaissance trumpets, unlike modern ones, had no valves and could play only a few notes, such as those used in fanfares. In the early 1400s a slide trumpet appeared, which used a movable slide to alter the length of the instrument and produce all the notes of the scale.

A more complex slide-based instrument, called the sackbut or trombone, emerged in the late 1400s. More versatile than the trumpet, the trombone was used in a variety of ways. Trombones appeared along with trumpets on ceremonial occasions, they formed a part of small groups with shawms, and they played with orchestras of strings and woodwinds in theatrical productions. They were also used for dance music and to support the lower voices in church choirs.

The cornet, which evolved from a medieval folk instrument, became a favorite instrument of the Renaissance. Made of wood and leather, it had a cup mouthpiece and was fingered like a flute. Popular in soprano and alto sizes, cornets performed with a wide variety of chamber and theater groups. They also supported the high voices in church choirs.

Keyboard Instruments. The main keyboard instruments of the Renaissance were organs, harpsichords, and clavichords. Organs used pipes to produce their sound, while harpsichords and clavichords used strings. The small portable organs of the Middle Ages, which could be held on the lap or placed on a table, remained fairly unchanged during the Renaissance. Large, stationary organs, by contrast, grew and developed dramatically during the 1400s and 1500s. Installed in all cathedrals and major churches throughout Europe, these large organs had many rows of pipes, and some had extra keyboards and foot pedals. These changes increased the range, volume, and variety of sounds that the organ could produce.

Harpsichords (with plucked strings) and clavichords (with hammered strings) first appeared in the late 1300s and grew increasingly popular over the next few hundred years. The clavichord, which played softly, appeared only in homes. The harpsichord, however, was far more versatile. By the mid-1500s it had become the most common instrument for solo performance, large and small groups, and accompaniment. Harpsichords varied greatly in size. Some had two or three strings per note and some featured extra keyboards, which enabled them to produce a variety of different tones. (*See also* **Music; Music, Instrumental.**)

* **classical** in the tradition of ancient Greece and Rome

A central feature of the Renaissance was the revival of interest in the cultures of ancient Greece and Rome. This revival brought classical* mythology—the stories of ancient gods and goddesses—into the popular imagination. Renaissance scholars translated and interpreted classical myths, giving new meanings to these pagan* tales. Artists and writers also turned to myths as a rich source of subject matter and sym-

The gods and goddesses of ancient Greek and Roman mythology often appeared in Renaissance art and literature. *The Birth of Venus,* painted by Sandro Botticelli in the late 1400s, features the Roman goddess Venus rising from the sea.

* **pagan**   referring to ancient religions that worshiped many gods, or more generally, to any non-Christian religion

* **epic**   long poem about the adventures of a hero

* **vernacular**   native language or dialect of a region or country

* **genealogy**   study of family origins and relationships

* **allegory**   literary or artistic device in which characters, events, and settings represent abstract qualities, and in which the author intends a different meaning to be read beneath the surface

bolism. By the late 1400s, pagan myths began to challenge the dominance of Christian subjects in literature and the arts.

Rediscovering Classical Myths. Scholars learned about classical mythology from four main sources. Two of these were Greek: the writings of the philosopher PLATO and the epics* of the poet Homer. The third, the *Aeneid,* was a Latin epic by the Roman poet VIRGIL about the founding of Rome. The verses of the Roman poet Ovid—particularly the *Metamorphoses,* a collection of myths—made up the fourth source.

Scholars of the Middle Ages had known the works of Virgil and Ovid. Renaissance readers inherited their texts along with a large body of commentary on the works. Homer's epics, however, were unknown except for scattered quotations in the works of ancient Roman writers. A major feat of Renaissance scholarship was the translation of Homer and Plato into Latin and the widespread publication of ancient Latin works. Later, scholars translated these classical texts into vernacular* languages. As a result of their activities, educated people of the Renaissance had access to a wealth of classical myths.

The Italian writer Giovanni BOCCACCIO pioneered mythography, the systematic study of myths. He devoted the final 25 years of his life to an encyclopedic work called *Genealogy** of the Gods. Boccaccio and other commentators claimed that myths contained multiple layers of meaning for readers. For example, one edition of Ovid's *Metamorphoses* presented four ways of reading the myth of Daedalus, the Greek inventor imprisoned by King Minos. Daedalus made wings to escape, but his son Icarus disobeyed him, flew too close to the sun, and died. The editor suggested that readers could view this story literally—as history—or as one of three allegories*. On the moral level, Daedalus could stand for a sinner imprisoned by the Devil. In religious terms, Daedalus might represent God and Icarus a Christian at risk of falling from grace. Finally, the story made a point about family life: that children should obey their

fathers. A popular history of the classical gods also offered historical, natural, and moral interpretations of the ancient stories.

Renaissance mythographers operated from the principle that classical mythology, although older than Christianity, was in harmony with Christian beliefs and morality. This principle led them to look for Christian themes beneath the surfaces of the myths. They also identified classical figures, such as heroes and gods, with Christian virtues and vices.

Mythology and the Arts. Some Renaissance mythographers emphasized physical descriptions of the gods or discussed the ways the ancient Greeks and Romans had portrayed them. One popular account, called *Images of the Gods,* described statues of the deities and included 85 illustrations. It was a useful source for artists and poets seeking to use classical mythology in their works.

In the 1400s, the Italian writer and architect Leon Battista ALBERTI advised artists to look to classical poetry for their subject matter. Many followed his advice and began painting scenes and figures from Ovid's poems and other ancient works. The first large-scale paintings of pagan gods made since antiquity* were Sandro BOTTICELLI's *Primavera* and *The Birth of Venus,* painted in the early 1480s. Both paintings focused on the nude figures of goddesses. Renaissance artists had a keen interest in human anatomy and sexuality. Classical myths, with their stories of the gods and their loves, offered many chances to explore these subjects.

The Italian artist TITIAN was the greatest mythological painter of the Renaissance. Early in his career he completed or added to mythological works by other artists, such as GIORGIONE DA CASTELFRANCO's *Sleeping Venus.* Between 1518 and 1523 Titian produced three large paintings on mythical subjects. He also made many paintings of Venus, the goddess of love, and he created a series of paintings that dramatized myths from Ovid for the Spanish king PHILIP II. However, Titian was not the only important artist inspired by classical myths. Scenes, images, and characters from myths appeared in countless works of art and decorations.

The influence of classical myths on Renaissance literature began with the Italian poet PETRARCH. He wrote sonnets* that described his own love affair in terms of the mythical relationship between the god Apollo and the nymph* Daphne. Another Italian poet, Angelo POLIZIANO, celebrated the powers of Venus and of the love god Cupid. His *Fable of Orpheus* (1480), based on the myth of Orpheus the singer, was the first pastoral* drama written in Italian. Poet Ludovico ARIOSTO used images from classical myths in his epic *Orlando Furioso,* which influenced many other writers. For example, he shows one character chained to a rock like the mythical princess Andromeda.

The Italian enthusiasm for mythology spread to France in the 1500s. Diane de Poitiers, a powerful woman at the court of King Henry II, sparked many references to the Roman goddess Diana in art and poetry. One French poet who drew upon classical myth was Pierre de RONSARD, who used the gods Apollo and Bacchus as symbols of poetic inspiration.

* **antiquity** era of the ancient Mediterranean cultures of Greece and Rome, ending around A.D. 400

* **sonnet** poem of 14 lines with a fixed pattern of meter and rhyme

* **nymph** in ancient mythology, a nature spirit who takes the form of a beautiful young woman

* **pastoral** relating to the countryside; often used to draw a contrast between the innocence and serenity of rural life and the corruption and extravagance of court life

The Renaissance arrived in England in full force in the late 1500s, introducing English writers to classical influences. Edmund SPENSER's long poem *The Faerie Queene,* published in the 1550s, contains elements drawn from Ovid and Virgil as well as from the tradition of chivalry*. William SHAKESPEARE drew characters and plots for several of his plays from Ovid. However, his most notable contribution to mythological literature was the poem *Venus and Adonis* (1593). It captures both the humor and the tragic tone of Ovid's poem about the doomed love of the goddess and a beautiful young man. (*See also* **Classical Antiquity; Classical Scholarship; Paganism.**)

* **chivalry** rules and customs of medieval knighthood

See color plate 5, vol. 3

* **Holy Roman Empire** political body in central Europe composed of several states; existed until 1806

* **illegitimate** refers to a child born outside of marriage

* **abdicate** to give up the throne voluntarily or under pressure

During the Renaissance, Naples was the capital of a kingdom that included the southern portion of the Italian peninsula and, at times, the island of Sicily. Many European powers fought for control of the kingdom, with France, Spain, and the Holy Roman Empire* ruling Naples at different times.

History and Politics. The kingdom of Naples emerged in the 1000s with the Norman French conquest of southern Italy and Sicily. In the next century, control passed to the Holy Roman Empire. The French allied with the pope to seize control of Naples in the 1200s, but a revolt in 1282 left Sicily under the control of the Spanish kingdom of Aragon. The greatest ruler of early Naples was Robert the Wise (ruled 1309–1343), who hoped to unite all of Italy. However, the kingdom plunged into turmoil when his successor and granddaughter failed to produce an heir.

In 1442 King Alfonso V of Aragon conquered and reunited Sicily and southern Italy into a single kingdom. He later established his court at Naples. Alfonso soon became involved in political affairs in Milan and Genoa. He also helped elect one of his favorite aides, Alonso de Borgia, as Pope Calixtus III. Alfonso's illegitimate* son Ferrante succeeded him as king. Ferrante supported Lorenzo de' MEDICI in Florence and allied himself with the Sforza rulers of Milan through marriage.

Ferrante's son Alfonso II became king of Naples in 1494. He encountered trouble when the French king Charles VIII invaded Italy. Although Alfonso sent an army to northern Italy to intercept Charles, the French managed to avoid Alfonso's forces and marched on Naples. Alfonso abdicated* in 1495, and Charles left the city three months later. Alfonso's son Ferrandino led Neapolitan forces to a victory over the French, but he died just over a year later. In 1499 King Louis XII of France invaded Naples, and the following year he divided the kingdom with his cousin, King Ferdinand II of Spain. Three years later Spanish forces conquered the kingdom and expelled the French.

Under Spain's rule, Naples became the center of Spanish military policy in Italy. The new leaders expelled Neapolitan nobles who favored France, replacing them with loyal followers of Spain. In this way Spanish kings weakened the power of local nobles and strengthened royal control over Naples. Spain ruled the city and the kingdom until 1713.

* **Black Death**   epidemic of the plague, a highly contagious and often fatal disease, which spread throughout Europe from 1348 to 1350

* **patronage**   support or financial sponsorship

Economy and Culture. Before the Black Death* struck, the kingdom of Naples had about 2.5 million inhabitants. That number fell sharply before recovering to almost 3 million by 1600. By then, the city of Naples had some 250,000 residents, rivaling Paris as western Europe's largest city. Most of the kingdom's inhabitants lived in cities and larger towns, rather than in the countryside. This hindered the kingdom's economic development, as did the kingdom's trade policies. Foreign merchants controlled Naples's wheat, silk, wool, and olive oil industries, and they usually sent these goods to cities in their own homelands.

Nevertheless, Naples developed a rich court life. Under French rule, the court extended patronage* to artists, writers, and architects from all over Italy. The rulers from Aragon and Spain did the same, and Naples remained an important center of culture throughout the Renaissance. (*See also* **Art in Italy; Borgia, House of; Sicily.**)

Nation-state, a modern term, refers to a form of political organization in which all the people of a nationality live in a nation-state ruled by members of that nationality. There is limited evidence of the existence of nation-states in the Renaissance. At the time, more people identified with a religion than with a nation. The ambitions of noble and royal families, not clashes between nationalities, caused most wars.

The organization of Renaissance states shows the weakness of the sense of national identity. Joint monarchs ruled several kingdoms, and members of one national group sometimes accepted rulers from a different group. Countries that elected their monarchs, such as Bohemia* and Hungary, often chose foreign princes to rule. Most states restricted citizenship to a small fraction of their people, which limited the growth of national identity.

Some countries, however, did have elements of the modern nation-state. The Swiss Confederation had a national identity, although it lacked a state of its own at the time. France also had a sense of historical national borders. The feeling of nationalism was perhaps strongest in England, Sweden, and Portugal. It can be seen in the plays of William SHAKESPEARE, which reflect a strong sense of English patriotism. Although evidence for the existence of nation-states is weak, national sentiment did develop over time. Religious struggles in the 1500s made people aware that they belonged to distinct ethnic groups. Scholars regard this knowledge as a key factor in the later creation of the nation-state. (*See also* **Political Thought.**)

* **Bohemia**   kingdom in an area of central Europe now occupied by the Czech Republic

Nepotism is the act of showing favoritism to one's family or friends, usually by granting them jobs, offices, or titles. Although the term *nepotism* emerged only in the later years of the Renaissance, the practice goes back to the ancient world. Ancient Romans believed that individuals could rely only on their relatives to protect their interests. They considered nepotism an act of *pietas,* the duty a child owed to its parents or the living owed to deceased relatives.

Nepotism was widespread in the Renaissance, and society tended to look down on powerful people who did not assist their own family members. Rulers and political leaders provided relatives with offices and riches. They believed that the relatives they favored would be more likely to support them. Besides, money and titles given to relatives remained in the family. Business owners also preferred to hire relatives.

High church officials used nepotism as well, both to secure power and to gain support. Popes often appointed nephews (*nipote,* the Italian word from which *nepotism* comes) as bishops and cardinals. One popular strategy was for a pope to grant titles and land in the Papal States* to relatives. This policy not only helped enrich the family, it put papal* relatives in a position to offer material, political, and military aid to the pope against his rivals. Most people expected the pope to support and promote his relatives.

Pope Sixtus IV (1471–1484) used nepotism extensively. Six of the 34 new cardinals he appointed were relatives. While many of these cardinals were notable for their immoral behavior, they helped support and maintain the papacy. However, Pope JULIUS II (1503–1513), a nephew of Sixtus IV, used nepotism solely to support his family.

Various church councils attempted to reform the system. For example, the Council of Trent tried to prohibit the use of nepotism by bishops and cardinals. However, a crisis in papal finances in the early 1600s spurred the first real reforms. Proposals at this time called for reducing the number of cardinals and fixing their salaries. The pope would control only a small amount of money, the rest being in the hands of the College of Cardinals. As a result, papal nepotism gradually died out by 1700. (*See also* **Councils; Popes and Papacy.**)

* **Papal States**   lands in central Italy under the authority of the pope

* **papal**   referring to the office and authority of the pope

Netherlands

* **duchy**   territory ruled by a duke or duchess

* **Low Countries**   region bordering on the North Sea, made up of present-day Netherlands and Belgium

During the Renaissance the Netherlands consisted of two distinct regions separated by the Waal and Meuse Rivers. The region to the south, which included the provinces of Flanders and Brabant, had ties to France and the duchy* of BURGUNDY. The region north of the rivers, which contained the provinces of Holland and Zeeland, leaned toward Germany and the BALTIC STATES. The two regions used different languages and operated within separate political and economic spheres.

Burgundian Rule.   The beginning of the Netherlands, also known as the Low Countries* or the Seventeen Provinces, dates from the time of the dukes of Burgundy. In 1384 Philip the Bold of Burgundy acquired Flanders through his wife, Margaret, the daughter of the count of Flanders. By 1428 the dukes of Burgundy had extended their territory to include the northern provinces of Holland and Zeeland.

In the 1400s, Duke Philip the Good of Burgundy attempted to unify his holdings in the Netherlands by creating new legislative bodies. These included the States General, an assembly, and the Chamber of Accounts. However, these bodies could not resolve the divisions among

1384
Philip the Bold of Burgundy acquires province of Flanders.

1428
Dukes of Burgundy gain control of Holland and Zeeland.

1477
Netherlands is linked to the Habsburg dynasty.

1506
Charles of Habsburg becomes prince of the Netherlands.

1555
Charles V abdicates in favor of Philip II.

1566
Great Revolt begins.

1579
Union of Utrecht and Union of Arras.

1648
Permanent separation of Dutch Republic and Spanish Netherlands.

1350
1400
1450
1500
1550
1600
1650

* **autonomy** independent self-government

* **Holy Roman Empire** political body in central Europe composed of several states; existed until 1806

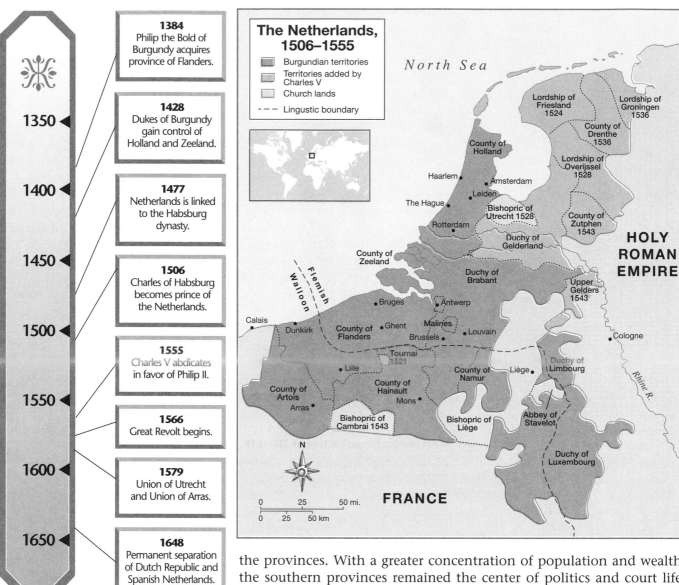

The Netherlands, 1506–1555

- Burgundian territories
- Territories added by Charles V
- Church lands
- --- Lingustic boundary

North Sea

Lordship of Friesland 1524
Lordship of Groningen 1536
County of Drenthe 1536
County of Holland
Lordship of Overijssel 1528
Haarlem
Amsterdam
Leiden
The Hague
Bishopric of Utrecht 1528
County of Zutphen 1543
Rotterdam
Duchy of Gelderland
County of Zeeland
Duchy of Brabant
HOLY ROMAN EMPIRE
Upper Gelders 1543
Flemish
Walloon
Bruges
Antwerp
Calais
Malines
County of Flanders
Ghent
Brussels
Louvain
Cologne
Dunkirk
Tournai 1521
Lille
County of Namur
Liège
Duchy of Limbourg
Rhine R.
County of Artois
Arras
County of Hainault
Mons
Abbey of Stavelot
Bishopric of Cambrai 1543
Bishopric of Liège
Duchy of Luxembourg
N
0 25 50 mi.
0 25 50 km
FRANCE

the provinces. With a greater concentration of population and wealth, the southern provinces remained the center of politics and court life. Many public officials came from the southern provinces, and northerners viewed them as foreigners. The towns and provinces in both regions remained stubbornly attached to traditional privileges and resisted giving up their own interests for the benefit of the Burgundian state.

In the 1460s and 1470s, Duke Charles the Bold tried to centralize government. However, his death in 1477 brought a reaction in favor of local autonomy*, forcing his daughter Mary to grant a set of privileges to the States General and the separate provinces. Each province also sought to exclude foreigners. Holland and Zeeland banned outsiders from government positions and called for the use of Dutch as the official language, rather than the French used in the southern provinces.

Habsburg Rule. In 1477 the marriage of Mary of Burgundy to Maximilian (later MAXIMILIAN I) of HABSBURG linked the Low Countries to the Holy Roman Empire* ruled by the Habsburgs. The towns of the

* **guild**   association of craft and trade owners and workers that set standards for and represented the interests of its members

* **civic**   related to a city, a community, or citizens

* **regent**   person who acts on behalf of a monarch who is too young or unable to rule

* **abdicate**   to give up the throne voluntarily or under pressure

* **heresy**   belief that is contrary to the doctrine of an established church

* **humanism**   Renaissance cultural movement promoting the study of the humanities (the languages, literature, and history of ancient Greece and Rome) as a guide to living

* **dissent**   to oppose or disagree with established belief

Netherlands continued to guard their privileges jealously, frustrating Habsburg efforts to centralize the government. Guilds* held considerable power in the towns of the Netherlands. Their functions ranged from monitoring the quality of goods to protecting consumers and controlling trade. Guilds could exert pressure on town councils. But those who held civic* offices, mainly individuals from great merchant and noble families, were often tied to the interests of the Burgundian and Habsburg dynasties. Habsburg rulers sometimes took advantage of civic unrest to strip the guilds of their political role.

By the time Maximilian I became Holy Roman Emperor in 1493, his son, Archduke Philip the Handsome, had been accepted as prince in each of the provinces of the Low Countries. Philip's young son Charles succeeded him in 1506. But Charles's aunt, MARGARET OF AUSTRIA, served as regent* until 1515 and again from 1517 to 1530, while Charles took up the duties of king of Spain and later of Holy Roman Emperor (as CHARLES V).

In 1555 Charles abdicated* the throne of the Netherlands in favor of his son, PHILIP II of Spain. After spending four years in the Low Countries, Philip returned to Spain and appointed his half-sister, Margaret of Parma, to serve as regent. She faced a growing rivalry between two great lords, William of Orange and the count of Egmont, and some faithful followers of the Habsburgs. Plans for reorganizing church administrative districts also caused problems for Margaret. In particular, resistance grew to the enforcement of Habsburg laws against heresy*.

Religious Conflict and Revolt.   Travel and other contacts with Italy brought humanism* to the Netherlands at the end of the 1400s. Desiderius ERASMUS of Rotterdam gained fame throughout Europe for his humanist writings and teaching. However, the new learning contributed to the growing division in matters of faith in the 1500s. The north became a haven for Protestants and religious dissent*, though churches devoted to the teachings of John CALVIN also emerged in the south.

Religious dissenters of all kinds in the Netherlands were targeted by the campaign against heresy begun by Charles V and continued by Philip II. As part of this campaign, the INQUISITION was introduced in the Netherlands with special courts to investigate charges of heresy. These courts tried and executed about 1,300 people between 1523 and 1566.

By 1565 the religious situation in the Netherlands had reached the boiling point. Fearful of growing unrest, government leaders asked Philip II to suspend the harsh measures against heresy. His refusal led to widespread protest, which included demands to end the Inquisition. The protest turned into a full-scale uprising known as the Great Revolt.

Philip II sent the Spanish army under the command of the duke of Alba to put down the revolt in the Netherlands. However, by the time Spanish troops arrived in 1567, the central government in Brussels had already begun to reestablish itself. Many nobles and Protestants who supported the revolt had fled the country. Alba's Council of Troubles investigated and sentenced almost 9,000 individuals for their part in the uprising.

"Shooting Guilds"

Many towns in the Netherlands had "shooting guilds," which were groups of armed citizens. These local militias often played a key role in determining the allegiance of a town to the Holy Roman Emperor or the States General, the legislative body of the Netherlands. A choice also had to be made between loyalty to the Catholic Church or support for one of the emerging Protestant faiths. The "shooting guilds" had so much influence because town councils needed their support to enforce the law.

The prospects of the revolt seemed poor, but in 1568 the prominent Dutch nobleman William of Orange declared his support for the rebellion. Despite his leadership, the efforts of the rebels to seize and hold fortified towns failed. However, the seizure of the port city of Brill in 1572 marked a turning point. Town by town, much of Holland and Zeeland fell to the rebels.

One more effort was made to unite the north and the south against Spain. In 1576 Spanish soldiers in the Netherlands mutinied and attacked ANTWERP, the greatest commercial and financial center of Europe. Northern and southern provinces reacted to this assault by signing an agreement to unite to drive out the Spanish. Their unity was short lived, however. It collapsed because of the unwillingness of Calvinists to tolerate Catholics in the southern cities they controlled and then because of Spanish military successes.

William of Orange proclaimed a religious peace, allowing freedom of worship to Catholics and Protestants. But his attempt to promote unity failed. In 1579 rebel provinces in the north established the Union of Utrecht and declared their independence from Spain as the United Provinces of the Netherlands (Dutch Republic) two years later. The rival Union of Arras that formed in the south was Catholic and loyal to Spain. It later became the Spanish Netherlands. Hostilities between the Spanish Netherlands and the emerging Dutch Republic continued for the next 30 years. The Twelve Years' Truce (1609–1621) recognized the split between the two countries, which became permanent with the Treaty of Westphalia (1648). (*See also* **Amsterdam; Art in the Netherlands; Holy Roman Empire.**)

Netherlands, Art in

See *Art in the Netherlands.*

Netherlands, Language and Literature of

During the Renaissance, the Dutch language and literature developed against the backdrop of the Netherlands' struggle for independence. The nation waged a long battle to overthrow the rule of Spain and its king, PHILIP II. Philip was a member of the HABSBURG DYNASTY, one of the most powerful political families in Europe in the 1500s. By the 1580s, war with Spain had divided the Netherlands into northern and southern territories.

After the Spanish recaptured the city of ANTWERP (in what is now Belgium) in 1585, a number of merchants, intellectuals, craftspeople, and artists left the southern Netherlands to settle in the north. These talented and educated immigrants contributed to a "Dutch golden age" marked by new growth in the economy, arts, and sciences. By 1588, people in the north had formed their own Dutch Republic, which officially gained its independence in 1648. The southern Netherlands remained under the rule of the Habsburg dynasty for almost another 150 years.

Renaissance City

Plate 1
Built on a series of islands in the waters of a shimmering lagoon, Venice was one of five major powers in Renaissance Italy. The city dominated trade in the Mediterranean and was an important center of learning and the arts. Its unique and very stable government was based on shared responsibility among 2,000 male nobles who served on the city's many councils. Artist Vittore Carpaccio painted this view of Venice around 1486.

Plate 2: Left
As the headquarters of the Roman Catholic Church, Rome played an important role in religion. Popes, cardinals, and religious orders sponsored grand artistic and architectural projects to glorify God and to serve their own purposes. Giacomo da Vignola designed the church of Gesù, shown here, for the Society of Jesus about 1568. Completion and decoration took about a century. It follows the Renaissance idea of an open interior without aisles. Much of the decoration reflects styles of the late Renaissance and early Baroque periods.

Plate 3: Below
Architects of the Renaissance first developed the concept of urban planning. This *View of an Ideal City*, probably created by Luciano Laurana, reflects the classical styles of ancient Greece and Rome with its use of columns and its combination of squares and circles, two shapes viewed as ideal. The painting is based on sketches by artist Piero della Francesca from his work *On Perspective in Painting*, written in the late 1460s.

Plate 4: Left
The Medici family controlled Florence through most of the Renaissance, at first behind the scenes and later as dukes of the city. Cosimo I, shown here in a portrait by Agnolo Bronzino, ruled Florence from 1537 to 1564. One of the Italy's most successful rulers, Cosimo I added the neighboring city-state of Siena to his rule and won the title of "grand duke of Tuscany."

Plate 5: Below
The city-state of Naples changed hands several times during the Renaissance. It came under the control of the Spanish house of Aragon in 1442, but in the 1490s it fell to the French. However, Spanish forces led by Ferdinand of Aragon recaptured Naples in 1503. The new Spanish rulers made the city a strategic center in Italy. This painting by Francesco Pagano shows Ferdinand's fleet in Naples harbor.

Plate 6: Left

The city of Urbino, in central Italy, prospered during the Renaissance under the rule of the Montefeltro family. One of the most famous Montefeltro dukes was Federico, who ruled the city from 1445 to 1482. A strong leader, he carried out major remodeling and brought new Renaissance styles to the city. Piero della Francesca painted this portrait of the duke in 1465.

Plate 7: Below

The painting *View of Perugia, Italy* dates from the early 1400s. Perugia was the leading city-state in the central Italian region of Umbria in the mid-1300s. Over the next 200 years, it gradually lost its political independence. However, it remained a thriving center of the arts and learning, home to the celebrated painter Perugino and a university.

Plate 8: Left
A major building boom occurred in Paris during the 1500s. One of the most ambitious projects was the redesign of the Louvre palace. Work on the Square Court of the Louvre, shown here, began in 1546. Architect Pierre Lescot blended classical styles with elements of traditional French design, such as slate roofs. The remodeled Louvre became a model for new French châteaus.

Plate 9: Below
The largest city in Renaissance England, London had around 200,000 residents in 1600. Francis Hogenberg created this view of London in 1576 to illustrate the work *Cities of the World*. The painting shows part of the city walls, the great bulk of St. Paul's Cathedral, and the Thames River off to the right.

Plate 10: Left

Poverty was widespread in European cities. Although few people relied on charity all the time, more than half the population might fall into poverty at some point in their lives. Religious organizations and city governments played important roles in poor relief, but a great deal of charity was personal. Giving to the deserving poor was considered a blessed act, as shown in this panel from the painting *Seven Acts of Mercy*, by the Master of Alkmaar (1504).

Plate 11: Below

The port of Amsterdam, shown in this engraving by artist D.G. Hucquier, was the key transfer point between northeastern and western Europe. Amsterdam's trade declined sharply when the northern part of the Netherlands broke away from Spanish rule and became a separate nation. But in 1578 Amsterdam joined the new Dutch nation. The city quickly became the home base of the Dutch commercial empire in Asia and the Americas and a major European financial center.

Vista General de la Ciudad y Puerto de Amsterdam.
Dedicada al Ex.mo Señor Marques Grimaldi Embajador y Ministro Plenipotenciario de S. Majestad Catholica cerca de sus Altipotencias de los Estados Generales.
Por su mas humilde Servidor D. G. Huquier Gravador en Paris, calle de Santiago, a S. Remigio, el grande.

Plate 12: Left
Antwerp was another major trading city in the Netherlands. The city prospered during the 1500s and developed a thriving artistic and literary culture. Antwerp's town clerk, Pierre Gilles (shown here in a 1517 portrait by Quentin Massys) was a friend to such noted scholars as Thomas More and Desiderius Erasmus.

Plate 13: Below
Madrid became the capital of Spain in 1561. The Renaissance arrived late in the city and never took firm root, but the dramatic Baroque styles of art and architecture blossomed there in the 1600s. These buildings in the public square called the Plaza Mayor were constructed in 1620. The statue at left, by Italian artists Giambologna and Pietro Tacca, portrays Philip III, who ruled Spain from 1598 to 1621.

Plate 14: Right

Moscow became the center of political and religious life in Russia during the 1400s. Renaissance styles of art and architecture had little impact on Russia, partly because the nation's Orthodox Church rejected most forms of western culture. The Cathedral of St. Michael the Archangel in the Kremlin, designed by Italian architect Alevisio the Younger, is one of a few buildings in the city that combined Renaissance forms with traditional Russian styles.

Plate 15: Below

Renaissance culture thrived in Prague, the capital of the kingdom of Bohemia. Rudolf II, who ruled Bohemia from 1575 to 1612, hired stonemasons and other workers from Italy to transform Prague Castle into a magnificent Renaissance palace. His example inspired many of the nobles to build splendid homes. This view of the modern city shows both Prague Castle and Hradcany (Hrad Castle), now the home of the president of the Czech Republic.

Pieter Cornelisz Hooft was one of the first Dutch authors to use classical material in his writing. His works include poetry, plays, and a highly celebrated history of the Netherlands.

* **rhetoric**   art of speaking or writing effectively

* **humanism**   Renaissance cultural movement promoting the study of the humanities (the languages, literature, and history of ancient Greece and Rome) as a guide to living

* **classical**   in the tradition of ancient Greece and Rome

* **sonnet**   poem of 14 lines with a fixed pattern of meter and rhyme

* **vernacular**   native language or dialect of a region or country

* **ode**   poem with a lofty style and complex structure

Language Developments. Under the Habsburgs' rule in the 1500s, the people of the Netherlands did not all speak the same language. Instead, they used several related dialects known as "Diets." In the second half of the 1500s, Dutch scholars sought to strengthen the Netherlands' written language and create a national literature. They worked to create standards of grammar and spelling and to remove foreign words from the vocabulary. In 1584, the poet Hendrick Laurensz Spiegel published the first Dutch grammar book. Other Dutch scholars developed new scientific terms and produced books on rhetoric*.

The Netherlands based its new national language on a dialect from the northern province of Holland—the political, economic, and cultural center of the Dutch Republic. However, the language developed too slowly for some. In the winter of 1622 a group of poets began to hold regular meetings on the subject of language and literature. They sought to create standards for such language issues as word order and spelling. They put their new rules into effect in 1625 in a Dutch translation of a play by the ancient Roman author Seneca.

One of the most important events in the development of the Dutch language was the publication of the State Bible in 1637. This Dutch translation—based on the teachings of the French Protestant reformer John CALVIN—became the chosen Bible of the Protestant population. This Dutch Bible has influenced the country's language for more than 300 years; many Dutch words and phrases come directly from the State Bible.

Dutch Renaissance Literature. During the 1500s, the literary life of Dutch towns took place mainly in the chambers of rhetoric. These theatrical and literary organizations helped to spread the ideas of humanism* throughout the Netherlands. Poets, artists, and intellectuals met at these chambers, or halls, and practiced using the newly formed national language. They also discussed one another's writings and staged plays. The chambers played a significant role in the public cultural life of Dutch towns. After 1585, the city of AMSTERDAM, the present-day capital, became the Netherlands' primary literary center.

One of the first Dutch authors to bring classical* influences into the national literature was the poet, dramatist, and historian Pieter Cornelisz Hooft. In his youth Hooft wrote a number of love sonnets* in Dutch. He later introduced to Dutch literature a form of tragic drama based on ancient Greek models. Hooft also wrote a widely acclaimed vernacular* history of the Netherlands.

Works by a number of the Netherlands' other literary figures also helped to establish Dutch as the official language. Although he did not belong to one of the chambers of rhetoric, Jan van der Noot wrote the first collection of Dutch poetry to reflect new Renaissance ideas. Noot introduced a number of new poetic styles to Dutch literature, including the ode*. The dramatist Joost van den Vondel began his career writing tragedies based on ancient Greek drama, then later turned to the Bible as the source for most of his material. As a tribute to his work, actors performed one of Vondel's plays each New Year's Day in Amsterdam until 1967. A collection of poems in Dutch, written by the poet and scholar

Daniel Heinsius, also showed that the language was fit for use in high-quality literature.

Only a few female writers in the Netherlands published their work before 1650. These included the sisters Anna and Maria Tesselschade Visscher, who enjoyed the praise of other poets in their circle. However, their poetry did not become available to the reading public until the 1800s.

Popular Literature. In the early 1600s, songbooks—collections of songs and poems—became one of the most popular forms of Dutch literature. The publishers intended these pieces for performance by the young sons and daughters of wealthy families. The verses of many Dutch poets, such as Hooft and Gerbrandt Adriaensz Bredero, first appeared in songbooks. Many of the songbooks focused on poems about love. After the rebellion broke out, politics and religion became common themes as well.

Another popular form of Dutch literature in the 1600s was the illustrated emblem book. An emblem is an allegorical* picture containing a verse or motto that presents a moral lesson. Three types of emblem books became popular in the Netherlands. Love emblem books featured light romantic poems written in the style of the Italian-born poet and scholar PETRARCH. Another form, religious love emblem books, became especially popular with Jesuit* priests in the southern Netherlands. Jesuits used these religious picture books as an aid in educating the young and spreading the faith. The third type, the realistic emblem book, took its subjects from everyday life. Realistic emblem books, which first appeared in 1614, offered advice on every stage of life from infancy to old age. Leading artists created the pictures for most of these books, which added to their appeal.

Various other forms of poetry became popular during the Dutch Renaissance as well. Country house poems, for example, praised life in the country and the estates of the well-to-do. The poems paid tribute to everything from houses and gardens to libraries. In 1655 the Dutch poet Jacob Cats wrote *Garden Thoughts* in honor of his country home in the town of Zorghvilet.

Poetry served a variety of purposes in the Dutch Renaissance. Almost every poet wrote religious poetry, with many members of the clergy publishing volumes of songs for the people in their churches. Poets also wrote popular verses to celebrate public and social events. In 1655, Vondel wrote a long poem praising the town hall in Amsterdam, which effectively made him the official poet of that city. Poets also used their poems to criticize Dutch society and to ridicule the customs and manners of the time. (*See also* **Art in the Netherlands; Netherlands.**)

* **allegorical** referring to a literary or artistic device in which characters, events, and settings represent abstract qualities and in which the author intends a different meaning to be read beneath the surface

* **Jesuit** refers to a Roman Catholic religious order founded by St. Ignatius Loyola and approved in 1540

Nicholas V

1397–1455
Pope

Pope Nicholas V played a major role in establishing Rome as a center of Renaissance culture. As the first pope with an appreciation for humanist* learning, Nicholas promoted efforts to rebuild the city of Rome along classical* lines. He also founded the Vatican Library and made the Vatican palace the papal* residence.

* **humanist**   referring to a Renaissance cultural movement promoting the study of the humanities (the languages, literature, and history of ancient Greece and Rome) as a guide to living

* **classical**   in the tradition of ancient Greece and Rome

* **papal**   referring to the office and authority of the pope

* **theology**   study of the nature of God and of religion

Born Tommaso Parentucelli de Sarzana, the future Nicholas V studied the arts at the University of BOLOGNA. When his family could no longer support him, he interrupted his studies to become a tutor for wealthy families in FLORENCE. Parentucelli returned to Bologna in about 1420. There he met bishop Niccolò Albergati, whom he served for more than 20 years.

While assisting Albergati, Parentucelli shifted his studies to theology*. He became a priest around 1422 and later served as a church official in the cathedral of Bologna. In 1444 Pope Eugenius IV appointed Parentucelli a bishop. One of his early tasks involved a mission to meet with the German king Frederick III and gain his support against the Council of Basel. This Council was an assembly of the church that was causing conflict by refusing to remain under papal control. The mission was a success, and the pope rewarded Parentucelli by making him a cardinal in 1446. About two months later, upon Eugenius's death, Parentucelli gained election to the papacy as Nicholas V.

Nicholas's first priority as pope was to secure the support of Germany. His colleagues negotiated a settlement with Frederick III, which recognized the pope's right to appoint most church officials in Germany, but which had little effect in practice. With Germany's support, Nicholas ended the conflict with the Council of Basel. By 1449 he was officially acknowledged as ruler of the Papal States*.

* **Papal States**   lands in central Italy under the authority of the pope

As pope, Nicholas worked to please most people. Unlike other popes of his time, he did not use his power to gain titles for his relatives. He also respected existing political relations. In addition, he pursued a tolerant policy toward Jews, prohibiting attempts to baptize Jewish children without their parents' consent and supporting the right of Jews and Jewish converts in various parts of Europe.

* **patronage**   support or financial sponsorship

The most distinctive feature of Nicholas's rule was his support of humanism and the new direction he gave to the urban development of Rome. Nicholas brought many humanists to Rome and provided financial support for them. He also made the papal court a center of scholarly patronage*. Most importantly, he founded the Vatican Library as an aid to all scholars. At his death the library contained nearly 1,200 Latin and Greek manuscripts. (*See also* **Councils; Libraries; Popes and Papacy.**)

**1401–1464
Philosopher, theologian, and reformer**

* **treatise**   long, detailed essay

* **theology**   study of the nature of God and of religion

Nicholas of Cusa (Nicolaus Cusanus) was a leading philosopher and religious reformer of the early Renaissance. From humble origins, he rose to great heights of power and influence. He wrote many treatises*, sermons, and works on political theory.

Early Efforts. Born in the town of Kues in the Moselle River valley, Nicholas studied at the universities of Heidelberg, Padua, and Cologne. He received degrees in church law, studied theology*, and became acquainted with the new humanist* learning. By 1432 Nicholas had become a priest and a successful lawyer. That year he presented a case before the Council of Basel on a matter of religious law. Although

* **humanist** referring to a Renaissance cultural movement promoting the study of the humanities (the languages, literature, and history of ancient Greece and Rome) as a guide to living

* **Byzantine Empire** Eastern Christian Empire based in Constantinople (A.D. 476–1453)

* **prince** Renaissance term for the ruler of an independent state

* **Holy Roman Empire** political body in central Europe composed of several states; existed until 1806

* **Ottoman Turks** Turkish followers of Islam who founded the Ottoman Empire in the 1300s; the empire eventually included large areas of eastern Europe, the Middle East, and northern Africa

* **diocese** geographical area under the authority of a bishop

Nicholas lost the case, it inspired him to write a famous treatise on questions related to church structure and reform.

By 1437 Nicholas was working with Pope Eugenius IV to unite Roman Catholics and Greek Orthodox Christians. To advance this cause, Nicholas sailed to Constantinople, the capital of the Byzantine Empire*. Later, Nicholas reported having an experience during the voyage that changed his view of the universe. It inspired him to try to explain how one might reach a truer knowledge of God.

Between 1438 and 1445 Nicholas often worked in Germany, trying to win the support of German princes* for the pope. During this period, he produced his first important philosophical work, *On Learned Ignorance*. In it, Nicholas wrote that individuals could only hope to understand God by going beyond human abilities. He also argued that the only way to find truth was through faith in the Word of God.

Cardinal and Bishop. In 1450, Nicholas became a cardinal of the church, and the pope sent him to discuss reforms with leaders of the Holy Roman Empire*. However, Nicholas found efforts at reform blocked at almost every turn. Two years later, Nicholas went to the city of Brixen as its new bishop. However, many people there resented having an outsider as bishop, especially one of low birth. They also resisted his efforts to impose religious reform. Nicholas carried on his reform struggle until 1457, when he sought refuge in a nearby castle. He remained there until called to Rome by the pope in 1458. Despite the resistance he encountered in Brixen, Nicholas continued to write. The fall of CONSTANTINOPLE in 1453 inspired him to write *On the Peace of Faith*, a tale in which various nations and religions achieved religious harmony.

On his return to Rome, Nicholas became involved in efforts by Pope PIUS II to organize a crusade against the Ottoman Turks*, who had seized Constantinople. When the pope left Rome to seek support from various princes, Nicholas stayed behind as his representative and tried to reform the diocese* of Rome.

Nicholas returned to Brixen in 1460, but once again he had to flee to Italy. There he resumed his efforts to promote reform. Although his health began to fail, he remained an active writer and reformer. When the pope left Rome in the summer of 1464 in hopes of leading a crusade against the Turks, Nicholas remained behind to resolve some unfinished business. However, while traveling to join the crusaders, he fell ill and died. (*See also* **Astronomy; Christianity; Individualism; Philosophy; Religious Thought.**)

Nostradamus

See *Magic and Astrology.*

Notaries

Duck uring the Renaissance, many types of agreements—including land sales, business contracts, and wills—needed to be written in Latin and set up in the proper legal form in order to be binding and valid. The

notary created the legal record of these agreements, making them public documents that others could consult when necessary. In many areas, notaries played a key role in the Renaissance legal system.

To become a notary in Italy, a person had to join a guild* that also included lawyers. Admission into the guild involved an examination, which people prepared for either through apprenticeship* or by attending classes for two years. Although notaries outnumbered lawyers, they were of a lower social class and held less political power.

The use of notaries spread north during the 1200s. Their legal role and social status varied from one country to another. In France notaries headed government departments and royal offices for public records. By the 1400s they had become hereditary nobles and cultural leaders. Notaries in England played a more limited role. They had almost no function in common law courts, which preferred oral to written evidence. However, they did serve in church and military courts. Notaries were also a vital part of the papal* curia, or administration. In 1507 Pope JULIUS II established a formal college of notaries who had an exclusive right to serve in the curia. (*See also* **Law.**)

* **guild** association of craft and trade owners and workers that set standards for and represented the interests of its members

* **apprenticeship** system under which a person is bound by legal agreement to work for another for a specified period of time in return for instruction in a trade or craft

* **papal** referring to the office and authority of the pope

Numerology

During the Renaissance, many people attached symbolic meanings to different numbers. Authors made use of this symbolism in the structure of their works—that is, their division into books and chapters, verses and lines. They also created patterns of numbers by repeating certain words, phrases, and images. Readers saw these patterns as pointing to hidden meanings beyond the actual content of the text.

The study of numbers dates back to ancient Greece, where philosophers often explained their views of reality in terms of numbers and the relationships between them. The philosopher PLATO, for example, noted that certain ratios between numbers determined which notes of the scale would harmonize with each other. He considered a 2-to-1 ratio ideal because it produced the most perfect harmony, the octave. He called this ratio a diapason. He saw this and other ratios formed by combining the first seven numbers as expressing the harmony of the world.

Thinkers of the Middle Ages and Renaissance attached Christian beliefs to the classical* tradition of giving meaning to numbers and ratios. They linked Plato's seven numbers, for example, with the seven days of creation described in the Bible. They also saw meaning in certain numbers found within the Bible, such as 33 (Christ's age at the time of his death) and 42 (the number of generations from Abraham to Jesus). Such Christianized number symbolism figured prominently in the works of many Renaissance philosophers.

Some Renaissance writers structured their works according to key numbers and ratios. In John MILTON's poem "At a Solemn Musick," changes in rhyme and sentence structure break the poem's 28 lines into units of 16, 8, and 4 lines. This double diapason reflects the heavenly harmony that is the subject of the poem. The poem *Epithalamion,* by Edmund SPENSER, contains 24 stanzas, each corresponding to one hour of the day. Its structure is so precise that in the poem, night arrives after 16

* **classical** in the tradition of ancient Greece and Rome

and one-quarter stanzas, exactly when it would fall in a 24-hour period. Authors could also use words to form patterns and ratios—for example, by repeating images of the sun at certain places throughout a verse or, in a longer work, presenting parallel scenes in the first and final sections.

Within the system of numerology, the same number could have many possible meanings. Also, a given meaning of a number could be either a positive or a negative sign within a work. Readers had to rely on the content of the writing to show which reading the author intended. The use of numbers to express hidden meanings made the structure of a work a vehicle for Renaissance writers' wit. (*See also* **Literature.**)

Nürnberg

* **Holy Roman Empire** political body in central Europe composed of several states; existed until 1806

* **patronage** support or financial sponsorship

The German city of Nürnberg was one of the largest and most important cities in the Holy Roman Empire*. It was a major economic and political center as well as a focal point for Renaissance art. Throughout the 1400s and early 1500s, Nürnberg grew in wealth and population. New construction and the expansion of older buildings provided work for architects and artists, and the town's churches and monasteries served as important sources of patronage*. Among the important artists to live in Nürnberg was Albrecht DÜRER, a native of the city.

By the 1500s Nürnberg was the second largest German town, after Cologne. More than 40,000 people lived within the city walls, and a similar number dwelled in the surrounding area. Twelve important trade routes came together near Nürnberg, linking the city to the commerce of the Rhine River valley and far beyond.

Nürnberg's leaders made sure that local products were part of the commercial traffic that flowed around the city. Important privileges—such as toll-free trading zones—helped its economy. The city's craft workers earned fame for the quality of their goods, especially metal products such as cannons, clocks, and armor.

The city's political life was closely tied to the Holy Roman Empire. Nürnberg's Great Charter freed it from all authority except that of the Holy Roman Emperor or his agent. In the late 1300s, Emperor Charles IV granted Nürnberg the honor of holding the first diet, or legislative assembly, for each newly elected emperor. In 1424 Emperor Sigismund moved the imperial regalia* from PRAGUE to Nürnberg, where they remained for the next 300 years.

* **regalia** symbols or ornaments of royalty

Emperor CHARLES V made Nürnberg the seat of the Imperial Chamber of Justice, the empire's highest court of law. However, the city's support for the Protestantism of Martin LUTHER led Charles V, a Catholic, to move the imperial offices to another German city in 1524. Although Nürnberg adopted the Lutheran faith, it remained loyal to the emperor. The city continued to send money and troops to support the wars between the Holy Roman Empire and the Ottoman Turks*. (*See also* **Cities and Urban Life; Clocks; Economy and Trade; Nürnberg Chronicle.**)

* **Ottoman Turks** Turkish followers of Islam who founded the Ottoman Empire in the 1300s; the empire eventually included large areas of eastern Europe, the Middle East, and northern Africa

Nürnberg Chronicle

* **humanist** Renaissance expert in the humanities (the languages, literature, history, and speech and writing techniques of ancient Greece and Rome)

* **woodcut** print made from a block of wood with an image carved into it

* **apprentice** person bound by legal agreement to work for another for a specified period of time in return for instruction in a trade or craft

The *Nürnberg Chronicle* is one of the finest examples of book design and production in the history of printing. This heavily illustrated work relates the history of the world, beginning with the biblical account of its creation and continuing up through the 1400s. Although later works outshone the *Nürnberg Chronicle* in terms of content, the text remains significant for its images and graphic design. Humanist* and doctor Hartmann Schedel assembled the work and had it published in Nürnberg, Germany, in 1493. As Latin was the language of scholars at the time, the text appeared in Latin as well as in a German translation. Anton Koberger, one of the best printers of scholarly works in the 1400s, produced approximately 1,500 copies of the Latin edition and 1,000 copies in German.

The *Nürnberg Chronicle* contained more than 1,800 illustrations printed from 645 woodcuts*. At the time, this was the largest number of woodcuts that had ever appeared in a printed book. The images, which the young artist Albrecht DÜRER helped to create as an apprentice*, were of high quality. They included portrayals of major events from the Old and New Testaments, stories from the lives of saints, portraits of famous rulers, and maps and images of cities. (*See also* **Printing and Publishing.**)

Opera

* **Baroque** artistic style of the 1600s characterized by movement, drama, and grandness of scale

* **humanist** referring to a Renaissance cultural movement promoting the study of the humanities (the languages, literature, and history of ancient Greece and Rome) as a guide to living

* **nymph** in ancient mythology, a nature spirit who takes the form of a beautiful young woman

The opera—a full-length musical drama, complete with costumes and staging, which is sung throughout—first arose in the 1590s. Its appearance marked a change from traditional Renaissance music to a new style known as Baroque*. Modern opera has its roots in late-Renaissance Italian music, literature, and theater, as well as humanist* thought.

Opera's Greek Influence. Tales from ancient Greek mythology inspired many early operas. The first known opera, *Daphne,* told the story of a nymph* whom the Greek god Apollo loved. Its first performance occurred in Florence, Italy, in 1598. Planned and sponsored by silk merchant Jacopo Corsi, the opera formed part of the city's Carnival celebrations. (Carnival was a festive event that took place before Lent, the solemn period leading up to Easter.) Italian composer Jacopo Peri wrote the opera's music to accompany the poet Ottavio Rinuccini's text. Only six short sections of this work survive.

Soon after creating *Daphne,* Peri and Rinuccini teamed up again to produce a second opera, called *Eurydice.* This work, also based on Greek mythology, focused on the wife of the musician Orpheus. It premiered in Florence in 1600 as part of the marriage celebration of MARIE DE MÉDICIS (of the ruling MEDICI family) to King Henry IV of France. A complete printed musical score from *Eurydice* still exists.

Interest in ancient Greece grew throughout the Renaissance, inspiring a group of musicians in Florence to create an informal academy called the Camerata. The amateur composer Giovanni de' Bardi organized the academy as a place where the city's most important musicians, intellectuals, poets, and philosophers could gather to discuss ancient

Greek music. They learned about the subject from the Italian humanist Girolamo Mei. Mei believed that the ancient Greeks had chanted their tragedies in a style midway between speaking and singing. He also thought that many Greek tunes had focused on a single note. The members of the Camerata decided that ancient Greek music could move listeners better than the music of their time because it was vocal, followed the text closely, and consisted of only one melody. They believed that Renaissance music failed to stir people because it often involved several melodies that moved against each other.

Renaissance Influences. A key factor in the development of opera was the musical style that came to be known as recitative in the early 1600s. Recitative stressed musical simplicity. By using the patterns of regular speech, the singer could communicate the emotion of the work's text. In the early recitatives, composers wrote only one note for every syllable of text. In addition, they kept the voice's range (its ability to hit high and low notes) narrow, and avoided patterns of rhythm and melody.

Existing forms of Renaissance drama also influenced opera. Early operas were similar to pastoral* tragicomedies—plays that combined elements of comedy and tragedy in a rural setting. Giovanni Battista Guarini established this style in 1590 with his work *The Faithful Shepherd.* Italian dramas called *intermedi,* short pieces shown between the acts of Renaissance plays, also affected opera. *Intermedi* had first appeared in the 1400s at the court of Ferrara. They combined music, drama, dance, and in most cases, costumes. The opera *Daphne* begins exactly like one of the *intermedi* performed at a Medici wedding in 1589. (*See also* **Baroque; Music; Music, Vocal.**)

* **pastoral** relating to the countryside; often used to draw a contrast between the innocence and serenity of rural life and the corruption and extravagance of court life

Orphans and Foundlings

Churches and governments in Renaissance society made efforts to protect and care for needy and helpless people, such as children without parents or guardians. A variety of organizations existed to help such children. However, the treatment children received sometimes depended on whether they were orphans or foundlings. Orphans were children whose parents had died, while foundlings were those abandoned by their parents. Society generally had less respect for foundlings than for orphans and in some cases treated them as less worthy of aid.

Some religious leaders saw foundlings born to unmarried women as being at special risk of sin because they had been "doubly conceived in sin." Although not all foundlings were born outside of marriage, their uncertain origins disgraced them in the public eye. Abandonment by poor families unable or unwilling to keep all of their children became increasingly common over the course of the Renaissance.

In spite of the social distinctions between the foundlings and orphans, they often ended up in the same large institutions. For example, the Hospital of the Pietà in Venice, originally established to house abandoned children, admitted many orphans after outbreaks of plague* in the 1350s and 1440s. During the 1500s it became more common to

* **plague** highly contagious and often fatal disease that wiped out much of Europe's population in the mid-1300s and reappeared periodically over the next three centuries; also known as the Black Death

Renaissance hospitals and other institutions cared for orphans and foundlings from birth to adulthood. This scene from the 1400s shows various activities at of the Foundling Hospital of St. Maria della Scala in Siena, Italy, including the baptism, nursing, education, and marriage of the foundlings.

place foundlings and orphans in separate establishments. Some orphanages belonged to hospitals, while others stood on their own.

One great danger was that mothers might kill unwanted children before baptism—murdering their souls along with their bodies. To prevent such crimes, hospitals and other charitable institutions in some parts of Europe offered an alternative to desperate women. They provided places for people to abandon their children anonymously and in relative safety by simply leaving them on a special shelf or a rotating wheel. Unfortunately, when hospitals were flooded with abandoned children, death rates rose so high that abandonment threatened to become little more than a legal form of child murder. England and other Protestant countries were generally reluctant to let people abandon their children openly. Many hospitals and orphanages accepted foundlings but did not call attention to the fact.

Institutions that cared for large numbers of infants and children employed wet nurses to feed them. A wet nurse was a woman, usually of the peasant class, paid to breast-feed another person's child. After a few weeks in the hospital, most orphans and abandoned children were sent to stay with foster parents, often in the surrounding countryside. Most of them died, but those who survived generally returned to the hospitals between the ages of four and seven. The institutions prepared these older children for places in society as laborers, servants, housewives, or crafts workers. Some orphans and foundlings ended up spending their lives in service to the hospitals that had taken them in. In other

OTTOMAN EMPIRE

* apprenticeship system under which a person is bound by legal agreement to work for another for a specified period of time in return for instruction in a trade or craft

cases, an apprenticeship* or an attachment to a foster family could lead to official adoption. Either way, the goal was to turn abandoned children into useful and productive adults, preventing them from becoming beggars or criminals. (*See also* **Childhood; Education; Hospitals and Asylums; Motherhood.**)

Ottoman Empire

* Holy Roman Empire political body in central Europe composed of several states; existed until 1806

* Ottoman Turks Turkish followers of Islam who founded the Ottoman Empire in the 1300s; the empire eventually included large areas of eastern Europe, the Middle East, and northern Africa

* Byzantine Empire Eastern Christian Empire based in Constantinople (A.D. 476–1453)

* siege prolonged effort to force a surrender by surrounding a fortress or town with armed troops, cutting the area off from aid

* sultan ruler of a Muslim state

* hierarchy organization of a group into higher and lower levels

For more than 600 years, the Ottoman Empire ruled large parts of southeastern Europe, the Middle East, and east Africa. Founded in the late 1200s, the empire achieved its greatest size and strength during the Renaissance, when it extended well into eastern Europe. Its efforts to expand farther brought it into conflict with the Holy Roman Empire* of the HABSBURG DYNASTY and with other European powers.

Historical Overview. By the late 1400s the Ottoman Turks* had created a vast empire. In 1453 their ruler MEHMED II (1432–1481) used overwhelming force to conquer CONSTANTINOPLE, the capital of the Byzantine Empire*. Within 30 years the Ottoman Empire had taken over several states in eastern Europe, including Serbia, Bosnia, and Herzegovina. It also dominated the states of Montenegro and Albania, but they remained independent. Venice surrendered some of its outlying land to the empire in 1479. Under SÜLEYMAN I (ca. 1495–1566), the Ottomans hoped to advance even farther into Europe. But in their attempt to do so, they encountered the Holy Roman Empire ruled by CHARLES V.

The two empires first confronted one another in HUNGARY, where the Turks destroyed the armies of Hungarian king Louis II in 1526. The Ottomans then laid siege* to Vienna in 1529. To end the siege and free the city, the Habsburg rulers had to recognize Ottoman rule over most of Hungary and parts of Romania. Ottoman conquest of other areas of eastern Europe and lands bordering the Black Sea followed.

The conflict between the Ottoman and Habsburg empires extended to the Mediterranean Sea, where the Turkish navy fought against the forces of Spain and Venice. These battles ended in the destruction of the Turkish fleet at the Battle of Lepanto (1571). Many scholars regard this defeat as the beginning of the decline of the Ottoman Empire.

The Ottoman State and Society. Ottoman rule brought a long period of peace to the lands controlled by the empire. Although Ottoman rulers held almost absolute power, they governed efficiently and allowed the practice of different religions.

The Ottoman sultan* acted as military chief, lawgiver, and religious leader. As the commander of the armed forces, the sultan led his armies in jihad, or holy war, against unbelievers. As lawgiver, he served as the head of legal and religious hierarchies* that controlled almost every aspect of human conduct. The sultan exercised these extensive powers through a system of government established by Mehmed II in the late 1400s.

The basic law of the Ottoman Empire—the *Kanoun Namé*—established the state structure and regulated the social order. A central coun-

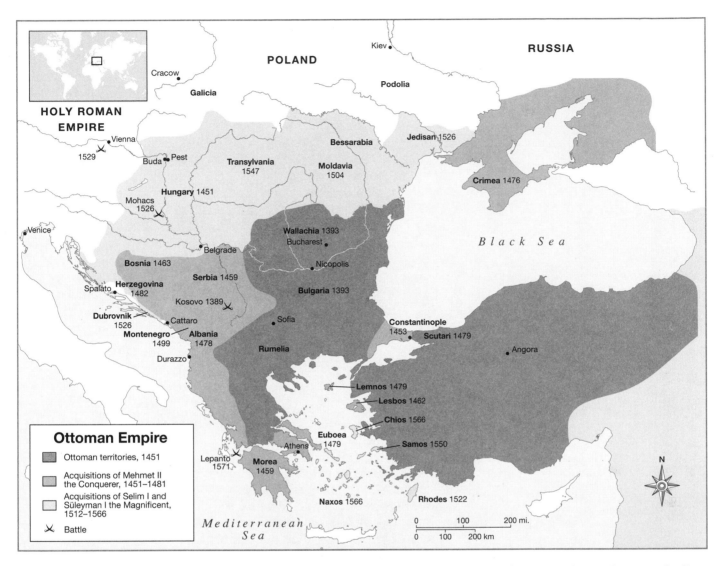

Ottoman Empire

- Ottoman territories, 1451
- Acquisitions of Mehmet II the Conquerer, 1451–1481
- Acquisitions of Selim I and Süleyman I the Magnificent, 1512–1566
- ✕ Battle

cil assisted the sultan. He appointed all the council members, including the grand vizier, who was the chief minister of state and leader of armies in the field. High-ranking administrators called pashas ran the large cities. These officials served only at the sultan's pleasure.

The Ottomans divided society into two main categories. The first distinguished Muslims from non-Muslims, while the second identified those connected with the state and its institutions—known as "professional Ottomans"—from the rest of the population. Most "professional Ottomans" came from a system of slavery in which Christian male children had to convert to Islam. These slaves served in the military, worked at the palace, or performed other tasks. Many became trusted government officials.

Under Ottoman rule religious groups could practice their faith freely. At a time when Jews suffered persecution throughout Europe, the Ottoman Empire welcomed them for their skills and for their contacts with the outside world.

Ottoman Impact on Europe. The Ottoman Empire's conquest of Constantinople and its control of the eastern Mediterranean undermined the dominant position of Venice and Genoa in regional trade. Merchants from these Italian cities were forced to look elsewhere for markets. The Ottoman expansion also increased Western fears of the Muslims and may have contributed to the Holy Roman Empire's decision in 1555 to recognize the legal rights of Protestants. Needing the support of Protestants in fighting the Turks, the Habsburgs took steps to come to terms with the followers of Martin LUTHER.

Many Europeans ignored the Ottoman Empire's advanced methods of government, its tolerance of ethnic and religious diversity, and its scientific and cultural achievements. Instead, they condemned the Ottoman conquests as brutal and viewed the Turks as a threat to Christian civilization. Others, such as Luther and Desiderius ERASMUS, saw the Turks as a sign of God's anger toward Europe and urged repentance and reform. However, as the Renaissance progressed, the threat of the Ottoman Turks became of less concern to Europe. (*See also* **Austria; Europe, Idea of; Habsburg Dynasty; Islam; Jews; Slavery; Venice.**)

* **pagan** referring to ancient religions that worshiped many gods, or more generally, to any non-Christian religion

* **classical** in the tradition of ancient Greece and Rome

Renaissance scholars took an intense interest in the cultures of ancient Greece and Rome. Because these pre-Christian societies had worshiped many gods, some Renaissance writers feared that studying them would lead Christian scholars and artists to develop pagan* beliefs. Even the Dutch scholar Desiderius ERASMUS, a noted supporter of classical* learning, saw this as a potential danger. Later historians who studied the Renaissance, such as Jakob BURCKHARDT, also saw signs of pagan influence among Renaissance scholars. Modern historians, however, have largely rejected these claims.

Although artists and writers referred to ancient gods such as Venus and Zeus in their works, they saw them not as true gods but as evil spirits, or as powerful men and women whose fame had led some people to view them as more than human. They also used pagan gods to represent abstract moral qualities. For example, the goddess Venus stood for love or lust. Most artists, writers, and scholars of the Renaissance took great care to distinguish the ancient gods they wrote about from the true God of Christianity.

A few Renaissance scholars, however, did adopt elements of pagan belief. In the early 1400s, the Greek thinker George Gemistus Pletho sought to revive the religious ideas of the ancient Greek philosopher PLATO. Eventually Plethos proclaimed his goal of reviving ancient paganism. Later scholars, such as Marsilio FICINO of Florence, tried to blend Plato's ideas with Christianity. Ficino claimed that certain pre-Christian figures, including Plato, had foreseen the major ideas of Christianity. Ficino did not see these ancient thinkers as "pagan" in their influence. Another Italian scholar, Giovanni PICO DELLA MIRANDOLA, drew on non-Christian sources in much of his work, including writings by Arabs and Jewish mystics*. However, his work also showed an intense belief in Christianity. (*See also* **Classical Antiquity; Humanism.**)

* **mystic** believer in the idea of a direct, personal union with the divine

Painting

See *Art.*

* **classical** in the tradition of ancient Greece and Rome

* **patron** supporter or financial sponsor of an artist or writer

* **facade** front of a building; outward appearance

* **medieval** referring to the Middle Ages, a period that began around A.D. 400 and ended around 1400 in Italy and 1500 in the rest of Europe

* **symmetry** balance created by matching forms on opposite sides of a structure

* **Gothic** style of architecture characterized by pointed arches and high, thin walls supported by flying buttresses

During the Renaissance, many wealthy individuals owned magnificent palaces and townhouses. The rise of a successful merchant class, along with a renewed appreciation for classical* architecture and design, led to a demand for grand private homes. The Renaissance palazzo, an elegant residence built in a specific style, first emerged in FLORENCE in the 1400s. Eventually, architects in other cities adopted the Florentine style and added new features to suit their patrons*.

Florence. During the Middle Ages, wealthy Florentine families lived in compounds consisting of clusters of buildings. The compounds often included defensive towers, covered walkways (loggias) overlooking the street, and shops on the lower level. By the mid-1400s this design gave way to the palazzo style—a single tall building with four wings surrounding a central courtyard. The facade* was covered with roughly finished stone and decorated with ornaments such as carved molding, the family coat-of-arms, or the patrons' personal symbols.

The palazzo was a more private place than the medieval* compound. The loggias faced the courtyard instead of the street, and the family's living quarters were located on the second floor (the *piano nobile*) away from the public areas. The courtyard provided a space for banquets and celebrations enclosed by the rest of the building. Because many Florentine palaces belonged to prosperous merchants, the ground floor often featured storerooms and other spaces connected with the family's commercial activities.

Various architects added new design elements to Florentine palaces. The Palazzo Rucellai (1450s), built by Leon Battista ALBERTI, included rows of classical columns on the facade. This became a popular feature in palace design, particularly outside Florence. The Palazzo Strozzi (1489–1490), built by Giuliano da Sangallo, introduced a strict symmetry* of design that influenced the placement of windows and other features and the arrangement of rooms around the courtyard.

Rome and Venice. Roman palaces evolved from medieval castles rather than from urban compounds. As a result, they were bulkier and contained less ornamentation than those in Florence. The facade and walls of Roman palaces had few openings and featured fortified towers that suggested military strength. The layout of Roman palaces varied but often included two or more wings around an open courtyard and rear loggias overlooking extensive gardens. By the 1500s, Florentine influence led to the increasing use of symmetry and classical elements.

Venice had a palace tradition well before the Renaissance. Gothic* palaces with irregularly spaced arcades (covered passageways) and brightly colored walls lined the city's canals. In the 1400s, Gothic and Renaissance elements combined to create a Venetian palazzo style. Many of Venice's powerful families admired ancient Roman culture and

The Palazzo Piccolomini in Pienza, in the Tuscan region of Italy, was built during the 1460s. It features the stone façade and carved moldings typical of Renaissance palaces.

See color plate 8, vol. 3

had close ties with the Roman nobility. For these reasons, Venetian palazzo design borrowed heavily from the Roman style.

France. The French equivalent of the Italian palazzo was the *hôtel particulier,* the townhouse of a noble family. But, unlike in Italy, the occupants of these townhouses did not include members of the middle class. Sharp social distinctions in France distinguished the residences of the upper class from the *maisons* (houses) of wealthy merchants.

In the Middle Ages the *hôtel particulier* was like a castle in the city, but in the mid-1500s the Italian style became popular. FRANCIS I (ruled 1515–1547) invited Italian designers, such as the Venetian architect Sebastiano Serlio, to his court. They applied Italian Renaissance principles to the French townhouse style.

French Renaissance townhouses consisted of a main block set between a courtyard and a garden. Wings enclosed two sides of the

courtyard and a wall separated the house from the street. The facade, often decorated with classical elements such as columns, featured a large door. As in Rome, the *hôtel particulier* was organized in suites of rooms, such as a main hall, a bedchamber, and a study. (*See also* **Architecture; Châteaus and Villas.**)

Palatinate

* **principality**   independent state ruled by a prince or count

* **patronage**   support or financial sponsorship

* **Holy Roman Emperor**   ruler of the Holy Roman Empire, a political body in central Europe composed of several states that existed until 1806

The Palatinate was a German principality* that became known for its patronage* of the arts during the Renaissance. Two territories made up the Palatinate. The Rhine or Lower Palatinate was in western Germany along the Rhine and Neckar Rivers. The Upper Palatinate consisted of an area north of the region of BAVARIA. Other lands separated the two territories. Heidelberg, the Palatinate's capital, gained a reputation as a literary and cultural center.

The region's ruler, known as the count palatine, served as one of seven German electors who chose the Holy Roman Emperor*. He also represented the emperor when the throne of the HOLY ROMAN EMPIRE was vacant. The borders of the Palatinate changed often. The principality expanded under Elector Frederick I, who ruled from 1449 to 1476, then lost territory as a result of the Bavarian War of Succession in 1504.

In the 1500s many residents of the Palatinate converted to Protestantism. However, their loyalty shifted between the churches established by Martin LUTHER and by John CALVIN. Elector Frederick V, a Protestant, became king of BOHEMIA in 1619. His rise to power troubled the Catholic HABSBURG DYNASTY, which ruled the Holy Roman Empire, and led to the first phase of the THIRTY YEARS' WAR. Frederick's army suffered defeat, and he lost his role in electing the emperor. The Peace of Westphalia in 1648 restored the electoral role to the Palatinate.

* **humanist**   Renaissance expert in the humanities (the languages, literature, history, and speech and writing techniques of ancient Greece and Rome)

Rulers of the Palatinate supported artists, writers, and scholars. In 1386 Elector Rupert I founded the University of Heidelberg, which became a center of scholarship and culture. Cultural life also flourished at the court of Frederick I and his nephew Philip. During the late 1400s, Philip's patronage attracted humanists* such as Rudolf AGRICOLA and Conrad CELTIS, who founded the Literary Society of the Rhine. Philip also sponsored German literature as well as translations of Latin and Greek works. Heidelberg had one of the best libraries in Germany—the Bibliotheca Palatina. By the early 1600s it contained thousands of books and priceless manuscripts. However, the ruler of Bavaria gave the library to the pope after the Palatinate's defeat in the Thirty Years' War. (*See also* **German Language and Literature; Libraries; Princes and Princedoms; Universities.**)

Palestrina, Giovanni Pierluigi da

ca. 1525–1594
Italian singer and composer

Giovanni Palestrina was one of the outstanding singers of the Renaissance and a leading composer of sacred music. He wrote a great deal of music for Catholic services, including 104 Masses and 250 motets*. Although copies of Palestrina's sacred works spread widely during the 1500s, his most popular works were his Italian madrigals*.

* **motet** sacred musical work for several voices, usually performed without instruments

* **madrigal** piece of nonreligious vocal music involving complex harmonies, usually for several voices without instrumental accompaniment

* **papal** referring to the office and authority of the pope

Palestrina began his musical career as a choirboy in the church of Santa Maria Maggiore in Rome. In 1551 he became master of choirboys there, and later he served as choirmaster at St. Peter's Cathedral. In 1555 Pope Julius III named Palestrina to the papal* choir, bypassing the rule that allowed the members of the choir to choose new singers. His time there was short lived, however, as Pope Paul IV had Palestrina and two other singers removed from the choir because they were married.

Palestrina began composing music as a young man, publishing his first book of Masses in 1554. His second publication was a popular book of madrigals, which he later said he was embarrassed to have written because they were not religious works. After Paul IV had him removed from the papal choir, Palestrina spent the rest of his life as chapel master for major churches and related institutions in Rome. In this role he produced music for the papal chapel and became, in effect, its official composer.

In addition to his reputation as a composer and singer, Palestrina was also a highly respected teacher. Those who wished to learn the art of Renaissance counterpoint (the interweaving of two or more melodies) used his style as a model. After his death Palestrina also became something of a mythical figure in the field of music. A legend from the 1600s claimed that he had prevented Pope Marcellus II from banning music in the 1500s. According to this story, Palestrina won over the pope by dedicating a unique Mass to him. (*See also* **Music.**)

Palladio, Andrea

1508–1580
Italian architect

* **classical** in the tradition of ancient Greece and Rome

* **apprentice** person bound by legal agreement to work for another for a specified period of time in return for instruction in a trade or craft

* **humanist** Renaissance expert in the humanities (the languages, literature, history, and speech and writing techniques of ancient Greece and Rome)

* **facade** front of a building; outward appearance

* **medieval** referring to the Middle Ages, a period that began around A.D. 400 and ended around 1400 in Italy and 1500 in the rest of Europe

Andrea Palladio (Andrea di Pietro della Gondola) was the most influential architect of the Renaissance. Famous for his use of classical* elements, he designed many villas (country homes) and public buildings in the region of northern Italy around VENICE and Vicenza. Hundreds of years after his death, modern architects still find inspiration in Palladio's work.

Early Life and Career. Born in the city of Padua, the young Palladio served as apprentice* to a local stonemason. He later moved to the town of Vicenza to join a workshop that specialized in architecture. By his late 20s, Palladio had attracted the attention of Gian Giorgio Trissino, a humanist* and former diplomat who had retired to Vicenza. Under Trissino's influence, Palladio was introduced to humanist ideas, discovered the writings of the ancient Roman architect Vitruvius, and made contacts in intellectual circles of northern Italy.

Palladio designed his first villas in the late 1530s and early 1540s, but these works show few signs of his mature style. His first real breakthrough came when he was asked to design a facade* for the Basilica, Vicenza's public palace. This complex of medieval* buildings had been reorganized into a single structure in the 1400s. Palladio's design incorporates the classical orders (styles of columns) he had studied on trips to Rome. It also employs simple decoration, rather than the complicated ornaments found on many buildings of the time.

Architect Andrea Palladio's most famous country house is the Villa Rotonda, located near Vicenza, Italy. The Rotonda contains large rooms at the corners, with a dome covering a central hall and columned porches flanking its four sides.

* **patron** supporter or financial sponsor of an artist or writer

Later Works. Although Palladio died before work on the Basilica was complete, the project gained him a solid reputation and important contacts. During the 1550s, he developed a villa design that was typical of his work. This design features a central hall with a high ceiling and a row of rooms on each side. The facades of the villas resemble Greek and Roman porticoes (columned porches).

Most of Palladio's projects from this period were located in the countryside, but by the mid-1560s he was again working on public buildings and palaces in Vicenza. His urban works displayed a new boldness that included the use of the colossal order, in which columns and other elements extend through two or more stories of a building. His most famous country house, the Villa Rotonda (near Vicenza), dates from this time. It features a circular central hall covered by a dome, with large rooms in the corners and identical porticoes on four sides.

Palladio's friend and patron* Trissino died in 1550, but the architect kept close contact with humanists in Vicenza and nearby Padua. He was particularly close to Daniele Barbaro, a prominent writer and patron of the arts. Barbaro introduced Palladio to clients in Venice and asked the architect to prepare illustrations for his Italian translation of the works of Vitruvius. Palladio also designed a villa for Barbaro and his brother. However, the house is not typical of Palladio's work and clashes with the decorations commissioned for it, suggesting that the brothers played a major role in the design process.

In the 1560s Palladio began to work on buildings for religious institutions. In his plans for the San Francesco della Vigna church in Venice, he solved the longstanding problem of combining the classical orders with the uneven ceiling heights used in Christian churches. Palladio's solution was adopted by many later architects.

In 1570 Jacopo Sansovino—architectural adviser to the Venetian Republic—died, and Andrea Palladio was appointed to replace him. Palladio devoted the last ten years of his life to the service of Venice. He worked on the building of the grand church of Redentore and acted as a consultant to other projects, including the restoration of the duke's palace. Palladio also designed buildings in other towns, such as churches in Bologna and a theater in Vicenza.

Influence. Palladio's buildings were widely copied and his unique solutions to design problems became common techniques. He wrote several texts on architecture, including *The Churches of Rome* and *Roman Antiquities* (both published in 1554) and his major work, *Four Books on Architecture* (1570). In the 1600s his ideas spread across northern Europe, thanks in part to the efforts of the English architect Inigo JONES. (*See also* **Architecture**.)

Papacy

See *Popes and Papacy.*

Paracelsus

1493–1541
German-Swiss physician
and reformer

* **mysticism**   belief in the idea of a direct, personal union with the divine

* **alchemy**   early science that sought to explain the nature of matter and to transform base metals, such as lead, into gold

* **theology**   study of the nature of God and of religion

Philippus von Hohenhiem, known by the adopted name Paracelsus, helped to establish the role of chemistry in medicine. Although his unusual religious views influenced few people, his ideas on how to treat illness transformed the practice of medicine.

Born in a Swiss village, Paracelsus grew up in Carinthia, now part of southern Austria. Details about his education are unclear; he claimed that his father, a physician, had tutored him. It is unlikely that he ever received a formal medical degree. His writings reveal a knowledge of mysticism*, alchemy*, and folk medicine. As an adult Paracelsus became one of many religious thinkers and reformers who wandered Europe during a time of social, religious, and intellectual turmoil. He narrowly escaped trial for supporting the rebels in the PEASANTS' WAR, an uprising in central Germany during the 1520s. Paracelsus also wrote many works on theology*. In some of these pieces he argued that the nature of God was fourfold, containing not only the traditional Trinity of Father, Son, and Holy Spirit, but also a female creative force.

The medical ideas of Paracelsus differed sharply from those of physicians trained in the universities of Europe. Paracelsus denied the basic principles of Renaissance medicine as put forth by ancient Greek physicians such as GALEN. In particular, he disputed the theory of humors, which held that the body contained four fluids and that a balance among them produced good health. His dislike of standard practices once led Paracelsus to throw an expensive medical textbook onto a bonfire. This stunt enraged the medical authorities, as did his attacks on their methods.

Although he had many odd ideas about human anatomy, Paracelsus offered a new approach to the treatment of illness. It focused on the use of powerful drugs tailored to specific ailments. Paracelsus made many of these drugs by refining poisonous minerals and plants. He also used chemical processes that were unfamiliar to most physicians. Such novel practices made him many enemies, but they also earned him a reputation as a pioneer of medical chemistry.

Because Paracelsus led a wandering life and lacked formal training, most scholars of his time ignored his work. In the two generations after his death, however, medical scholars paid greater attention to his ideas. They published and wrote commentaries on his works. His ideas spread, and the concepts and drugs developed by Paracelsus became the basis of chemical medicine. By the 1600s traditional physicians began to accept his methods, and soon the idea of treatment based on chemistry became part of a new approach to medicine. (*See also* **Alchemy; Medicine.**)

Parades and Pageants

* **civic**   related to a city, a community, or citizens

* **classical**   in the tradition of ancient Greece and Rome

Parades and pageants were a major part of civic* life during the Renaissance. Frequent, lavish, and costly, these public events took place in the city streets, where all residents could view the spectacle. Although displays of this type had been common during the Middle Ages, the revival of classical* culture during the Renaissance gave many of these events a new look.

Renaissance cities often held processions to celebrate the arrival of royal visitors. Here, a parade marches past Henry II of France in honor of his visit to the French city of Rouen in 1550.

Occasions for Display. Parades and processions were held on several different occasions. For example, nearly every city held an event each year in honor of its patron saint. On the saint's feast day, priests and town officials formed an elaborate public procession through the streets, either to visit the local church that bore the saint's name or to display items associated with the saint to the population. Events honoring patron saints became particularly important in the city-states of Italy as a way of building civic identity. In some places the law required all citizens to participate.

Processions also occurred to mark the arrival of distinguished visitors to the city, such as foreign rulers, diplomats, or high church officials. Such formal entries were called *receptions* when local officials treated the entering guest as a formal equal. A *triumph,* by contrast, honored a guest who ranked above the hosts, such as a visiting king or pope. The name referred to a type of procession held in ancient Rome to honor a general returning to the city after a victory. Renaissance triumphs pointed up this link with ancient Rome through their decorations, which might include classical arches, columns, and chariots. The arches constructed for triumphal entries were temporary structures, often labeled with Latin mottoes or verses. Monarchs and popes sometimes made several such entries in the course of a long journey.

Some of the grandest processions occurred during events such as royal marriages, funerals, and coronations. In England, for example,

* Holy Roman Emperor ruler of the Holy Roman Empire, a political body in central Europe composed of several states that existed until 1806

new monarchs paraded through the streets of London on the day before they were crowned. Noble brides arriving in their new homes also received grand entries, often followed by courtly entertainments such as comedies. Solemn processions often formed a part of funeral ceremonies. Many cities even held elaborate processions to honor rulers who had died and been buried elsewhere. The grandest funeral procession of the Renaissance occurred in Brussels (then part of the Netherlands) in honor of the Holy Roman Emperor* CHARLES V, who had died in Spain. This event featured a chariot in the shape of a ship, decorated with painted scenes. The Italian city of Florence also staged many lavish funerals for foreign rulers. In 1564, however, it held an equally magnificent funeral for MICHELANGELO BUONARROTI, one of the city's most famous artists.

Features of Public Displays. Since the Middle Ages, public processions had involved ceremonial costumes and precedence—a specific order in which the participants appeared. A person's position in the procession reflected his or her rank or public role. The link between precedence and power was so strong that any change in the ranking seemed to be a political statement and could cause a public dispute.

Many civic processions, especially during the 1400s and 1500s, included a type of drama called a pageant. There were three main types of pageants. In a *tableau vivant,* or "living painting," the actors stood silently, arranged in poses to illustrate a scene from the Bible, mythology, or ancient history. In pantomime pageants, the actors moved to enact a scene but did not speak. Only the third type, known as a set piece, included spoken lines—usually verses recited in the local language, rather than in Latin. Pageants could take place on floats that moved along the procession route or on fixed stages that the people in the procession would see as they passed by. More than mere entertainment, pageants became the chief way for civic officials to promote ideas to the public and to make political announcements to outsiders.

Public displays also sometimes included complex devices designed to amaze viewers. LEONARDO DA VINCI is thought to have created a moving mechanical lion for the entry of the French king Louis XII into the Italian city of Milan in 1507. About 20 years later, Genoa received Emperor Charles V with a globe of the world that opened to release perfume.

* humanist referring to a Renaissance cultural movement promoting the study of the humanities (the languages, literature, and history of ancient Greece and Rome) as a guide to living

Parades and pageants were vast, living works of art. Humanist* scholars helped plan and design them, poets wrote verses for pageants, and cities hired large numbers of artists to create decorations on short notice. After the development of printing, a tradition arose of preserving these splendid events through books of descriptions and illustrations. About 250 such books survive for Italy alone from the years 1475 to 1600. Planners of entertainments began collecting these festival books as sources of ideas for their own events. (*See also* **Fairs and Festivals.**)

Paré, Ambroise

1510–1590
French surgeon

* **patronage**   support or financial
sponsorship

The most famous surgeon of the 1500s, Ambroise Paré introduced a number of changes in the art of surgery, such as the use of salve to treat wounds. He shared his knowledge with his colleagues through illustrated case histories drawn from his experiences on military campaigns and his medical practice in Paris. Paré's writings, which combined modern and ancient knowledge, had a great influence on the development of surgery.

Paré received training as a barber-surgeon—a profession that, at the time, was separate from the rest of medicine and held a lower status. Around 1533 he became the resident surgeon at the main hospital in Paris. Paré spent much of his career as an army surgeon, accompanying the French military on campaigns over a 30-year period. He also enjoyed royal favor, serving as a court surgeon for several kings.

One of the most readable of Renaissance medical writers, Paré had a great breadth of experience and knowledge. He wrote on surgical techniques as well as anatomy, poisons, and many other medical topics. He was also famous for his invention of artificial noses, tongues, hands, and iron legs. Royal patronage* helped promote Paré's ideas, as well as protect him from attacks by critics. His success served as an example of how a low-status barber-surgeon could achieve both learning and honor. (*See also* **Medicine.**)

Paris

See color
plate 8,
vol. 3

* **elite**   privileged group; upper class

* **guild**   association of craft and trade owners and workers that set standards for and represented the interests of its members

Paris, the largest city in northern Europe in the 1500s, was the commercial, financial, and intellectual center of France. Although the French royal court continued the custom of traveling around the kingdom, the nation's king Francis I made Paris his main residence in 1528. His action added political strength to the city's economic and cultural power.

In the first half of the 1500s the population of Paris nearly doubled, reaching 250,000 to 300,000 at midcentury. The number of residents fell in the 1560s and 1590s during times of war, but recovered during periods of peace. Most people lived in the crowded city center. However, buildings sprawled beyond the city walls despite repeated bans on construction. Royal officials erected large townhouses on the right bank of the river Seine away from the city center. The first signs of Renaissance architecture in Paris appeared in this neighborhood. The left bank of the river contained the city's printing shops, the University of Paris, and religious buildings.

Economy and Society. Agriculture, trade, and manufacturing formed the basis of the city's economy. As home to the nation's elite*, Paris supported a growing market for luxury goods. The production of such items became the city's leading industry. Over time, however, many wealthy merchants abandoned commerce to seek royal offices that promised greater income and the chance to advance into the nobility. They also invested heavily in land, which was associated with noble status, rather than in commerce or industry. In the long term, this hurt the French economy. Guilds* controlled most industries in Paris,

Paris, the financial and cultural center of Renaissance France, lay along the banks of the Seine River. This view of the city from the 1600s shows the Seine with the Nevers Hotel and Nesle Tower on the left bank, and the Louvre, at that time a royal palace, on the right.

* **civic**   related to a city, a community, or citizens

* **militia**   army of citizens who may be called into action in times of emergency

although work performed by women fell outside of the guilds' rule. As the 1500s wore on, the guilds offered less opportunity for advancement. Besides guild members, the city had a large pool of unskilled laborers who often turned to begging during times of scarcity. The city established a public office to help the "worthy" poor, but those considered unwilling to work faced expulsion from Paris.

Government and Politics. A corporation of merchants governed many civic* functions. It built ports and roads, regulated trade, raised the militia*, and collected taxes. Although the merchants' corporation was an elected body, most of its highest officers came from a few wealthy families. These families often held on to their offices, even after abandoning trade and taking positions in government. Merchants who had little chance to move up in the ranks of the corporation filled most of the lower offices. Despite the presence of the corporation, the king often took personal control of city government. He delegated power to an appointed director, known as the provost, and a military governor, who ruled with the help of lesser officers. The king also used the merchant corporation and the high court of the French assembly, or Parlement, to carry out royal policies.

Taxes and forced loans on the city paid for many of France's wars in Italy and the civil wars of the late 1500s. However, the city's financial power enabled it to protect local privileges or to protest royal policies.

Parmigianino

1503–1540
Italian painter

* **Mannerism** artistic style of the 1500s characterized by vivid colors and exaggeration, such as elongated figures in complex poses

* **fresco** mural painted on a plaster wall

* **altarpiece** work of art that decorates the altar of a church

* **Huguenot** French Protestant of the 1500s and 1600s, follower of John Calvin

* **siege** prolonged effort to force a surrender by surrounding a fortress or town with armed troops, cutting the area off from aid

Paris leaders displayed this leverage during the Wars of Religion, a prolonged struggle between Catholics and Huguenots*. The Catholic loyalties of the city's leaders made it difficult for French monarchs to negotiate and enforce peace treaties after several of the religious wars.

The Holy League, a militant group of Catholic leaders, eventually led the city in a revolt against King Henry III. The king formed an alliance with the Protestant Henry of Navarre to oppose the league. Before his death in 1589, Henry III named Henry of Navarre his heir. Navarre claimed the throne as HENRY IV and laid siege* to Paris for several months during 1590. However, the league fell apart when its leaders began to argue among themselves. In 1594 Parisians allowed Henry's forces to enter the city. Henry showed mercy on most of the league's leaders but tightened royal control over the government of Paris. He also began a building program that boosted the city's economy and tied it more firmly to the crown. (*See also* **France; Wars of Religion.**)

The Italian artist Parmigianino (Giorlamo Francesco Maria Mazzola) painted in a sophisticated and elegant style later known as Mannerism*. His graceful portraits and religious images won him high praise and influenced many other Renaissance artists.

The son of a painter in the city of Parma, Parmigianino was taught by his uncles, Pier Ilario and Michele Mazzola. The young Parmigianino showed early talent and completed his first painting at age 16. Three years later he completed two frescoes* for the chapel of Parma's San Giovanni Evangelista church. The frescoes, along with several of the artist's other early works, reveal the influence of the Italian master CORREGGIO.

In 1524 Parmigianino and his uncle Pier Ilario went to Rome to study the ancient ruins and the highly regarded works of MICHELANGELO and RAPHAEL. Impressed by Parmigianino's grace, good manners, and artistic style, critics began to compare him to Raphael. While in Rome, he experimented with printmaking techniques such as etching. He also completed a small number of paintings, including an altarpiece*—the *Vision of St. Jerome*—for the chapel of a local nobleman. According to the Renaissance art historian Giorgio Vasari, the painter was working on this altarpiece when the army of emperor CHARLES V sacked Rome in 1527. Soldiers broke into Parmigianino's studio and captured him. Rather than harming him, though, they demanded some of his drawings as ransom.

In 1530 Parmigianino returned home to Parma to create a pair of altarpieces for the church of Santa Maria della Steccata. He never completed these paintings, but the many drawings he made in preparation for them show that he spent a great deal of time developing his ideas. In about 1534 Parmigianino began his most famous work, an altarpiece called the *Madonna of the Long Neck*. Created for the chapel in the Servite church of Parma, it depicts the Virgin Mary holding the infant Jesus across her lap. Again Parmigianino prepared a large number of sketches in search of the right design. Although he never finished the painting,

PASTORAL

the completed sections show the elongated lines and elegant poses typical of his work.

In the late 1530s, the church members who had commissioned the paintings for the Steccata church became frustrated with Parmigianino's lack of progress. They had the painter jailed briefly, and then barred him from working on the project. Parmigianino fled to the nearby town of Casalmaggiore, where he worked on various other pictures. Still hoping to return to Parma and finish the Steccata altarpieces, he died at age 37. (*See also* **Art; Art in Italy.**)

Pastoral

* **Flemish** relating to Flanders, a region along the coasts of present-day Belgium, France, and the Netherlands

* **medieval** referring to the Middle Ages, a period that began around A.D. 400 and ended around 1400 in Italy and 1500 in the rest of Europe

* **genre** literary form

* **romance** adventure story of the Middle Ages, the forerunner of the modern novel

* **epic** long poem about the adventures of a hero

Artists and writers of the Renaissance often portrayed the countryside as a perfect place, far from the corrupt life of the city and the court. This style, known as the pastoral, became one of the most popular forms for art and literature. Such noted Renaissance figures as English playwright William SHAKESPEARE, Spanish author Miguel de CERVANTES SAAVEDRA, and Flemish* painter Peter Paul RUBENS all created works in a pastoral style.

The pastoral developed out of a variety of ancient and medieval* forms. In particular, it drew on the ancient Roman poems called eclogues, which focused on conversations between shepherds. In the 1200s and 1300s, the Italian poets Dante Alighieri, PETRARCH, and Giovanni BOCCACCIO created new Latin works in this form. Later writers produced eclogues in Italian, and in time the pastoral form spread throughout Europe. Artists also adopted pastoral themes in their works, often placing biblical stories in a country setting.

The Renaissance pastoral was not really a single distinct genre*. Writers used pastoral themes in a variety of forms, including poetry, prose, and drama. For example, Italian playwright Giovanni Battista Guarini used the pastoral style in his play *The Faithful Shepherd* (1590). Guarini believed that the pastoral's rural setting, far removed from the customs of city life, made it an ideal form for social, political, and even sexual experimentation. Other works, such as Cervantes's *Don Quixote*, combined the pastoral style with elements of the romance* form.

The pastoral became extremely popular in England in the late 1500s. English writers produced many famous pastoral works in a variety of literary forms. Edmund SPENSER created a book of eclogues called *The Shepheardes Calender* and also used pastoral themes in his epic* *The Faerie Queene*. Philip SIDNEY produced *Arcadia*, a pastoral romance, and Shakespeare adopted the pastoral style in his comedy *As You Like It*. (*See also* **Drama, French; Italian Language and Literature; Poetry, English.**)

Patronage

Much of the glorious outpouring of art in the Renaissance was the result of *patronage*. The term traditionally refers to the support that people of wealth and influence provided to artists, scholars, and writers. Rulers, popes, and prosperous merchants hired artists to adorn

THE RENAISSANCE

their homes and public spaces, and scholars to translate ancient Greek and Roman texts. *Patronage* can also apply to other types of social and political ties. Many aspects of Renaissance life involved bonds of mutual support between individuals and groups.

PATRONS AND CLIENTS

Patrons, usually individuals or groups with power and substance, assisted their clients—those who followed or served them—in various ways. They might provide clients with jobs in the church or government or supply them with a steady income. Patrons also offered protection and helped clients if they were in trouble with the law. Clients, in turn, gave patrons their loyalty and support. The same person could be a patron (provider of assistance) in one situation and a client (someone needing assistance) in another.

The Renaissance system of patronage evolved out of ancient and medieval* traditions. The words *patron* and *client* came from the Latin terms *patronus* and *cliens,* which date back to ancient Rome. In the late 1400s, some Italians with classical* training began using these words to refer to the patron-client relationships of their day.

In many cases, client-patron relations included strong elements of friendship or even kinship. Members of the English gentry* often referred to their close associates as "cousins," while Italians spoke of their "kinsmen, friends, and neighbors." In some cases, patronage extended or made formal the ties that already existed among neighbors and relatives. Although clients and patrons usually came from different ranks of society, their relationship could include a degree of equality.

Patronage played an important role in the Italian republics* of Florence, Venice, and Genoa, where changes of government or regime* were frequent. To protect their position in these shifting societies, people attached themselves to the *gran maestri,* or "big shots," who dealt in political power. Patron-client relations could become the basis for stable political factions*. Ambitious party leaders and rulers used their patronage to draw power to themselves. For example, the MEDICI family ruled the city-state of Florence by building one-party regimes made up of their friends and clients.

Beginning in the 1460s, Italians began to use the term *maestro della bottega* (boss of the shop) to describe leaders, including rulers and private citizens, who were masters of the art of political patronage. As these political figures grew in power, their relationships with their clients became increasingly unequal. Clients showed greater deference toward them and spoke of them in more respectful, even fawning, terms. Nonetheless, patronage remained a two-way relationship. Great lords frequently went out of their way to "serve" quite humble friends and supporters, knowing that they needed their clients' devotion to maintain their reputations and perhaps their armed support to defend their regimes.

Women, who had little formal power in Renaissance politics, managed to exert quite a bit of influence through the informal workings of

* **medieval**   referring to the Middle Ages, a period that began around A.D. 400 and ended around 1400 in Italy and 1500 in the rest of Europe

* **classical**   in the tradition of ancient Greece and Rome

* **gentry**   people of high birth or social status

* **republic**   form of Renaissance government dominated by leading merchants with limited participation by others

* **regime**   government in power at a particular time

* **faction**   party or interest group within a larger group

Artists, scholars, and writers often depended on the support of wealthy patrons to produce their works. English playwright William Shakespeare dedicated two major works to his patron Sir Henry Wriothesley, the earl of Southampton.

* **humanist**   referring to a Renaissance cultural movement promoting the study of the humanities (the languages, literature, and history of ancient Greece and Rome) as a guide to living

* **prince**   Renaissance term for the ruler of an independent state

* **Holy Roman Emperor**   ruler of the Holy Roman Empire, a political body in central Europe composed of several states that existed until 1806

patronage. Most female patrons focused on helping other women or the poor. Noblewomen, wives and mothers of party leaders, and women who headed important convents all used the culture of patronage to their advantage.

ARTISTIC PATRONAGE

Patronage of the arts took place within the larger context of social and political patronage. Most patrons commissioned artworks not for the art itself, but because it contributed to the splendor of their domains. They sought works that would proclaim their wealth and rank to the world. Patronage could raise the status of the artist as well as the patron. Those who served powerful patrons often acquired prosperity and fame.

Patrons possessed considerable influence, even control, over the artists they hired. Because they were paying, they had the right to dictate the subject matter and style of a piece. Patrons often requested works in their honor. However, patrons and artists could also influence each other through shared ideas, and the works produced under such a partnership are sometimes associated with the names of both patron and artist. The politician Giorgio Trissino, for instance, introduced the architect Andrea PALLADIO to humanist* education and promoted his career. Similarly, artists sometimes functioned as patrons. When MICHELANGELO BUONARROTI worked on the church of San Lorenzo in Florence, he chose boyhood friends, relatives, and neighbors to assist him in the task.

Royal and Papal Patrons. Rulers and popes were the leading patrons of the arts during the Renaissance. Not only did they have the most wealth at their disposal, but they also had the greatest need for artworks. They relied on the splendor of their courts and their possessions to display their power to their subjects and to other princes*. To demonstrate their magnificence, Renaissance rulers commissioned and built grand palaces, churches, and monuments. They also purchased costly decorative items such as jewelry, dishes, luxurious tapestries, and richly embellished armor and weapons. They adorned their clothes with pearls, gems, and embroidery, and their homes with paintings, statues, and manuscripts in lavish bindings.

Among the greatest Renaissance patrons were the dukes of BURGUNDY, who ruled northern France, Belgium, Luxembourg, and the Netherlands. Two of these dukes, Philip the Good (ruled 1419–1467) and Charles the Bold (ruled 1467–1477), gained fame for their magnificent courts and ceremonies. Many masters of arts and crafts served the dukes, including painter Jan Van EYCK. The dukes also collected books and assembled an exceptionally fine choir of musicians.

Several Holy Roman Emperors* of the HABSBURG DYNASTY were noted patrons of the arts. Emperor MAXIMILIAN I (ruled 1493–1519) sought to glorify his family through art. He planned a vast monument that was to feature more than 40 life-size statues of his ancestors, including Julius Caesar, as well as 100 statues of Habsburg family saints. Maximilian also

wrote literature praising his own deeds and had the works illustrated by major artists. In addition, he collected tapestries, gold work, and armor—he was probably the greatest patron of armor-makers in his day. Maximilian's grandson, CHARLES V, preferred science and technology. He collected globes and maps, scientific instruments, and illustrated books on astronomy and anatomy.

Popes emerged as powerful patrons of the arts in the 1500s, and the papal* court became a leading center of culture. Perhaps the most ambitious was Pope JULIUS II (ruled 1503–1513), who sought to restore the lost glories of ancient Rome. He hired architects and artists to turn medieval Rome into a classical city, rebuilding entire sections of town and creating broad avenues bordered with palaces. His successor, LEO X (ruled 1513–1521), was a member of the Medici family. Leo devoted great energy and resources to restoring his family's power through artistic projects. He commissioned Michelangelo to build a huge marble facade* for the church of San Lorenzo in Florence and RAPHAEL to decorate his private dining room in the Vatican. Popes, like worldly rulers, commissioned artworks not only for personal use but also as diplomatic* gifts. Leo X sent the king of France two of Raphael's paintings.

Other noted patrons of the Renaissance included the monarchs of England, France, Naples, and Spain, the dukes of Milan, and the influential ESTE and Medici families. HENRY VIII of England (ruled 1509–1547) spent great sums on his palaces. His 55 residences were furnished with more than 2,000 tapestries, 2,028 items plated in silver or gold, and 1,800 books. FRANCIS I (ruled 1515–1547) of France turned an old hunting lodge into the glorious Renaissance château of Fontainebleau. He bought many Italian artworks and attracted artists, such as LEONARDO DA VINCI and Benvenuto CELLINI, to decorate his flourishing court. Several female rulers also gained fame as patrons. The Spanish queen ISABELLA OF CASTILE (ruled 1474–1504) supported architecture, art, and literature. MARGARET OF AUSTRIA, the daughter of Maximilian I, collected tapestries, gold work, manuscripts, and paintings by such artists as Hieronymus BOSCH. Isabella d'Este of Mantua commissioned a variety of pieces, ranging from floral tapestries to musical instruments.

Other Patrons. Members of the nobility imitated the grand rulers by practicing artistic patronage on a smaller scale. They built mansions, decorated their homes with artworks, and wore expensive clothes and jewelry. They also assembled libraries and sponsored religious architecture, especially private chapels for their families.

Many merchants, bankers, and court officials rose to wealth and prominence in the service of powerful rulers and became patrons themselves. Agostino Chigi, a banker in the Italian city of SIENA, provided funds to three popes and managed business for the papal court. He owned a palace in the center of Rome and a lavish suburban residence modeled on the villas* of ancient Rome. Another notable patron, Nicolas Rolin, rose from a middle-class background to enormous power in the service of the dukes of Burgundy. He commissioned an elaborately adorned hospital in the city of Beaune and Jan van Eyck's painting *Virgin with Chancellor Rolin*.

* **papal**   referring to the office and authority of the pope

* **facade**   front of a building; outward appearance

* **diplomatic**   having to do with formal relations between nations

* **villa**   luxurious country home and the land surrounding it

* **guild** association of craft and trade owners and workers that set standards for and represented the interests of its members

* **epic** long poem about the adventures of a hero

* **masque** dramatic entertainment performed by masked actors, or a ball or party at which all guests wear masks or costumes

Even members of the middle class served as patrons of the arts on a modest scale. People with limited means bought artworks made of inexpensive materials, such as wood, pewter, clay, paper, and brass. Most such items, however, were not commissioned but produced on speculation—that is, to be sold at public markets or in the artist's workshop. As a result, the personal connection between patron and client, so important at the higher levels of artistic patronage, did not exist.

Some patrons were not individuals but groups. Local governments, guilds*, churches, and various religious groups commissioned a variety of artworks and buildings. Town officials were responsible for the construction of bell towers, town halls, fountains, and city walls. Guilds and religious organizations built meetinghouses and chapels and adorned them with artworks. Michelangelo's colossal statue *David*, for example, was a commission from the board of directors of the Florence cathedral. In addition, guilds and other groups ordered decorations, floats, and entertainers for public events.

LITERARY PATRONAGE IN ENGLAND

A complex system of literary patronage developed in Renaissance England, where booksellers paid very small sums to the authors whose works they published. As a result, most writers who were not independently wealthy had to seek a patron to support them. The luckiest authors found positions as secretaries or librarians, either with noble patrons or with the government, which allowed them to pursue their literary efforts as part of their job. Those who could not obtain regular employment struggled along by writing poems or other works on request for the wealthy.

Some authors dedicated their literary works to prominent figures in the hope of being rewarded with money or work. English monarchs—most notably ELIZABETH I and JAMES I—often received such dedications. This method sometimes met with success. After dedicating the first three books of his epic* *The Faerie Queene* to Elizabeth I, Edmund SPENSER received a yearly pension of 50 pounds for life. John DONNE was less fortunate. Dismissed from his patron's service because of a marriage regarded as unsuitable, Donne spent 14 years unable to find steady work. He eked out a living by writing poems to or for various patrons.

Another form of literary patronage involved the theater. Because authorities in London often took a hostile attitude toward plays and the acting profession, acting companies had to seek the aid of powerful nobles or even monarchs. Royal and noble patrons extended their protection to the actors and sometimes hired playwrights directly to provide entertainment for public occasions. The best example of this practice is the elaborate court masques* of the early 1600s.

The patronage system was one of the most important influences on literary production in Renaissance England. It affected the types of works that writers produced, causing some of them to concentrate on works most likely to flatter or please possible patrons. It also led to fierce competition among authors. Patronage not only made the profession of

writing possible but also helped determine the form that profession would take. (*See also* **Architecture; Art; Art in Italy; Books and Manuscripts; English Language and Literature; Literature; Luxury; Parades and Pageants.**)

Peasantry

About 90 percent of the people in Renaissance Europe were peasants—rural laborers who planted crops and tended animals. Agriculture was the most important economic activity throughout Europe, and the peasantry produced the food consumed by people living in cities.

During the Middle Ages most European peasants were serfs, legally bound to the land they worked. Serfdom began to decline in western Europe in the 1300s, and by the late 1500s it had largely disappeared. As a result, Renaissance peasants enjoyed much greater freedom. Many peasants moved to other villages, to other regions, or to towns and cities in search of a better life. Those most likely to migrate were the young and the landless. Adult peasants often became seasonal migrants, helping to harvest crops in areas far from their own villages—or even in foreign countries.

Peasant villages served as the economic and political foundation of Renaissance society. Each village had a local assembly or council to govern it. Outside authorities, such as nobles and the church, granted villages a large degree of local self-rule because they recognized the need for local decisions about some issues. In theory, all citizens could participate in village government on equal terms. However, wealthy landowners or merchants often dominated local assemblies.

Village councils regulated the use of local resources such as forests, pastures, and farmland. They also took charge of building and maintaining roads, wells, and anything else that would benefit the community as a whole. Village governments also played a role in the hundreds of peasant rebellions that took place in the Renaissance. These revolts often resulted from the growing power of nation-states, which cut into time-honored peasant rights.

* **artisan**   skilled worker or craftsperson

Rural society during the Renaissance was quite varied. Many peasants not only worked in agriculture, but also labored as shopkeepers, artisans*, or traders. Furthermore, the boundaries between rural and urban society were often unclear. All towns and cities had residents who worked in the surrounding countryside. The social and economic life of the villages often overlapped with that of nearby cities. Beginning in the 1400s, many peasants started growing cash crops for sale, rather than merely producing enough for their own needs. A few of these peasants became wealthy and bought up their neighbors' lands, while others moved into trade and other businesses. These changes made rural society more diverse and weakened traditional peasant life. (*See also* **Agriculture; Artisans; Daily Life; Economy and Trade; Nation-state; Peasants' War; Population; Revolts; Social Status.**)

Peasants' War

* **artisan**   skilled worker or craftsperson

* **Holy Roman Empire**   political body in central Europe composed of several states; existed until 1806

* **mercenary**   hired soldier

* **prince**   Renaissance term for the ruler of an independent state

The Peasants' War was an uprising in southern and central Germany in the 1520s. A wide range of common people, including tillers of the soil, village artisans*, and poor townspeople, supported the uprising. The rebels did not want to overthrow the government or the Holy Roman Empire*. Rather, they hoped to end certain practices of nobles and the Roman Catholic Church. The war lasted from May 1524 to July 1526, involved up to 300,000 people, and claimed as many as 100,000 lives.

The revolt began as protests against lords to force them to treat common people justly. The rebels managed to seize supplies from monasteries and to dismantle several castles. They also forcibly occupied a number of German towns. More commonly, however, they captured cannons and supplies from towns that they did not enter. Violence against individuals by the rebels was rare. Battles did not begin until after April 1525, when armies of mercenaries* serving German princes* assembled to crush the uprising. In the one-sided battles that followed, thousands of peasants died.

The Peasants' War occurred in the most urbanized region of the Holy Roman Empire. Since about 1450, western Europe had experienced sizable population growth and an economic upswing. These changes led to greater differences of wealth and status among rural residents. Peasants who owned land controlled village governments and had a better life than landless peasants, laborers, and servants. However, they still owed rents and other payments to landlords, the government, and the church.

Peasants presented their complaints to the nobles in 1525. They resented the efforts of landlords and rulers to take away their time-honored privileges, such as attempts to exclude them from using the products of forests, waterways, and meadows. These products, especially game and fish, were sources of much-needed extra income. Other objects of protest included labor owed to landlords and rulers, excessive rents, and penalties that varied from customary laws.

The Peasants' War did not resolve the peasants' complaints, and smaller uprisings lasted into the 1600s. Because the revolt began with attacks on monasteries, German princes connected it to the religious upheaval sweeping the region. They feared the effects of the lawlessness on their authority and took firm control of the practice of religion. As a result, the PROTESTANT REFORMATION in Germany lost some of its early energy. (*See also* **Artisans; Mercenaries; Peasantry; Revolts.**)

Perugino

ca. 1450–1523
Italian artist

See color plate 7, vol. 3

Perugino (Pietro Vannucci) was one of the most sought-after artists of the late 1400s. The first painter to work almost exclusively in oils, he was probably the teacher of the great RAPHAEL.

Born in a small town near Perugia in central Italy, Perugino moved to Florence about 1470. He may have worked under the painters Andrea del VERROCCHIO and PIERO DELLA FRANCESCA. Perugino's early works, which show the influence of these artists, display an abundance of detail, bright colors, and a sense of harmony and openness.

In about 1480 Perugino began his best-known work, *Christ Giving the Keys to St. Peter,* in the Sistine Chapel in Rome for Pope Sixtus IV. For the next 25 years, Perugino was the most popular artist in central and northern Italy. He worked for prominent patrons* such as Lorenzo de' MEDICI, Cardinal Giuliano della Rovere (later Pope JULIUS II), and Isabella d'ESTE. In the *Portrait of Francesco delle Opere* (1494), the artist achieved a perfect balance between the figure of the subject and the background. A few years later, his frescoes* in the Audience Chamber of the Guild of the Exchange in Perugia (1496–1500) combined images from pagan* and Christian traditions and impressed even the most severe critics.

Perugino's success came to an abrupt halt in the early 1500s. First, a major project completed in 1505 displeased Isabella d'Este, who had commissioned it. Then Pope Julius II dismissed Perugino and hired Raphael to paint the ceiling of the Vatican apartments. Perugino continued to paint, but demand for his work declined. Yet, the delicate figures and pastel colors of his later paintings helped pave the way for the artistic movement known as Mannerism*. (*See also* **Art; Art in Italy.**)

* **patron** supporter or financial sponsor of an artist or writer

* **fresco** mural painted on a plaster wall

* **pagan** referring to ancient religions that worshiped many gods, or more generally, to any non-Christian religion

* **Mannerism** artistic style of the 1500s characterized by vivid colors and exaggeration, such as elongated figures in complex poses

Peruzzi, Baldassare

1481–1536
Italian painter and architect

One of the leading architects of the 1500s, Baldassare Peruzzi is also known for his magnificent drawings. Among his earliest architectural projects was the Farnese Palace in ROME, built between 1505 and 1511. He also worked as a painter around this time and as a designer.

Peruzzi's breakthrough as an architect came in 1520, with his appointment as second architect of St. Peter's Church in Rome. Two years later, he went to BOLOGNA to create designs for the stonemasons' lodge. Back in Rome around 1523, Peruzzi designed burial places for important individuals. During this period his own distinctive architectural style became evident.

Peruzzi's career as an architect reached its peak in SIENA after 1527. There he created innovative designs for rebuilding the city's cathedral and also worked on the Palazzo Pollini with its monumental facade and the fortress Rocca Sinibalda. Returning to Rome in about 1534, Peruzzi produced magnificent designs for St. Peter's and worked on various other projects, including an apartment in the Vatican. A highly inventive artist, Peruzzi used both the art of antiquity* and that of the leading artists of his time. His work had considerable influence on the architects of the late 1500s, including MICHELANGELO and Andrea PALLADIO. (*See also* **Architecture.**)

* **antiquity** era of the ancient Mediterranean cultures of Greece and Rome, ending around A.D. 400

Petrarch

1304–1374
Italian poet and scholar

* **classical** in the tradition of ancient Greece and Rome

The poet and scholar known as Petrarch played a major role in launching the Renaissance in literature. One of the great scholars of his age, Petrarch had a deep commitment to the revival of classical* learning and culture. The products of his imaginative mind played a central role in Renaissance cultural life. His poetry, in particular, not only reflected the changes in the world around him but also influenced the work of many later generations of writers.

* **elegy**   type of poem often used to express sorrow for one who has died

Early Life. Francesco Petrarca was born in Arezzo, in central Italy, in 1304, but his family eventually moved to southern France. When Petrarch was 12 years old his father sent him to study law at the University of Montpellier. While Petrarch was there, his mother died, and he wrote an elegy* in Latin, the earliest of his works that still survives. Petrarch continued his law studies in Bologna, Italy, before deciding that he did not want to pursue a legal career.

In 1327 Petrarch saw and fell in love with a woman who inspired his poetic imagination for the rest of his life. In his poems he called her Laura—a name suggesting both the evergreen laurel tree, which was sacred to the Greek god Apollo, and the crown of poetic glory made from the leaves of the laurel tree. Petrarch gathered his love poems to Laura in a collection known as the *Canzoniere* (Book of Songs). In these poems, which he worked on all his life, Laura symbolized Petrarch's vision of ideal love.

Petrarch spent much of the 1330s working as a member of the staff of a Roman Catholic cardinal. In this position, Petrarch traveled around Europe and began his lifelong search for the manuscripts of works by ancient Greek and Roman authors. A trip to Rome in 1336 fed Petrarch's love for classical culture. In a letter he said that he found the city "greater than I thought" and full of "abundant marvels."

* **papal**   referring to the office and authority of the pope

* **epic**   long poem about the adventures of a hero

Although he admired Rome and felt an attachment to Italy, Petrarch settled in southeastern France, near the papal* court at Avignon. There he began a number of works inspired by his classical readings. These writings included his epic* poem *Africa* and more of his poems in the *Canzoniere*. In 1341 the Roman Senate crowned Petrarch as poet laureate, an honorary title that reflected their esteem for his work. Petrarch's acceptance speech, known as the *Oration,* revealed his broad knowledge of classical authors. In the speech, he referred to such ancient Roman writers as VIRGIL, Ovid, and CICERO.

The honor of becoming poet laureate turned Petrarch into one of the first true celebrities of the Renaissance. He became an honored guest in cities throughout Europe. His fame led to the development of what scholars refer to as "Petrarchism"—the imitation of Petrarch's style in poetry.

Later Works. In 1345, during another period of travel throughout Europe, Petrarch discovered and copied the letters of Cicero. These letters inspired Petrarch to begin his own collection of letters addressed to friends and to classical authors. This series included *Letters on Familiar Matters, Letters of Riper Years,* and *Book Without a Name.* One of his most famous letters, the *Letter to Posterity,* described Petrarch's interests and views for future generations of readers. This letter reveals that Petrarch was well aware of his unique place in history and actively sought to promote himself. His focus on his own identity hints at the emphasis on INDIVIDUALISM that would surface in the next few centuries.

During a visit to Florence in 1350, Petrarch first met the Italian author Giovanni BOCCACCIO, who became his friend. The two writers shared a passion for classical culture and for collecting books. Over the years, Petrarch amassed what may have been the largest private library in Europe. When Boccaccio, believing his life was near an end, considered abandoning his studies, Petrarch persuaded him not to do so—although he also expressed an interest in buying his friend's books if he chose to sell them.

From 1353 until 1361, Petrarch lived mostly in the northern Italian city of MILAN with the support of the wealthy Visconti family. One of the projects Petrarch began in Milan turned into his longest work, two books about morality titled *Remedies for Good and Bad Fortune*. Petrarch organized this work as a series of dialogues between characters who represented certain ideas. In the first book, Joy and Hope debate the dangers of good fortune with Reason. In the second book, Sorrow and Fear oppose Reason, discussing the perils of bad luck. Petrarch also continued to revise the *Canzoniere* during his eight years in Milan.

In 1367 Petrarch composed *On His Own Ignorance and That of Many Others*. This piece was a response to four Italian philosophers who had described Petrarch as "a good man, but uneducated." The work attacked outdated modes of thinking and pointed the way toward the new learning of humanism*. Petrarch argued that the source of true knowledge lay in a strong awareness of the self, an idea central to Renaissance thought.

During the last years of his life, Petrarch completed the final revisions to the *Canzoniere*. The finished version contained 366 poems, which the author separated into two sections. One part honored the life of his beloved "Laura," while the other honored her death. The poems treat some of the most important themes of the Renaissance, including love, art, morality, and religion. Their unique blend of the psychological and the poetic became a central feature of Petrarchism.

Lasting Influence. Petrarch's verses, especially his sonnets*, had a great influence on later writers. Although Petrarch did not invent the sonnet, he developed a distinct version of it that became the standard form for Italian sonnets. In the first half of the 1500s many writers of sonnets and other types of poems followed Petrarch's style for love poetry, which presented the beloved in ideal terms. After the Catholic Counter-Reformation* began in Italy, poets turned more toward Petrarch's work on religious themes. Many writers took inspiration from his thoughts on such topics as suffering, sin, and death.

Petrarch's works inspired several female poets in Europe during the Renaissance. These authors adapted Petrarch's style to a female viewpoint. For example, the Italian poet Gaspara Stampa closely followed Petrarch's use of symbolism in her poems. She also used Petrarch's lyric style to describe a woman's experiences of ecstasy, sorrow, jealousy, and passion. Another Italian poet, Vittoria Colonna, modeled love poems to her dead husband after Petrarch's sonnets in praise of Laura.

For more than three centuries, scholars throughout Europe praised Petrarch as the ideal poet to imitate. Petrarch's influence spread far beyond Italy. In England, for instance, noted authors such as Edmund SPENSER and William SHAKESPEARE turned to the humanist scholar for

The influence of Petrarch, the poet and scholar who played a leading role in the Renaissance, lasted long after his time. Petrarch's emphasis on the ancient cultures of Greece and Rome ushered in an era of classical learning, and his poetry inspired writers for centuries.

---

* **humanism** Renaissance cultural movement promoting the study of the humanities (the languages, literature, and history of ancient Greece and Rome) as a guide to living

* **sonnet** poem of 14 lines with a fixed pattern of meter and rhyme

* **Counter-Reformation** actions taken by the Roman Catholic Church after 1540 to oppose Protestantism

inspiration. (*See also* **Classical Scholarship; Humanism; Italian Language and Literature; Latin Language and Literature; Poetry.**)

Philip II

1527–1598
King of Spain

* **patronage** support or financial sponsorship

* **regent** person who acts on behalf of a monarch who is too young or unable to rule

Philip II of Spain was an ambitious ruler whose empire stretched across Europe and into the Americas. Although he faced many challenges during his reign, his support for the arts, learning, and literature helped create a golden age in Spain.

Philip II ruled Spain at a time when it reached its greatest power. A member of the HABSBURG DYNASTY, he oversaw an empire that included nations in Europe and colonies in the AMERICAS. Although Philip failed to achieve his foreign policy goals in the Netherlands and in England, his patronage* of the arts helped create a golden age in Spain.

Ruling an Empire. The son of CHARLES V and Isabella of Portugal, Philip took control of Spain as regent* in 1545, during his father's absence. From 1548 to 1551, Philip traveled around Italy, Germany, and the Netherlands. The tour gave him experience in European politics and a taste for Flemish* and Italian Renaissance culture. Philip married four times—to Maria of Portugal, MARY I of England, Elizabeth of Valois, and Anna of Austria.

As husband of Mary I, Philip was co-ruler of England, where he lived for about a year after their marriage in 1554. He left England to join his father's wars against France. When Charles V abdicated* the throne of Spain in 1556, Philip became king and inherited an empire that included American colonies, the Netherlands, and several smaller European territories.

Philip faced many challenges during his reign. Although the tumult linked to the Protestant Reformation* threatened the stability of his empire, he hesitated to use force to combat heresy*. However, he used the full power of the Spanish Inquisition* against Protestant groups in Spain.

Philip attempted to reform the structure and finances of the Spanish government. Charles V had left huge debts that forced his son to stop payments from the royal treasury several times. Most spending went to war and to building ships in the Mediterranean Sea. The major threat there came from the Ottoman Turks*, who defeated Spain at the island of Djerba off the coast of North Africa in 1560. However, combined Spanish and Italian forces won a decisive naval victory over the Turks in 1571 at the battle of Lepanto off the coast of Greece. Philip also faced a revolt in the Netherlands, which sought independence from Spain. Philip hoped to crush the uprising with tough measures, but he failed to put down the revolt. As a result, military costs continued to grow.

A succession crisis caused Philip to invade Portugal in 1580 to support his claim to the Portuguese throne. He established his capital at LISBON, ruling in Portugal as Philip I until his death. He then decided that England posed a major threat to his empire. In 1588 he attempted a naval invasion of England, which resulted in the costly defeat of his fleet, the Spanish ARMADA. The huge costs of running the empire drained the nation's economy throughout Philip's reign.

Although foreign affairs demanded much of his attention, Philip did not neglect governmental matters at home. He reformed the treasury

* **Flemish**   relating to Flanders, a region along the coasts of present-day Belgium, France, and the Netherlands

* **abdicate**   to give up the throne voluntarily or under pressure

* **Protestant Reformation**   religious movement that began in the 1500s as a protest against certain practices of the Roman Catholic Church and eventually led to the establishment of a variety of Protestant churches

* **heresy**   belief that is contrary to the doctrine of an established church

* **Spanish Inquisition**   court established by the Spanish monarchs that investigated Christians accused of straying from the official doctrine of the Roman Catholic Church, particularly during the period 1480–1530

* **Ottoman Turks**   Turkish followers of Islam who founded the Ottoman Empire in the 1300s; the empire eventually included large areas of eastern Europe, the Middle East, and northern Africa

See color plate 13, vol. 4

and negotiated tax agreements with the Cortes, Spain's national assembly. Philip also reorganized the government to allow more effective control of war and built a fleet for the Mediterranean Sea. Because Spain had no capital city, he chose MADRID in 1561.

Philip worked tirelessly to suppress revolts in his far-flung empire. At the same time, he respected the autonomy of different provinces in Spain, and most of them remained peaceful throughout his reign. However, tensions increased in the province of Castile during Philip's later years, mainly due to opposition to higher taxes. In 1591 he also faced the threat of rebellion in the Spanish province of Aragon.

Reputation and Achievement. Philip's actions abroad made him many enemies. His suppression of the revolt in the Netherlands unleashed hostility from the Dutch, while the English mocked him for the failure of the Armada. Sinister rumors circulated abroad about Philip murdering a son and wife. Even Spanish officials found fault with the king's fondness for paperwork.

Despite the many problems and responsibilities of ruling the Spanish empire, Philip made substantial contributions as a patron of the arts. He built or restored splendid palaces and gardens and supported leading Renaissance painters throughout Europe. Philip also invited foreign musicians to his court, collected rare books and manuscripts, and financed scientific studies and geographical surveys.

Philip II was a steadfast Catholic, yet he modified laws that discriminated against JEWS. He also accepted the need for some religious toleration in the Netherlands. He supported reform of the Catholic Church and played an important role in the success of the last sessions of the Council of TRENT. Yet, he also consistently opposed church policies with which he disagreed. (*See also* **Architecture; Art in Spain and Portugal; England; Netherlands; Ottoman Empire; Spain.**)

Philosophy

* **theology**   study of the nature of God and of religion

* **humanism**   Renaissance cultural movement promoting the study of the humanities (the languages, literature, and history of ancient Greece and Rome) as a guide to living

The study of philosophy changed a great deal over the course of the Renaissance. During the Middle Ages, philosophy had strong links to theology*. Although Renaissance philosophers continued to think about the general subjects of God, nature, and humanity, they no longer viewed their studies as focusing chiefly on God. With the rise of the scholarly movement known as humanism*, human beings took center stage in philosophy, as they did in most areas of culture and thought.

These changes in philosophy began in Italy and worked their way into northern Europe. The leading figure of the Italian Renaissance was the poet and philosopher PETRARCH (1304–1374), who turned to the ancient Greeks and Romans for inspiration. He believed that philosophy should focus on the human struggle to achieve dignity as a creature of God. Rudolf AGRICOLA (1444–1485) was an early leader of the northern Renaissance. He stressed the importance of discovery, rather than judgment, in gaining knowledge. He also made advances in the study of logic. The most important figure of the northern Renaissance was

Desiderius ERASMUS (ca. 1466–1536). His philosophical works focused on the issue of human freedom.

Moral Questions. Renaissance scholars viewed philosophy as a practical subject, useful in everyday life. They believed that philosophy could promote virtue in the individual, the family, and society as a whole. They divided practical philosophy into three main areas of study: ethics, economics, and politics. Ethics focused on the question of how to become a good person. Economics taught people how to manage a household, and politics showed them how to be good citizens. Many scholars viewed ethics, which focused on the individual, as the most basic of these three disciplines.

Renaissance scholars based their study of ethics on the writings of ancient thinkers, especially the ancient Greek philosopher ARISTOTLE. His work *Ethics* became the main university textbook on the subject. This text influenced generations of scholars, inspiring classroom lectures, translations into Latin and other languages, and even an epic*. To Aristotle, leading a moral life meant avoiding extremes. Each moral virtue, in his view, occupied a middle position between the two extremes of too little and too much. Courage, for example, was the balance between being rash and being a coward.

Aristotle lived in the pagan* culture of ancient Greece. However, Renaissance scholars adapted his ideas to their Christian society. For instance, Aristotle had claimed that people could achieve their highest purpose—to gain wisdom—during their life on earth. Christians, by contrast, believed that humans could reach a higher goal: to enter heaven after death. Philosophers in the Middle Ages dealt with this conflict by arguing that Aristotle's supreme good was a step on the way to the ultimate goal of union with God in the next life.

Natural Philosophy. The ideas of Aristotle inspired work in other fields as well, such as natural philosophy. This discipline, also known as natural science, involved the study of the physical world. Students of natural philosophy drew on the work of other thinkers as well, including the ancient Greek philosopher PLATO and various Christian and Islamic scholars. Like ethics, natural philosophy became a major part of university studies in the Renaissance.

The basic ideas of natural philosophy came from two works by Aristotle: *Physics* and *On the Soul*. The discipline covered such topics as matter, form, chance, motion, time, and space. For some scholars, the study of these subjects led to larger questions about theology and the nature of being. Others saw links between natural philosophy and the sciences of mechanics, astronomy, and medicine. Patronage* by royal courts promoted studies in these fields and encouraged the search for practical results. In this way, natural philosophy served as the seedbed of modern science.

Over time, Renaissance scholars began to question classical* ideas about the natural world. For example, they disputed Aristotle's ideas about falling bodies. Aristotle had claimed that the speed of a falling body changes according to its weight and the resistance it encounters as

* **epic**   long poem about the adventures of a hero

* **pagan**   referring to ancient religions that worshiped many gods, or more generally, to any non-Christian religion

* **patronage**   support or financial sponsorship

* **classical**   in the tradition of ancient Greece and Rome

Renaissance philosophers Marsilio Ficino and Giovanni Pico della Mirandola sought to link the ideas of the ancient Greeks, Romans, and Hebrews with Christian thought. This detail from a 1486 wall painting shows the two thinkers with fellow scholar Angelo Poliziano.

it falls. However, as early as 1544, the Italian scholar Giovanni Battista Benedetti argued that this theory was wrong. Eventually scientists in Italy, including Galileo GALILEI, disproved Aristotle's claims through experiments. Their discoveries marked the beginning of the "new science" of nature, which relied on careful observation.

Metaphysics. Unlike natural philosophy, which deals with the physical world, metaphysics deals with those things that are beyond human experience. Aristotle described metaphysics as a "divine science" that studies those aspects of reality that never change. He also claimed that it served as the basis for all special sciences.

Renaissance studies in metaphysics took an important turn with the Council of Florence, held by the Roman Catholic Church between 1438 and 1445. One member of the council, the Greek philosopher George Gemistus Pletho, argued that the Latin theologians at the council had been misled by the teachings of Averroes, an Islamic thinker of the Middle Ages. Averroes had claimed that Aristotle's works contained all of human wisdom. Pletho argued that scholars had fallen into error by not paying enough attention to the teachings of Plato. His claim triggered a debate over the relative merits of these two ancient thinkers.

Several Italian philosophers developed new approaches to Plato's thought. For example, Marsilio FICINO combined Plato's ideas with Christian views. He argued that human beings could, through thought, achieve union with God and the universe. Ficino saw everlasting life in heaven as the true fulfillment of human nature. Another Italian scholar, Giovanni PICO DELLA MIRANDOLA, tried to link Christian ideas with

* **mystical**   based on a belief in the idea of a direct, personal union with the divine

* **Jesuit**   refers to a Roman Catholic religious order founded by St. Ignatius Loyola and approved in 1540

ancient wisdom. Along with Greek and Roman sources, he drew on the Jewish Kabbalah, a mystical* religious system that involved reading encoded messages in the Hebrew Scriptures.

Some Catholic scholars, such as the Jesuit* Benito Perera, tried to use metaphysics to prove that the soul was immortal. They built a science of metaphysics based on the idea that God had created the world. Perera divided traditional metaphysics into two sciences. His "first philosophy" discussed the nature of being, and his "divine science" dealt with matters such as God and the soul.

Protestant scholars also studied metaphysics. The German religious reformer Martin LUTHER rejected most of Aristotle's ideas. However, some of his followers turned to Aristotle's theory of truth to prove that faith could exist in harmony with reason. They used this theory to counter the beliefs of extremists who saw faith as contrary to reason.

Scholasticism. Although Renaissance scholars revived classical ideas in philosophy, they also preserved some traditions of the Middle Ages. One such method was Scholasticism, or the Scholastic method. This term literally meant a way of teaching and learning used in schools, but it referred more generally to a system of solving problems by examining the arguments for and against an idea. Its goal was to reach a scientific solution that fit the facts and that did not contradict accepted authorities, human reason, or Christian faith.

Many humanist thinkers criticized the Scholasticism of the Middle Ages. They argued that it relied too much on tiny distinctions and that it paid too little attention to sources. Other Renaissance scholars responded to these charges by making changes in the Scholastic method. They created a rigid system of laying out arguments and stressed the importance of using accurate translations of Greek texts, such as the Bible. This new form of Scholasticism became popular in Italy, Spain, France, Germany, the Netherlands, and Britain.

Both Catholic and Protestant clergy members promoted Scholasticism. The Jesuits became the strongest supporters of the movement. Jesuit scholars blended Scholasticism with humanism and developed new systems of thought that influenced both Catholic and Protestant thinkers throughout Europe. Some early Protestant schools even used Jesuit texts to teach metaphysics. Eventually, however, they replaced these books with new texts written by Protestants. By the 1600s, Scholastic thought had taken a central place in Protestant universities.

Scholasticism often came into conflict with humanism. The two movements took very different approaches to the search for truth. Humanists sought practical knowledge to guide human life. Scholastics, by contrast, focused on abstract truths. Humanists and Scholastics engaged in violent disputes about such issues as doctrines, teaching methods, and how to interpret the Bible. (*See also* **Councils; Education; Humanism; Science.**)

Philosophy 101

Most Renaissance universities took a similar approach to teaching philosophy. Preparation began with basic instruction in grammar, mainly in Latin but also in Greek and, in a few cases, Hebrew. Students read classics in Latin literature and also received an introduction to rhetoric (the art of speaking and writing effectively) either in secondary school or at the university. Their formal training in philosophy covered three years. During the first year students studied logic; in the second they took natural philosophy, which dealt with the physical world; and in the third they studied metaphysics, which dealt with higher reality and the soul.

Pico della Mirandola, Giovanni

1463–1494
Italian philosopher

* **mystical**   based on a belief in the idea of a direct, personal union with the divine

* **medieval**   referring to the Middle Ages, a period that began around A.D. 400 and ended around 1400 in Italy and 1500 in the rest of Europe

* **pagan**   referring to ancient religions that worshiped many gods, or more generally, to any non-Christian religion

* **astrology**   study of the supposed influences of the stars and planets on earthly events

* **rhetoric**   art of speaking or writing effectively

A bold and creative thinker, Giovanni Pico della Mirandola sought to join the best aspects of all schools of philosophy into a single system of thought. Pico also became the first Christian scholar to use the Kabbalah to support Christian thought. The Kabbalah is a mystical* Jewish religious system that involves reading encoded messages in the Hebrew Scriptures.

Pico's Life.   Born to a noble family in northern Italy, Pico went to Bologna to study church law at the age of 14. Two years later he moved to Ferrara and then to Padua, where he encountered the teachings of the ancient Greek philosophers ARISTOTLE and PLATO. He also exchanged letters with important Italian Renaissance figures such as the statesman Lorenzo de' MEDICI. After spending time in Paris, Pico returned to Italy, where he caused a scandal by running off with a young woman named Margherita, who had previously been engaged to a member of the powerful Medici family.

At this time Pico began one of his life's major projects: to create a philosophy that found harmony among all schools of thought. At its core, the project aimed to unite the teachings of Plato and Aristotle. He wrote that he meant to include "all teachers of philosophy" and "all writings" in "every school."

Pico planned to hold a large conference in Rome in 1487 to introduce his ideas. To prepare for the meeting, he collected 900 theses (positions to be debated) on different points of philosophy taken from many different schools of thought. He included ancient, medieval*, pagan*, Christian, Muslim, and Jewish writings. Through debates with other scholars he aimed to prove that these diverse texts had similar principles at their cores. Pico had his 900 theses, known as the *Conclusions*, printed in Rome in 1486. To introduce the *Conclusions* he wrote his most famous work, now known as the *Oration on the Dignity of Man.*

However, the Roman Catholic Church blocked Pico's plans. The church objected to some of the theses because they combined Christian and pagan philosophies. When Pico tried to justify his work in an *Apology,* Pope Innocent VIII responded by condemning all 900 of the theses. Pico left Italy for Paris, where French authorities jailed him briefly. Within a year he returned to Florence and wrote *Heptaplus,* an account of the six days of creation from Genesis, the first book of the Bible. In it, Pico placed humans, created in the image and likeness of God, at the center of the universe.

In 1493 Pope ALEXANDER VI pardoned Pico for his earlier offenses. By that time, Pico had begun to withdraw from the world. He gave away much of his property to relatives and the church and grew close to the outspoken Italian preacher Girolamo SAVONAROLA. Pico died a year later, at age 31, while working on his last major project, a work opposing astrology*. Some people claimed that poison had helped bring about his death.

Pico's Thought.   The idea of human dignity and freedom played a major role in Pico's work. In the *Oration on the Dignity of Man,* one of the finest examples of Renaissance rhetoric*, Pico developed a new creation

myth that presented Adam as a being with unlimited choices. He stressed that although human beings were free to rise or fall as they chose, their freedom came from God. The goal of this human freedom, he claimed, was to die in the body in order to let the mind live in the supreme Mind of God. Later, in the *Heptaplus*, Pico described humans as miraculous beings made in the image of God. He identified Christ, who was God in human form, as a model for humanity. He urged people to deny the body, as Christ had done, and to raise themselves through learning.

Pico believed that all wisdom came from three sources: ancient learning, the Bible, and the Kabbalah. The *Conclusions* contained more than 100 theses about the Kabbalah. One of Pico's greatest achievements was the invention of a Christian Kabbalah. He introduced this idea in the *Oration*, defended it in the *Apology*, and applied it in the *Heptaplus*. Aided by his great gift of intellect, especially in languages, and by the help of many learned JEWS, Pico uncovered links between Jewish and Christian theology*.

Pico viewed the Hebrew alphabet as the key to the Kabbalah. He read its signs as both letters and numbers and used NUMEROLOGY to find hidden meanings in them. He also viewed the shapes of the letters as symbols. For example, he saw a letter whose shape resembled a cross as a foretelling of the coming of Christ. Pico believed people could read both nature and Scripture as books that revealed God's creation.

However, Pico also believed that every system of philosophy—whether pagan or Christian, ancient, medieval, or modern—contained something of value. Even if the rest of the belief system was false, he claimed, some statements were true, and these true statements reflected a single eternal truth. According to Pico, the basic truths in every philosophy came from God, the ultimate source of truth, understood in different ways by different thinkers. (*See also* **Humanism; Magic and Astrology; Man, Dignity of; Philosophy.**)

* **theology** study of the nature of God and of religion

Piedmont-Savoy

* **duchy** territory ruled by a duke or duchess

* **regent** person who acts on behalf of a monarch who is too young or unable to rule

Piedmont-Savoy, a duchy* located in what is now northern Italy, southeastern France, and western Switzerland, was ruled by the dukes of Savoy, a powerful dynasty. In the early Renaissance, the French town of Chambéry served as the duchy's capital, but in the 1500s the dukes moved the capital to Turin, in Italy.

History and Government. Piedmont-Savoy grew in influence during the late 1300s and early 1400s. Dukes Amadeus VI (ruled 1343–1383) and Amadeus VII (ruled 1383–1391) acquired new lands and began to play a major role in European affairs. In the mid- to late 1400s, political tension broke out between the leading families of Savoy and Piedmont. The duchy went through an unstable period politically, with several dukes reigning briefly or through regents*. Then, in 1536 Swiss, French, and German armies invaded Piedmont-Savoy and occupied it. After 21 years of foreign rule, Duke Emmanuel Philibert

(1553–1580) won a stunning victory against the invaders, and regained most of the land.

Piedmont-Savoy established a variety of governmental bodies to manage the affairs of the duchy. Beginning in the late 1200s, regional assemblies made up of nobles, clergy, and townspeople met to negotiate with the dukes for privileges and a degree of self-government. By the 1300s the duchy had several courts and a traveling council that administered justice. In the early 1500s, the French replaced the courts with assemblies called *parlements*. However, when Emmanuel Philibert resumed control he stopped summoning the assemblies and negotiated taxes directly with individual groups instead.

Economy and Culture. By the late 1500s Piedmont had a population of about 520,000; Savoy was slightly smaller. Livestock raising, mining, weaving, and banking were the most important economic activities in Savoy. Piedmont produced grains and textiles, including silk. The dukes supported industry and commerce by passing laws favorable to merchants, enacting banking reforms, and building canals. Taxes on salt, meat, and wine, as well as revenue from feudal* lands, provided the duchy with most of its income.

The court of the dukes of Savoy became a rich cultural center that attracted musicians, historians, artists—especially those skilled in illumination*, and scholars. Professors at the University of Turin began teaching about 1411 and included prominent intellectuals. Duke Emmanuel Philibert and his successors promoted advances in science, engineering, architecture, and mathematics. His wife, Margaret of France, supported various poets and was a voice of religious moderation in the duchy. She persuaded her husband to call off a war against a religious minority in Piedmont and to allow limited tolerance toward Protestants. (*See also* **Princes and Princedoms.**)

* **feudal**   relating to an economic and political system in which individuals gave services to a lord in return for protection and use of the land

* **illumination**   hand-painted color decorations and illustrations on the pages of a manuscript

Piero della Francesca

ca. 1412–1492
Italian painter and mathematician

* **perspective**   artistic technique for creating the illusion of three-dimensional space on a flat surface

* **apprentice**   person bound by legal agreement to work for another for a specified period of time in return for instruction in a trade or craft

* **fresco**   mural painted on a plaster wall

A skilled painter who made advances in the use of perspective*, Piero della Francesca was also an important figure in the history of MATHEMATICS. He left a rich legacy, both through his works of art and his writing on various mathematical subjects. Born into a prosperous merchant family in a small town in Tuscany, Piero probably attended an "abacus school," which taught mathematics to boys destined for careers in commerce or banking. In addition, he served as an apprentice* under Antonio da Anghiari, a local painter.

Painting. Unlike many Renaissance artists, Piero della Francesca never ran a workshop. Furthermore, he probably relied more on income from his family's merchant business than on painting for his livelihood. Nevertheless, he did accept commissions to produce works of art. His first major project was the *Madonna della Misericordia* (1445), a set of painted panels. Around 1455 he began work on a series of frescoes*, *The Legend of the True Cross,* for the Church of San Francesco in Arezzo. His last painting, the *Nativity of Christ* (1480s), was left unfinished.

Scholars have difficulty dating Piero della Francesca's pieces because he worked slowly, sometimes taking years to complete a picture. It is thought that he used damp cloths to keep the plaster of his frescoes wet so he could continue working on them. Piero's paintings show the influence of earlier artists, especially DONATELLO, MASACCIO, and Domenico Veneziano. They also reveal evidence of elaborate drawings beneath the paint, suggesting that he worked hard to perfect the design before adding layers of color. He was especially skillful at balancing the background and foreground of scenes and depicting delicate details.

Piero may have trained various other artists, including Luca Signorelli (ca. 1450–1523) and Melozzo da Forlì (1438–1495). In the 1500s, changing artistic tastes led to a decline in Piero's reputation as a painter. However, in the early 1900s art historians rediscovered his work, noting his many contributions.

Mathematics. Giorgio Vasari, the Renaissance artist and historian, wrote that Piero della Francesca produced many mathematical treatises*, but only three have survived. The *Abacus Treatise*, probably written before 1460, is a textbook for teaching arithmetic, algebra, and geometry. The *Short Book on the Five Regular Solids*, probably written after the *Abacus Treatise*, is devoted to geometry. Piero's *On Perspective for Painting* (late 1460s) is the earliest known work on the mathematics of perspective. It explains basic principles and describes the construction of both regular shapes and complex figures, such as the human head.

Although Piero della Francesca never taught mathematics, his books on the subject had a significant impact on other scholars. In the late 1400s, the mathematician Luca Pacioli used the *Abacus Treatise* extensively in writing his own *Treatise on Arithmetic*. Moreover, many Renaissance works on perspective echo Piero's ideas. (*See also* **Art; Art in Italy.**)

A pilgrimage is a journey to a shrine, or a site that the traveler considers sacred. Renaissance pilgrims made these trips for a variety of reasons. Many pilgrims wanted to feel closer to the divine or to celebrate a particular saint's feast day. Others went to ask for help and to receive indulgences*. Some made pilgrimages for worldlier reasons. A pilgrimage typically involved some sort of sacrifice or hardship, such as walking the entire distance.

Reasons for Pilgrimage. A variety of factors besides religious passion motivated Renaissance pilgrims. For example, a town suffering from a disaster might hire a pilgrim to travel to a shrine and pray for the entire town. Local priests and courts occasionally sentenced offenders to undertake a pilgrimage as punishment for their sins or crimes. Towns sent residents with leprosy, an incurable illness in those days, on pilgrimage. If they did not recover, these sick pilgrims would probably die elsewhere, not infecting anyone else in the town.

At shrines, pilgrims prayed for aid, forgiveness of sins, or improvement in physical health. Pilgrims often left an ex-voto, or memento, as

* **treatise** long, detailed essay

* **indulgence** in Catholic practice, a means by which a sinner could reduce the punishment for a sin by repenting (being sorry for the sin) and performing a good deed

Many pilgrims to holy sites traveled long distances on foot. This sculpture from the 1400s shows a group of pilgrims equipped with walking sticks and small sacks for carrying supplies.

* plague highly contagious and often fatal disease that wiped out much of Europe's population in the mid-1300s and reappeared periodically over the next three centuries; also known as the Black Death

a sign of thanks. Many people who took pilgrimages hoped to witness—or even experience—a miracle.

People wanted to know that their prayers were being answered. Even if they did not experience a miracle, they earned indulgences by going on pilgrimages. During the plague*, the number of indulgences grew rapidly. Excessive indulgences, such as those shortening punishment in the afterlife by 33,000 years, became common.

Pilgrims often timed their journeys so that they would arrive at their destinations in time for particular events. A shrine might celebrate a saint's feast day with special celebrations or activities. If the feast fell on a Sunday, the Church might offer more powerful indulgences to pilgrims. In 1300, Pope Boniface VIII established a practice of holding jubilee years in Rome every 50 years, complete with indulgences. These were extremely popular, drawing millions of visitors to the seat of the Catholic Church.

Making the Journey. A pilgrimage could be a difficult physical ordeal, and at least 10 percent of all pilgrims died on their journeys. Among other dangers, they faced wild animals, thieves, storms, and pirates. A pilgrim who tried to visit the Holy Land might be forbidden to enter Jerusalem or held for ransom. Nevertheless, the Renaissance interest in travel helped to keep pilgrimages popular. The concept of vacation did not yet exist, and pilgrimages offered a rare excuse to see the world. Some people chose not to return home afterward.

Pilgrimages attracted people from all stations in life, from kings to beggars. Compared to the pilgrims of the Middle Ages, a greater propor-

* **Protestant Reformation** religious
movement that began in the 1500s as a
protest against certain practices of the
Roman Catholic Church and eventually
led to the establishment of a variety of
Protestant churches

* **Counter-Reformation** actions
taken by the Roman Catholic Church
after 1540 to oppose Protestantism

tion of Renaissance pilgrims were poor. They often traveled to take advantage of the charity available to them on the way. However, the system of charity declined during the Protestant Reformation* and the Catholic Counter-Reformation*.

Many pilgrims wrote accounts of their experiences, often as guides to future pilgrims visiting the same sites. The number of guidebooks to the three main pilgrimage sites—Jerusalem, Rome, and Santiago de Compostela in Spain—more than doubled each century after the 1200s. Some pilgrims' accounts became the first travelogues, noting the customs of the regions visited along the way. Pilgrimages also inspired artists. Prayer books for the rich often featured images drawn from or related to these journeys.

Decline of Pilgrimages. Pilgrimages were extremely popular during the Middle Ages. Some shrines could attract more than 100,000 visitors in a single day. However, the number of pilgrims declined during the Protestant Reformation, when early Protestant leaders opposed pilgrimages. Martin LUTHER objected to the worship of images and the sale of indulgences, both of which played major roles in the tradition. John CALVIN mocked the practice as superstitious.

Areas that became Protestant had the sharpest drop in pilgrimages. However, pilgrimages to some shrines in Protestant lands, like that of St. Winefred in Wales, remained popular despite official opposition. Many new shrines were established in Catholic areas, but most of them remained minor. At the same time, Christians in the Spanish New World began making pilgrimages to Guadalupe, Mexico, after reports that the Virgin Mary had appeared there. (*See also* **Americas; Catholic Reformation and Counter-Reformation; Protestant Reformation.**)

Piracy

Although piracy existed before the Renaissance, the practice of robbing vessels at sea became more widespread during that period. After 1350, as trade increased in the Mediterranean Sea and the eastern Atlantic Ocean, pirates attacked merchant ships with alarming frequency. They often sailed or rowed small, swift vessels and attacked with lightning speed. They took their loot to uncontrolled or friendly harbors where they were safe from the law.

Pirates often chose their victims based on such factors as nationality and religion. For example, some attackers had permission from their own governments to strike the vessels of enemy states. This form of piracy, called privateering, was most common at times of war between nations. Piracy sometimes took a religious slant as well. In the Mediterranean region, Christian pirates often attacked Muslim ships and vice versa. Piracy in this area involved not only looting but also kidnapping. Spanish writer Miguel de CERVANTES was among those captured and held for ransom by Mediterranean pirates. In the 1500s and 1600s, Protestant pirates looted Spanish and Portuguese ships in the eastern Atlantic, the Caribbean, and Brazil. However, piracy was not purely a religious matter. For example, the pirates whose attacks caused Venice to fall into decline in the early 1600s were mostly from fellow Christian states, including Florence, Malta, Spain, and England.

Piracy in the Atlantic grew rapidly after 1500, when Portugal and Spain increased their overseas trade. The ships carrying valuable goods such as spices and gold back to Europe made tempting targets for raiders. Spain's settlement of the Americas led to even more shipments of precious metals across the Atlantic (and later across the Pacific, to Spain's colony in the Philippines). Pirates preyed on this profitable, unprotected traffic.

In the early 1600s the Dutch dominated piracy in the Americas, the Mediterranean, and the Portuguese Indies. By the close of the Renaissance, a worldwide "age of piracy" had begun. Pirates from all backgrounds formed bands to raid whatever ships or towns they thought worthwhile, regardless of nationality or religion. Sometimes called buccaneers or freebooters, these pirates flourished during the second half of the 1600s, with strongholds in the Caribbean and the Indian Ocean. After the 1680s England came close to wiping out piracy in the Atlantic and Indian Oceans, and by the 1720s piracy in these seas had largely died out. Sea raiders in the Mediterranean, however, kept piracy alive there for another century. (*See also* **Americas; Economy and Trade.**)

Pirckheimer Family

* **humanism** Renaissance cultural movement promoting the study of the humanities (the languages, literature, and history of ancient Greece and Rome) as a guide to living

The Pirckheimers, a leading family in the German city of Nürnberg, played an important role in promoting the ideas of humanism* and in making Nürnberg a center of Renaissance culture. The best-known members of the family, Willibald and his sister Caritas, were the last to bear the Pirckheimer name.

Franz Pirckheimer (1388–1449) received a humanist education and ensured that his children did also. His daughter Katharina was notable for her time. Neither married nor a nun, she ran her own household and was admired because of her education. Her brother Hans studied law, served on the Nürnberg Council, and wrote a work on moral philosophy based on ancient Roman texts. Hans's son Johannes (ca. 1440–1501) served the bishop of Eichstätt and was a founder of the School of Poets in Nürnberg in 1496. He also possessed one of the most important private libraries in Germany.

* **abbess** female head of an abbey or convent

* **sacrament** religious ritual thought to have been established by Jesus as an aid to salvation

Johannes's eldest daughter Barbara (1467–1532) entered Nürnberg's convent of Santa Klara in 1479 and changed her name to Caritas. Endowed with an amazing talent for Latin, she helped write the Latin version of the convent's history and its German translation. In 1503 Caritas was elected abbess* of the convent. Humanists cited her as the ideal of a learned woman. When the Nürnberg Council adopted Protestantism as the official religion, she came out in opposition. She kept the convent open with the aid of her brother Willibald (1470–1530) and the scholar Philipp MELANCHTHON. However, city authorities would not allow the nuns to receive any sacraments* of the Roman Catholic Church.

Willibald, the most important member of the family, was trained at the court of the bishop of Eichstätt and studied law in Italy. From 1496 to 1523 he served on the Nürnberg Council, made several diplomatic journeys, and served as a captain in a war with Switzerland. Willibald had five daughters, whom he raised on his own after the death of his wife in 1504. Only the eldest daughter married and had children. The others entered convents when they were young.

Willibald is best known for his humanist studies and writings. He taught himself Greek and published his first translation from Greek to Latin in 1513. He translated 16 other Greek works including material by the historian Plutarch and the ancient Egyptian scientist PTOLEMY. Of greater interest are his personal letters, which give a lively portrait of the humanist circle in which he lived. Among his friends were the German artist Albrecht DÜRER and the Dutch scholar Desiderius ERASMUS. But the Protestant Reformation* caused this humanist group to break apart. Although Willibald supported the Reformation at first, he remained faithful to his Catholic beliefs. (*See also* **Humanism; Nürnberg; Protestant Reformation.**)

* **Protestant Reformation** religious movement that began in the 1500s as a protest against certain practices of the Roman Catholic Church and eventually led to the establishment of a variety of Protestant churches

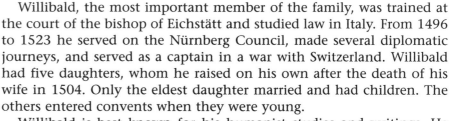

Pisa

The northern Italian city of Pisa was an important commercial center in the Renaissance and home to one of Europe's leading universities. It also served as the seaport of Tuscany, the region around Florence. Pisa had been an independent commune during the Middle Ages, but it fell under the control of Florence in the early 1400s.

Before losing its independence, Pisa was ruled by a group of consuls elected by urban guilds* such as the wool workers and the order of merchants. The consuls appointed the members of the Senate, an assembly that had authority over political affairs, but they retained responsibility for legal matters. Both the consuls and the members of the Senate came from the city's noble and merchant classes. The common people were represented by a council of elders.

Since the 1200s the city had been split into two factions*—the merchants and the other major guilds. Pisa's merchants opposed the policy that allowed the textile merchants of Florence to use the port of Siena without paying taxes. However, the other guilds supported it. The dispute over this matter led to war with Florence from 1356 to 1364. When the war ended, Florence kept its tax exemption. By the end of the 1300s, Duke Gian Galeazzo Visconti of Milan had gained control of Pisa. However, he died suddenly in 1402, and four years later his son sold Pisa to Florence for 206,000 gold florins.

Florence ruled Pisa harshly until the time of Lorenzo de' MEDICI. The Medici family helped rebuild Pisa by replacing trade income with investments that improved Pisa's defenses and drained the marshes that surrounded the city. Lorenzo revived the university, which had closed in the early 1400s. He moved the University of Florence to Pisa and ordered his subjects to study there. With Medici support, the University of Pisa became a major center of learning. The influence of the Medici family ended in 1494, when Charles VIII, the king of France, invaded

* **guild** association of craft and trade owners and workers that set standards for and represented the interests of its members

* **faction** party or interest group within a larger group

Italy. He expelled the Medici from Florence, and Pisa rose up in rebellion. Pisa suffered through three sieges* before surrendering to Florence in 1509.

In the 1530s Pisa became a favorite residence of Alessandro de' Medici, the first duke of Florence. The painter and writer Giorgio Vasari designed a palace and church for Pisa's Order of the Knights of St. Stephen. The Medici created this order to help Pisa recover some of its income from sea trade. In addition, the well-known scientist Galileo GALILEI taught at the university during the late 1500s. (*See also* **Florence; Universities.**)

Pisanello, Antonio Pisano, Il

ca. 1395–1455
Italian artist

The painter and sculptor Pisanello (Antonio Pisano) is celebrated for his remarkable drawings and sculpted medals. He was the first Renaissance artist to create portrait medals. These minature bronze pieces contained the subject's face on one side and images highlighting the person's achievements on the reverse.

Early Life and Career.   Born in PISA, Pisanello trained in northern Italy and spent his early career there. He probably painted a fresco* in the Doge's Palace in VENICE in the early 1400s. Around 1426 he produced a fresco for a tomb in the church of San Fermo Maggiore in Verona. This work shows the influence of Gentile da Fabriano, the most accomplished northern Italian painter of the time.

In the 1420s, Pisanello settled into a lifelong pattern of moving among various Italian courts, especially those of FERRARA and MANTUA. His patrons* included the duke of MILAN and Pope Eugenius IV, for whom he completed a cycle of paintings begun by Gentile da Fabriano. In 1448 Pisanello left northern Italy for NAPLES, where King Alfonso V appointed him a member of the royal household.

Medals and Drawings.   Pisanello also visited Rome, where he studied the ancient ruins and developed an interest in classical* art. This inspired him to reinvent the ancient art form of portrait medals. He began with a medal of the Byzantine* emperor John VIII Palaeologus. During the 1440s, Pisanello created medals for most of the major political figures in northern Italy. Many distributed the small, portable portraits to their friends.

Few of Pisanello's medals and paintings have survived. However, he left a large collection of magnificent drawings, considered his most important legacy. Many of the drawings are careful studies of objects that Pisanello may have planned to incorporate into larger works. Others are more freely sketched, suggesting that the artist drew them directly from nature rather than copying images from other works, a common practice of the time.

Pisanello's drawings give an excellent idea of the range of tasks undertaken by a court artist's workshop in the early Renaissance. The subjects include military objects, such as helmets, armor, and cannons; personal items, such as rings, crowns, and tableware; animals, such as horses,

dogs, falcons, monkeys, and camels; and portraits of his patrons and their elaborate costumes. (*See also* **Art in Italy; Sculpture.**)

1405–1464
Pope and author

* **Ottoman Turks** Turkish followers of Islam who founded the Ottoman Empire in the 1300s; the empire eventually included large areas of eastern Europe, the Middle East, and northern Africa

* **humanist** Renaissance expert in the humanities (the languages, literature, history, and speech and writing techniques of ancient Greece and Rome)

* **Holy Roman Emperor** ruler of the Holy Roman Empire, a political body in central Europe composed of several states that existed until 1806

Pope Pius II led the Roman Catholic Church from 1458 to 1464. He tried to unite Europe in a crusade against the Ottoman Turks*. He also left a legacy as a humanist* and writer.

Pius II was born Enea Piccolomini, the son of poor nobles from the Italian city of Siena. He studied at the University of Siena before serving as secretary to several church leaders. After attending the Council of Basel (1431–1449), he came to believe that church councils, rather than the pope, should decide the policies of the Roman Catholic Church.

Piccolomini traveled throughout Europe and learned a great deal about the nations of Europe and their leaders. In the 1440s he served Frederick III, the Habsburg ruler of Germany and Austria who later became Holy Roman Emperor*. Around this time Piccolomini abandoned his support for church councils and embraced the idea that the pope and the Holy Roman Emperor should join forces to unite Christian Europe. He feared that rivalry between countries was tearing Europe apart.

Piccolomini left Frederick's service to enter the priesthood, and he became bishop of Trieste in 1447. Nine years later Pope Calixtus III made him a cardinal. In 1458 he was elected Pope Pius II and made plans for a military campaign against the Ottoman Turks. However, few European leaders supported the cause and the expedition fell apart before leaving Italy. Pius, who was seriously ill by the time he reached the fleet's departure port of Ancona, died there in 1464.

Pius II was the most important literary figure among all the popes. As a young man he wrote light pieces, including a novella (a short novel) that became one of the most popular works of the 1400s. His memoirs became one of the classics of Renaissance literature. (*See also* **Habsburg Dynasty; Ottoman Empire; Popes and Papacy.**)

1499–1565
Roman Catholic pope

* **patron** supporter or financial sponsor of an artist or writer

Pope Pius IV led the Roman Catholic Church from 1559 to 1565. His greatest achievement as pope was to conclude the work of the Council of TRENT. Pius IV was also an important patron* of the arts. He was born Giovanni Angelo Medici in Milan, Italy. His family, though noble, was not related to the powerful MEDICI family of Florence. Giovanni studied civil and church law and began his legal career while Clement VII was pope.

Medici developed his skills as a lawyer and worked his way up the church ladder of offices. He became an archbishop in 1545, even though he had never been ordained as a priest, and a cardinal four years later. In 1559 Catholic cardinals elected him pope after debating for almost four months. As Pope Pius IV, Medici's first act was to remove the former pope's relatives from office and to have two of them—a cardinal

and a duke—sentenced to death for their crimes. Pius IV then granted his own relatives positions loaded with honors.

Pope Paul III had called the Council of Trent in 1545 to address problems within the Catholic Church following the spread of Protestantism. However, wars and political pressure caused long delays between sessions of the council. Pius IV called the council back into session after an interval of ten years. When the council called for thorough reforms, the pope established a permanent group of cardinals to enforce the decision.

An accomplished Latin scholar, Pius enjoyed reciting entire passages of classical* works from memory. As a patron of the arts, he promoted many projects in the Vatican. Among others, he supported MICHELANGELO BUONARROTI as architect for St. Peter's Cathedral and hired him to build the church of Saint Mary of the Angels. (*See also* **Catholic Reformation and Counter-Reformation; Nepotism; Popes and Papacy.**)

* **classical** in the tradition of ancient Greece and Rome

Pizan, Christine de

1364–ca. 1430
French writer

* **chancellery** office of the chancellor, a high government official who composed official letters and assisted the ruler

* **humanist** referring to a Renaissance cultural movement promoting the study of the humanities (the languages, literature, and history of ancient Greece and Rome) as a guide to living

* **allegorical** referring to a literary or artistic device in which characters, events, and settings represent abstract qualities and in which the author intends a different meaning to be read beneath the surface

Christine de Pizan was the first independent professional female author in Europe, and perhaps in the world. Though she wrote about education and French politics, Pizan's reputation rests mostly on her feminist writings. Her works on women's issues, such as the role and status of women in society, remain significant to modern readers.

In 1369 Pizan's family moved from Italy to Paris, France, where her father served as a medical adviser to the French king. At the age of 15 Pizan married Étienne du Castel, who worked in the French court. After 10 years of marriage, Castel died, leaving Pizan to raise their three children alone. She later wrote that she had to become like a man in order to survive this difficult period. In time, she created a new life for herself through reading and writing.

Literary Works. Pizan's poetry was greatly influenced through contact with the group of poets known as the Court of Love. Her writing attracted attention when she became involved in a debate regarding the work of Jean de Meun, a member of this group. Though poets in the Court of Love claimed to write in honor of women, Pizan accused de Meun of unfairly attacking women in his works. She argued her point in one of her longer poems, *The Letter to the God of Love* (1399). In 1402 she discussed her ideas about women publicly with several young men who were members of the royal chancellery*.

The humanist* ideas of these young men inspired Pizan's allegorical* poem *The Book of the Long Road of Study* (1403). In it, Pizan described a meeting with four mythical queens of the universe who were discussing the qualities of an ideal ruler. Scholars believe that this work reflects the early Renaissance idea that a writer has a duty to influence the thinking of political leaders.

Pizan's involvement in the debate surrounding de Meun's work inspired her to write *The Book of the City of Ladies* in 1405. This poem, influenced by Italian author Giovanni BOCCACCIO's work *On Famous Women,* offered a new interpretation of the role of women in history.

She followed that work with *The Book of the Three Virtues* (1406), in which she advised young women on how to achieve a proper life in society. This book is thought to have influenced young women for more than 100 years after its publication.

Political Writings. Scholars consider Pizan's political works valuable resources for understanding the France of her day. One of her earliest political writings was a biography of the late French ruler Charles V. She composed *The Book of the Deeds and Good Customs of the Wise King Charles V* (1404) to honor Charles and preserve his fame.

As France entered a period of political tension in the early 1400s, Pizan's works became critical of French rulers. In one book, she complained that the nation's leaders were not maintaining a stable government and offered suggestions on how to create a well-organized society. In another work, Pizan expressed the need to calm warring groups and restore the welfare of the country. She also addressed works to specific leaders, reminding them of their responsibility toward France.

Pizan's late works began to focus on how the country's political problems were affecting French women. As France continued its decline, she withdrew from society, though she continued to write. One of her last works was a tribute to France's national heroine, Joan of Arc. (*See also* **French Language and Literature.**)

Plague

The plague—a highly contagious and often fatal disease—swept across Europe repeatedly throughout the Renaissance. It struck every region in Europe at least once in every generation, and there was no effective treatment or cure. The first and deadliest outbreak, the Black Death, struck between 1348 and 1350. The last large-scale epidemic of plague occurred at Marseilles, France, in 1720.

No war, disease, or famine has killed as large as percentage of the population as the Black Death. It wiped out between 30 and 50 percent of the population wherever it appeared and left some places almost uninhabited. The Italian poet PETRARCH survived the Black Death and described its horrific effects: "When was anything similar either seen or heard? In what [history] did anyone ever read that dwellings were emptied, cities abandoned, countrysides filthy, fields laden with bodies, and a dreadful and vast solitude covered the earth?"

The Disease. The plague took two main forms, pneumonic and bubonic. Pneumonic plague, a severe and often fatal lung infection, caused its victims to spit up blood. The characteristic symptoms of bubonic plague were swellings in victims' groins or armpits. According to one witness, they could grow to be as large as an egg or an apple. This form of the disease took its name from buboes, the word Renaissance Europeans gave these lumps.

Modern medical researchers have identified the bubos as swollen lymph nodes and the plague as infection with the bacterium *Yersina pestis*. Normally the bacterium lives in rodents and their fleas. In

Artist Marcantonio Raimondi captured the death and despair of the plague in this work from the early 1500s. Outbreaks of the plague struck every part of Europe repeatedly during the Renaissance, increasing death rates to as much as ten times as high as normal.

humans, however, its effects are devastating. It can spread rapidly to people from rodents such as the common house rat.

People of the time might refer to any episode of widespread disease as a plague or pestilence. Bubonic plague was at the center of these waves of death, although other diseases may have been involved as well. Outbreaks usually occurred during warm summer months and struck suddenly. They affected both urban and rural people and raised the death rate to levels two to ten times normal.

Plague Prevention. Communities tried to organize measures to protect themselves in times of plague. Even during the Black Death, leaders in some cities tried to enforce laws about street cleaning and other forms of sanitation, thinking that filth somehow fueled the plague.

Between 1350 and 1500 Italian cities developed new public-health approaches to plague based on keeping healthy people apart from individuals or goods that might carry plague. Over the next 150 years the

rest of Europe adopted these practices. One method was the quarantine—an attempt to prevent the spread of plague by banning trade or travel from areas where there had been an outbreak of the disease. To protect a port city, passengers on incoming vessels stayed under observation to see whether they developed plague. Although "quarantine" refers to a period of 40 days, the actual length of isolation varied. Another protective measure was the *lazaretto,* or plague hospital, sometimes called a pesthouse. It was a place set aside for individuals thought to have plague in order to isolate them from the healthy.

During the 1400s, local authorities began tracking outbreaks of plague. Their operations gave rise to permanent organizations. By the 1600s, monitoring plague had become a sensitive government activity. It required governments and merchants across regions to work closely together.

Effects of the Plague. The Black Death, and the lesser outbreaks of plague that followed it, had a long-lasting effect on Europe's population. For a century after the first outbreak, the population steadily declined in both rural and urban areas. Before 1348, for example, more than 100,000 people lived in the city of Florence. By 1430 plague had reduced the city's population to about 40,000. In the late 1400s the population of Europe began to rise gradually. However, the patterns of settlement and land use during this time differed from those before the Black Death. Europeans now preferred to live in cities, and most of the great urban areas of modern Europe emerged between 1500 and 1700. Even brutal outbreaks of plague during those years did not halt the growth of Europe's cities.

Most of the people who survived the Black Death and wrote about it were churchmen. They viewed the plague as a warning or a punishment from God for the sins of the world. Religious responses to the plague included appeals to saints and public processions of sorrowful sinners. After the Protestant Reformation*, Protestants abandoned these practices and turned to private prayer. However, all Christians continued to see sin as the primary cause of the plague.

The plague had strong effects on Renaissance medical beliefs. Medical scholars who wrote about plague during the Renaissance believed, according to traditional ideas, that the plague resulted from an imbalance in the body's natural order. As time went on, however, some Renaissance researchers reviewed ancient accounts of other plagues and began to consider how such diseases might come into existence or change over time. These discussions contributed to new ideas that challenged the traditional view of illness as an internal imbalance. (*See also* **Death; Medicine.**)

* **Protestant Reformation** religious movement that began in the 1500s as a protest against certain practices of the Roman Catholic Church and eventually led to the establishment of a variety of Protestant churches

Plato, Platonism, and Neoplatonism

Plato (ca. 428–348 B.C.) was one of the leading philosophers of ancient Greece. His system of thought, known as Platonism, gained favor with many scholars during the Renaissance. Among those who

studied Plato were NICHOLAS OF CUSA, Marsilio FICINO, and Giovanni PICO DELLA MIRANDOLA.

At the beginning of the period, Italian scholars knew little of Plato's work. Because Latin was the language of educated people, few could read or translate Greek. During the 1400s, however, many Greek scholars came to Italy. Some of them brought with them Greek texts previously unknown to western Europe. With their arrival, more scholars became aware of Plato's importance and tried to translate his works. Humanists*, who were eager to learn Greek and promote its use, began translating Plato's work for literary, educational, and political purposes. In 1462 Ficino began a project to translate all of Plato's works into Latin for his patron* Cosimo de' MEDICI. Ficino published the *Complete Works of Plato* in 1484, and in 1496 he added his *Commentary on Plato*. These two works helped to spread Platonism.

Neoplatonism. Most Renaissance scholars approached Plato's works through the writings of Plotinus, an ancient philosopher who had lived several centuries after Plato. Plotinus had developed a school of thought called Neoplatonism, which built on the ideas of Plato. Ficino, in particular, relied heavily on the ideas of Plotinus.

A form of Neoplatonism unique to the Renaissance emerged with the work of the Greek educator George Gemistus, who adopted the name Pletho to link himself more closely with Plato and Plotinus. Pletho dreamed of reviving Neoplatonism as a form of theology* and even wrote hymns to Platonic ideas such as light and goodness. His critics accused him of trying to replace Christianity with a pagan* religion based on Plato. Nonetheless, Pletho influenced many Christian thinkers through his writings. His argument that Plato's reasoning was superior to that of ARISTOTLE, another ancient Greek thinker, sparked a lively debate among philosophers.

One of Pletho's most important supporters was the Greek humanist Bessarion. In his four-part defense of Plato, Bessarion tried to show that Plato's thinking was consistent with Christian teachings. He also argued that the ideas of Plato and Aristotle had much in common. This work introduced Italians to the debate about the merits of the two ancient Greeks. It went through many printings and became an important source for scholars.

The Nature of Reality. Renaissance scholars took special interest in Plato's idea of a perfect, eternal reality outside of the physical world. Although Plato had lived in a pagan culture, Renaissance thinkers examined his writings through Christian eyes. Ficino, for example, tried to prove that there was no conflict between Plato's philosophy and the basic ideas of Christianity. Ficino argued that the belief systems of the ancient Greeks and Romans, such as Plato, were similar to those of the ancient Hebrews and had sprung from the same source. Scholars such as Ficino and Pico hoped to use Plato's ideas to mend the long-standing divide between religion and philosophy.

Renaissance thinkers revived the Neoplatonist idea that all of nature has a soul. In exploring this idea, they drew on theories of MAGIC hand-

* **humanist**   Renaissance expert in the humanities (the languages, literature, history, and speech and writing techniques of ancient Greece and Rome)

* **patron**   supporter or financial sponsor of an artist or writer

* **theology**   study of the nature of God and of religion

* **pagan**   referring to ancient religions that worshiped many gods, or more generally, to any non-Christian religion

ed down from the Middle Ages and from Arab scholars. However, their goal was not to control nature, as magicians tried to do, but to find a connection between the human soul and a larger "World-Soul." They sought this connection through such different fields as music, number symbolism, and astrology*. Critics of this view claimed that it linked human souls to demons and spirits.

* **astrology**   study of the supposed influences of the stars and planets on earthly events

Students of Plato focused on the idea of human beings as the image and likeness of God. They believed that each human soul longed to reunite with the universal soul of nature. Scholars such as Ficino and Pico believed that human beings could, through intellect and will, reach a godlike state and achieve union with God and the universe.

Philosophers also explored Plato's ideas about love, which they saw as the longing or desire for beauty. The Neoplatonists' thoughts about love and desire had a great influence on other fields, such as art and literature. They inspired, among others, the Italian painters Sandro BOTTICELLI and MICHELANGELO BUONARROTI, the English poet Edmund SPENSER, and the Italian scientist Galileo GALILEI. (*See also* **Greek Émigrés; Humanism; Numerology; Philosophy.**)

Poetics

See *Literature; Poetry.*

Poetry

* **medieval**   referring to the Middle Ages, a period that began around A.D. 400 and ended around 1400 in Italy and 1500 in the rest of Europe

* **sonnet**   poem of 14 lines with a fixed pattern of meter and rhyme

* **humanism**   Renaissance cultural movement promoting the study of the humanities (the languages, literature, and history of ancient Greece and Rome) as a guide to living

* **vernacular**   native language or dialect of a region or country

* **classical**   in the tradition of ancient Greece and Rome

The Renaissance was a time of explosive growth for poetry. Renaissance poets revived the poetry of ancient Greece and Rome and expanded the medieval* traditions of religious poetry. They also developed a new poetic form—the sonnet*—that swept through Europe.

CLASSICAL POETRY

As part of the educational backbone of humanism*, Greek and Latin poetry played a central role in the Renaissance. During this time, the word *poetry* referred to the verse of ancient Greece and Rome rather than to vernacular* poetry.

Access to Classical Poetry. Anyone who hoped to study classical* poetry first had to learn Latin and Greek. Latin had been the language of learning throughout the Middle Ages, but the version that many scholars of the early Renaissance knew differed from the Latin of ancient Roman poetry. Scholars had to relearn elements of the language in order to study the poetry on its own terms.

The Italian scholar PETRARCH (1304–1374) realized that ancient Greek literature would be essential to the rebirth of classical culture that he hoped to create. However, like most people west of Greece, he had not mastered Greek. Instruction in Greek had begun to spread throughout Europe by the 1400s, but the majority of Europeans never became skilled in the language. Still, the recovery of ancient Greek literature is one of the great achievements of Renaissance humanism.

This painting by the artist Pinturicchio shows Emperor Frederick III crowning Enea Silvio Piccolomini as imperial poet laureate. This practice dates back to the ancient Greek and Romans, who honored poets with a crown of laurel, a tree sacred to Apollo, the god of poetry.

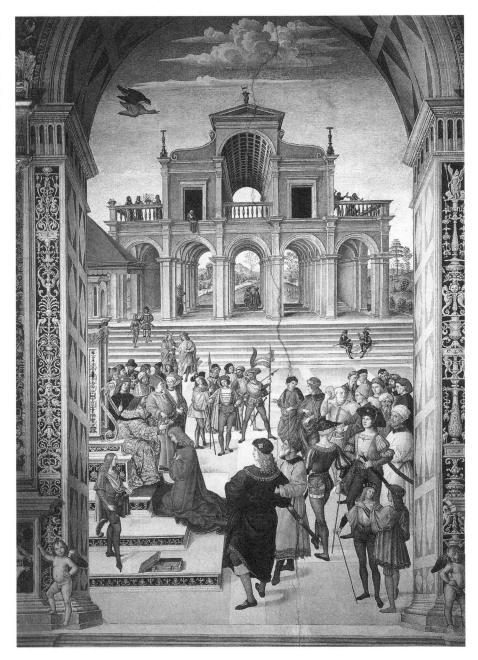

Many people had an in-depth knowledge of a great deal of classical literature during the Renaissance. Most of these people learned to read ancient Greek and Roman poetry in humanist schools. Cheap printed editions also helped to make classical texts accessible. Other people became familiar with classical stories and ideas indirectly. For example, they might learn the elements of a story from paintings or sculptures.

Interpretation and Imitation. Renaissance schoolmasters often instructed their students to keep two notebooks, called commonplace books, while studying classical literature. In one notebook, students copied lines that explained virtues, common feelings, and social prac-

* **allusion**   indirect reference to historical or fictional characters, places, or events

tices. In the other, they listed expressions that they might use in their own writing. This practice may have affected the way that students approached classical texts. Notes that they made in their books suggest that they were on the lookout for items for these notebooks as they read. Allusions* to classical poetry became a common language for Renaissance artists and authors and artists. Writers who composed in Latin and in the vernacular expected their readers to know the classical texts that formed the basis of their works. Even the English playwright William SHAKESPEARE (1564–1616), who wrote for all levels of society, could be confident that his audience would understand basic references to classical literature.

RELIGIOUS POETRY

English Protestant writers produced a great deal of religious poetry. Their writings reflected English literary trends as well as the issues of the time. The first publication of English Protestant religious songs was Miles Coverdale's *Ghostly Psalms and Spirituall Songes* (ca. 1538). Coverdale based it on German reformer Martin LUTHER's book of hymns (1524). Verse translations of the Psalms began to appear in the 1570s. These works aimed to make Scripture accessible to people from all levels of society.

Thomas Wyatt's *Certayne Psalmes* (1549) brought Renaissance verse forms—especially the sonnet—to English sacred poetry. In the 1590s the popularity of English sonnet sequences inspired collections of religious sonnets. Biblical translation remained another major type of sacred poetry. Many of England's Renaissance poets tried their hands at verse translations of the Psalms, including Philip SIDNEY, Francis BACON, and John MILTON. Their works often included experiments in meter and personal expressions of faith.

* **epic**   long poem about the adventures of a hero

Some religious verse combined secular forms and religious themes. In the 1570s the French poet Guillaume Du Bartas created two epics* based on biblical stories, *La Judit* and *La Sepmaine*. Both works were translated into English and inspired a series of English biblical epics. In another popular form, the sacred complaint, biblical sinners tell the stories of their lives and explain how their misdeeds led to guilt and pain. Edmund SPENSER (ca. 1552–1599) brought Christian allegory and the Italian romantic epic together in *The Faerie Queene* (1596). Later poets drew on Spenser's religious themes, especially those of inner spiritual conflict.

* **Baroque**   artistic style of the 1600s characterized by movement, drama, and grandness of scale

* **theology**   study of the nature of God and of religion

The 1600s saw two distinct styles emerge in religious verse. The first was the passionate style of John DONNE's *Poems* and George Herbert's *The Temple,* both published in 1633. These works include detailed, deeply personal reflections on the soul. Sacred verse in the Baroque* style, by contrast, focused on complex issues of theology*. It also used highly emotional language. For example, in *Salve Deus Rex Judaeorum* (Hail God, King of the Jews; 1611), Aemelia Lanyer described Saint Lawrence, "Yielding his naked body to the fire, / To taste this sweetness, such was his desire." Poets such as Herbert and John Milton (1608–1674) also wrote in this style.

In the mid-1600s the English monarchy collapsed and the Church of England temporarily ceased to be the nation's official church. These changes helped to bring the period of Renaissance sacred verse to an end. The religious works of Robert Herrick (*Noble Numbers,* 1648) and Henry Vaughan (*Silex Scintillans,* 1650, 1655) show a defeated attitude. Their poems speak of the lost innocence of Eden, of infancy, and of England.

SONNETS

First created in the 1200s, the sonnet form spread across Europe during the Renaissance. It enjoyed popularity of one kind or another for almost 500 years. Although it began as straightforward love poetry, the sonnet had become a highly technical form of rhetoric* by the end of the Renaissance.

The First Sonnets. The sonnet began as the invention of Giacomo da Lentino, a member of the court of Holy Roman Emperor* Frederick II, in the first half of the 1200s. Lentino's sonnet had two parts—an octave (a group of eight lines) followed by a sestet (a group of six lines). Lentino may have used either an Italian peasant song or an existing poetic form as the basis for the octave. In each of the fifteen sonnets that he wrote, he used only four or five different end-of-line rhymes.

The sonnet's history as an important literary form began in the last decade of the 1200s, when the Italian poet Dante Alighieri chose to include sonnets in his *The New Life.* He combined the poems with a prose story to declare his narrator's love for Beatrice, a beautiful and virtuous woman. In the story, Beatrice never returns the poet's love, and she dies young.

Petrarch soon set out to surpass Dante in writing sonnets. His *Canzoniere* (Book of Songs) told the story of his unreturned love for Laura, another beautiful and virtuous woman who died early in life. Beatrice and Laura quickly became the models for sonneteers across Italy, as poets grieved the death of nearly perfect women who had not returned their love. Petrarch's friend, the Italian poet Giovanni Boccaccio (1313–1375), and the English poet Geoffrey Chaucer (ca. 1342–1400) became some of Petrarch's earliest imitators. More than 170 versions of the *Canzoniere* went to print between its first edition (in 1470) and 1600.

In all of these sonnet sequences, readers learn more about the hopelessness of the poets' love for these women than about the women themselves. In fact, it is difficult to identify most of these ladies historically. Today's scholars see these poems not as true accounts of love and devotion but as displays of the poet's skill. While these poems outwardly focused on love, many poets used their works to point out moral issues—especially the greed of the court and the church.

Petrarchan Sonnets. Petrarch's name soon became an adjective—Petrarchan—to describe sonnets about a lover whom the poet could not

* **rhetoric** art of speaking or writing effectively

* **Holy Roman Emperor** ruler of the Holy Roman Empire, a political body in central Europe composed of several states that existed until 1806

have and the poet's resulting agony. Two major Petrarchan writers surfaced in Italy in the 1400s and 1500s. The first, Il Cariteo, and his followers put many of Petrarch's sonnets to music and also composed original sonnet sequences. However, it was Pietro Bembo's *Rime* (1530) that set the standard for Petrarchan imitation in a sonnet. In 1545 nearly 100 writers published Petrarchan sonnets in the style of Bembo in a collection called *Diverse Rimes*. The book sold well—especially to foreign travelers. It also made the Petrarchan sonnet the accepted form for Italian sonnets.

During the early 1500s, writers in France, Spain, Portugal, and England began creating sonnets in their own languages. In 1552, another Italian sonnet collection appeared in Naples: *Rimes of Various Illustrious Neapolitans*. After its publication, a rush of sonnets spread across Europe.

Birth of the English Sonnet. English writers began experimenting with the sonnet form around 1527. As a young man, Sir Thomas Wyatt (1503–1542) began writing English sonnets after a trip to France. In these first English sonnets, he changed the sestet by making its last two lines a couplet*. His friend Henry Howard, earl of Surrey (ca. 1517–1547), revised the English sonnet further. He divided the octave into two quatrains (groups of four lines). The first four lines of the sestet made a third quatrain. Like Wyatt, he ended each sonnet with a couplet. This became the accepted form of the English sonnet.

Wyatt's and Surrey's sonnets did not appear in print during their lifetimes. Their first publication was in 1557, when publisher Richard Tottel included them in his enormously popular *Songes and Sonettes*. The book popularized the sonnet as an English literary form.

The Sonnet Craze. Around 1582, Sir Philip Sidney (1554–1586) wrote *Astrophel and Stella*. In this Petrarchan sequence, Sidney pined for "Stella"—his name for a real woman, Penelope Devereux. In 1591, five years after his death, the publication of *Astrophel and Stella* kicked off a craze for English sonnet sequences that lasted for nearly twenty years. The fashion for sequences, in turn, made individual sonnets popular. Philosophical, moral, and satiric* sonnets, as well as sonnets for special occasions, often appeared in small groupings or as independent works.

The most popular writers immediately following Sidney were Samuel Daniel (*Delia,* 1592) and Michael Drayton (*Ideas Mirrour,* 1594). Both had a mournful quality that other writers imitated. As time went on, however, Drayton adopted a more sarcastic and self-mocking tone.

Edmund Spenser's complicated *Amoretti* (1595) won much admiration in its time. In this sequence to his fiancée, Spenser revised the English sonnet's rhyme scheme and forced himself to rhyme more lines with the same sounds. Spenser's new form proved to be too difficult for most poets to imitate.

In some ways, the *Sonnets* of William Shakespeare, published in 1609, were traditional. Although his wordplay was especially witty, it clearly reflected the rhetoric of his time. He also used Sidney's form and Petrarch's themes. However, he questioned established ideas by twisting

* couplet pair of rhyming lines that appear together, as at the end of a sonnet or stanza of verse

* satiric involving the use of satire, the ridicule of human wickedness and foolishness in a literary or artistic work

Sonnets and Politics

Like other art forms, sonnets became an important measure of culture in Renaissance courts. Therefore, rulers took an interest in the poets of their nations. In Scotland, James VI (who later became James I of England) wrote a sonnet sequence (*Essayes of a Prentise in the Divine Art of Poesie,* 1584) and encouraged Scottish poets to do the same. In England, it became fashionable for the nobility to support poets.

some Petrarchan elements. For instance, instead of yearning for one person in his sonnets, Shakespeare addressed his poems to two different people. The first is a young man. Today's scholars still debate whether the sonnets that Shakespeare wrote to him are about a close friendship or a romantic relationship. The second is a woman, but she has few of the qualities of Beatrice and Laura. She is married to someone else, yet she and the speaker are involved in a bitter, sexual relationship. Because of Shakespeare's fame, the English sonnet also became known as the Shakespearian sonnet.

Decline of the English Sonnet. After Shakespeare, only a few major writers continued to write sonnets. These poets experimented with the form. Scottish poet William Drummond mixed the Italian and English forms of the sonnet. George Herbert and John Donne (1572–1631) both wrote religious sonnets. Their works introduced new techniques, such as running sentences across the ends of lines and placing words in an unusual order.

The poems of John Milton were the final burst of brilliance for the sonnet form in Renaissance England. Milton wrote sonnets mostly to friends or to public figures. Unlike other English writers, he usually used the Italian form of the sonnet. Milton was also one of only a few British Renaissance authors who wrote sonnets in Italian. Instead of writing as a suffering Petrarchan lover, Milton often spoke as a humanist in his poems. After his death, the sonnet fell out of fashion in England for a century. (*See also* **English Language and Literature; Humanism; Italian Language and Literature.**)

Poetry, English

* **medieval**   referring to the Middle Ages, a period that began around A.D. 400 and ended around 1400 in Italy and 1500 in the rest of Europe

* **humanism**   Renaissance cultural movement promoting the study of the humanities (the languages, literature, and history of ancient Greece and Rome) as a guide to living

Until HENRY VIII came to power in 1509, most of England's poetry resembled medieval* literature. As literature from other parts of Europe filtered into England, English poets began to experiment with European influences. The result was an explosion of new forms, styles, and voices in English poetry. English poetry had close ties with both culture and politics during the Renaissance. Three English monarchs—Henry VIII, ELIZABETH I, and JAMES I—were also poets.

POETRY IN LATIN

The first stirrings of humanism* in England appeared in the work of English poets who began composing verses in Latin. Latin poetry was most popular between 1540 and 1640. Universities taught their students to compose Latin poetry as a way to improve their skill in the language. In the 1580s, both Cambridge and Oxford Universities began to print the Latin verses of their graduates.

Most of the poets who wrote in Latin were university students or graduates, although a small number of privately educated women also published volumes of Latin poetry. Some writers composed Latin verse for their own enjoyment, while others hoped to attract a wealthy

* **patron**   supporter or financial sponsor of an artist or writer

patron*. However, only a handful of writers, including Sir Thomas MORE (ca. 1478–1535), earned lasting or widespread fame because of their Latin writings. More also wrote some poems in English, but like many humanists of the time, he believed that Latin was the proper language for serious literature.

The Latin poetry of the English Renaissance reflects a wide variety of influences. It includes elements of mythology, history, biblical stories, saints' lives, obituaries, and politics. Latin poems celebrated great national events and introduced books of all types. Many poems used "artificial," or cleverly crafted, forms that involved elaborate language patterns, riddles, and wordplay.

POETRY OF THE EARLY RENAISSANCE

Throughout most of the 1500s, English poets mixed forms, styles, and themes from the late Middle Ages and the Renaissance. For poets, it was a time of experimentation.

* **sonnet**   poem of 14 lines with a fixed pattern of meter and rhyme

English Poetry Before Elizabeth I. When Henry VIII took the throne, humanists and scholars such as Sir Thomas More saw an opportunity for the advancement of poetry. During Henry's marriage to CATHERINE OF ARAGON, poets began to import, translate, and adapt new poetic forms from across Europe, including the sonnets* of the Italian poet PETRARCH.

John Skelton (ca. 1460–1529) was one of the most inventive poets of the early Renaissance. Some of his writing was political—he wrote two dangerously pointed attacks on one of the king's powerful advisers, yet he also wrote in praise of an English victory in battle. Skelton also defended vernacular* poetry against critics who considered it trivial. He experimented with poetic forms, creating a form of rhymed English verse that drew on the traditions of medieval Latin poetry. His poems show a keen ear for sound and a love of realism.

* **vernacular**   native language or dialect of a region or country

The most important source of the English Renaissance style, however, lay in the work of Sir Thomas Wyatt (1503–1542). Wyatt translated many of Petrarch's sonnets into English using iambic pentameter*, which became a very popular meter for English verse. Some of Wyatt's lyrics illustrate the close relationship between the poetry and the politics of his time. This relationship was also obvious in Wyatt's life. In 1541, after being jailed for treason, he used his skill with rhetoric* to win his freedom.

* **iambic pentameter**   line of poetry consisting of ten syllables, or five metric feet, with emphasis placed on every other syllable

* **rhetoric**   art of speaking or writing effectively

* **couplet**   pair of rhyming lines that appear together, as at the end of a sonnet or stanza of verse

Henry Howard, earl of Surrey (1517–1547) perfected the style Wyatt had created. A skillful translator, he established what became the standard English sonnet form. He divided sonnets into three groups of four lines, or quatrains, and a couplet*. This form allowed for seven different rhymes rather than the repeated rhymes of Italian sonnets. Surrey also pioneered the use of English blank verse*.

* **blank verse**   unrhymed verse, usually in iambic pentameter—lines of poetry consisting of ten syllables, or five metric feet, with emphasis placed on every other syllable

In the mid-1500s some poets left England for religious reasons. Nonetheless, a number of printed collections of poems appeared during this time, including the popular *Songes and Sonnettes* (1557) by Richard

Edmund Spenser helped change the shape of English poetry by experimenting with new forms and themes. His *Shepheardes Calender,* published in 1579, combined new and old styles and used language in ways that reflected English literary tradition.

* **classical** in the tradition of ancient Greece and Rome

* **pastoral** relating to the countryside; often used to draw a contrast between the innocence and serenity of rural life and the corruption and extravagance of court life

Tottel. One of the most popular forms for poetry during this period was iambic septameter, which contained seven strong syllables and seven weak syllables per line. Many poets saw this meter as resembling the long lines of classical* poetry. However, these long lines sounded to many ears like pairs of shorter lines, with eight syllables followed by six. This "eight and six" form, also known as common meter, was used in a popular translation of the Psalms, which helped make Scripture in English easier to set to music.

Early Elizabethan Trends. Collections of works by several poets remained popular during the early years of Elizabeth's reign, which lasted from 1558 until 1603. At the same time, poets began to publish complete volumes of their own verses—often for profit. Many writers embraced the new ideas of the Renaissance in their work. They wrote poems on Renaissance themes, translated classical poetry, and drew on their experiences abroad.

During the 1560s, Isabella Whitney became the first female poet in England to publish her works. Whitney's poems followed many of the standards of the period, mixing classical and personal references and dealing with common themes. Her work is a sign of the increasing interest in writing among women at this time.

The bold, autobiographical writings of George Gascoigne reflect another trait of writers of this time—ambition. Although critics attacked the first edition of *The Posies of George Gascoigne, Esquire* (1573) for immorality and slander, Gascoigne published a second version two years later. He referred to himself by name in several of his poems, including the self-flattering "Gascoigne's Woodmanship." Gascoigne's career contrasts with that of Thomas Sackville, earl of Dorset. Sackville was one of the first authors to produce original works in blank verse. He went on to a distinguished career as a courtier—unlike Gascoigne, who remained on the outskirts of respectable society.

ELIZABETHAN POETRY

Popular collections of poetry from the reign of Henry VIII had a strong influence on many early Elizabethan writers. As a result, much Elizabethan poetry is similar to the poetry of an earlier generation. It was not until Edmund Spenser and Philip Sidney, both born in the 1550s, began experimenting with new forms and themes that Elizabethan poetry took on a distinct style of its own. Spenser, Sidney, and other Elizabethan poets blended humanism with Protestant beliefs and English nationalism.

Elizabethan Styles. Edmund Spenser's the *Shepheardes Calender* (1579) marked a turning point in English poetry. In this complex work, Spenser combined the pastoral* poems of the ancient Roman writer Virgil with a book of agricultural instructions from his own time. Like other pastoral poetry, this piece placed value on contentment rather than on personal ambition. It was also a political work. It expresses

* epic long poem about the adventures of a hero

* metaphor figure of speech in which one object or idea is directly identified with a different object or idea

* allegory literary or artistic device in which characters, events, and settings represent abstract qualities and in which the author intends a different meaning to be read beneath the surface

* satiric involving the use of satire, the ridicule of human wickedness and foolishness in a literary or artistic work

Spenser's nationalism at a time when many English feared that their Protestant queen would marry a French Catholic prince.

Spenser's use of language often carried hidden political meanings. His choice of outdated English spellings and words reminds his readers of history and England's literary traditions. In both the *Shepheardes Calender* and *The Faerie Queene* (1596), an epic* in honor of Elizabeth I, Spenser brought English creative writing to a new level of sophistication.

Philip Sidney, the poet to whom Spenser dedicated *Shepheardes Calender,* adapted classical poetic structures to English in his own works. In *Astrophel and Stella* (1591), he used both sonnets and Greek forms to revisit some of Petrarch's themes. Sidney's poems show a mastery of meter and rhetoric. They also reflect Protestant values, most obviously in the translation of the biblical Psalms that he left unfinished at his death.

Elizabethan poets frequently used extended metaphors* and allegories* in their work. Sidney built layers of metaphor into *The Faerie Queene,* and metaphors lie at the heart of many Elizabethan sonnets. Although William SHAKESPEARE (1564–1616) questioned the value of metaphor in sonnets 18 ("Shall I compare thee to a summer's day?") and 130 ("My mistress' eyes are nothing like the sun"), he relied on metaphor in these and other works. The verses of John DONNE (1572–1631) used metaphor to create logical puzzles and dense arguments. Such figurative language was less popular in religious and satiric* verse, which more often used a plain, straightforward style.

Forms of Elizabethan Poetry. Elizabethans valued imitation. Poets often drew on models from classical, Italian, and French literature. In addition, they commonly worked within standard forms, such as the complaint, the satire, the sonnet, and the epic.

Complaints, like pastoral poetry, stress the dangers of ambition and the virtues of a simple life. However, they tend to be more pointed and obviously political than pastoral works. Many complaints follow a common format—the ghost of a famous person asks the poet to describe how he or she fell from grace in life. Complaints might follow the misadventures of a ruler or a royal mistress in order to warn readers against misbehavior. Another form that often took a political slant was the satire, which became popular in the 1590s. In 1599, the government passed an order suppressing satiric works. However, this order seems to have had little effect. Numerous writers published satires before the end of the century.

The sonnet form became popular with writers after the appearance of Sidney's *Astrophel and Stella,* a sonnet sequence. Every would-be poet in the 1590s tried his hand at writing sonnets. Many of these verses, such as those of Shakespeare, are dark and complex. Donne's *Songs and Sonnets* (1633) also includes satiric love poetry. The sonnet form not only required poets to follow strict rules of meter and rhyme but also inspired them to use Petrarch's themes. For example, they often focused on a love interest—usually a lady—whom the speaker of the poem could

not have. The speaker might discuss this lady's many virtues and complain that she would not yield to him.

Renaissance poets considered the epic the highest form of poetic achievement. However, writers disagreed about what distinguished an epic from other forms of writing. Some believed that epics should reflect historical events. Others felt that poetry and history were separate and that poets needed to write with their own ideas. A related, shorter form was the Ovidian minor epic, a love poem based on the work of the ancient Roman poet Ovid. These pieces included elements of classical mythology as well as episodes from true epics. Examples of the form include Christopher MARLOWE's *Hero and Leander* (published after Marlowe's death in 1593) and Shakespeare's *Venus and Adonis* (1593).

ENGLISH POETRY IN THE 1600S

Neither English poetry nor English politics was as unified after 1603 as it had been during Elizabeth's reign. Civil war divided England, and English poets developed distinct styles that set them apart from one another. The most influential poets of the early 1600s were John Donne and Ben JONSON.

Metaphysical Poetry. The term *metaphysical* describes English poetry of the 1600s that did not separate emotion from reason. Metaphysical poems centered on complex ideas called "conceits" and used dramatic language. The main subject in these poems was love—romantic, sexual, or divine. Metaphysical poets used shocking metaphors and wild exaggeration to express their passions.

The leading metaphysical poet was John Donne. His writings about romantic and sexual love are both playful and dramatic. Unlike poems in the style of Petrarch, in which speakers pine for lovers they cannot have, Donne's poems focus on the mutual experience of love. His poetry shows a powerful connection between soul and body. Religious poet George Herbert (1593–1633) mastered many of Donne's effects in his own writing. In poems such as "The Collar," Herbert wrote of "the many spiritual conflicts that have passed [between] God and my soul."

Jonson's Influence. The poetry of Jonson and his "sons" (the poets he influenced) was more social than the highly personal writings of poets such as Donne. Jonsonian poems performed a variety of social and moral purposes such as glorifying the dead, instructing the living, honoring places and events, and praising pleasures. They often relied on classical traditions and took the form of letters to friends. Jonson's *Works* (1616) included two collections of poems in a classical style, as well as elegant translations and adaptations of classical poetry.

The work of Jonson's followers was varied. Thomas Carew (ca. 1595–ca. 1640) wrote verse letters to Jonson and an elegy* to Donne. On a lighter note, Robert Herrick (ca. 1591–1674) wrote "His Farewell to Sack" and "The Welcome to Sack," in which the speaker first swears off and then embraces alcohol. As England entered into civil war in the

Conventional Elizabethans

Elizabethan readers expected authors to use existing literary traditions from Europe and from ancient Greece and Rome. Part of the author's task was to blend these traditions with his or her own ideas and inventions. Elizabethans didn't think it was odd to find nymphs singing in an epic or a lover making himself miserable in a sonnet because they were used to seeing these elements in literature. Instead, they tried to see how authors used traditions creatively to convey their own ideas.

* **elegy** type of poem often used to express sorrow for one who has died

POLAND

* Puritan English Protestant group that wanted to simplify the ceremonies of the Church of England and eliminate all traces of Catholicism

1640s, Jonson's "sons" took the side of the royalty against the Puritan* reformers. Although some of their poems are anti-Puritan only in flavor (such as Herrick's "Delight in Disorder"), others are more direct. While in jail for supporting the king, Richard Lovelace (1618–1657) wrote "To Althea from Prison." In it, he boldly declared, "Stone walls do not a prison make / Nor iron bars a cage."

Spenserian and Female Poets. Although many poets of the 1600s used Spenser's themes and styles, these writers often had little else in common. Many of them wrote, as Spenser had, in the pastoral mode. Michael Drayton (1563–1631) and other writers also followed in Spenser's footsteps by using their pastoral writings to offer political criticism. Andrew Marvell also wrote pastoral poetry during this time, but he did not focus on allegory as many other Spenserians did. Instead, his work explored psychological and playful themes.

In the early 1600s collections of female poets' work began to appear in print. Most of these women followed the poetic forms of their time. Mary Wroth (ca. 1587-ca. 1651), Sidney's niece, continued her uncle's legacy of copying Petrarch's style in her sonnet sequence *Pamphilia to Amphilanthus* (1621). However, she introduced a female speaker. Jonson and others praised Wroth for her accomplishments. Aemelia Lanyer (1569–1645) included the beginnings of feminist viewpoints in her complaint *Salve Deus Rex Judaeorum* (Hail God, King of the Jews; 1611). Today, recently discovered poems in manuscript are helping to revive interest in these and other female authors of the period. (*See also* **Drama, English; English Language and Literature; Humanism; Latin Language and Literature; Poetry.**)

Poland

* humanist referring to a Renaissance cultural movement promoting the study of the humanities (the languages, literature, and history of ancient Greece and Rome) as a guide to living

* Ottoman Turks Turkish followers of Islam who founded the Ottoman Empire in the 1300s; the empire eventually included large areas of eastern Europe, the Middle East, and northern Africa

The Renaissance marked a golden age for Poland. Located at the crossroads of routes linking western Europe with central Asia and Muscovy with southern Europe, the country enjoyed a thriving trade in agricultural exports. In the 1500s Poland stretched from the Baltic Sea to the Black Sea, and its population reached about 11 million. The University of Cracow earned a reputation as an intellectual center, and literature and science flourished under the influence of humanist* ideas from Italy.

The Jagiellon dynasty that ruled Poland had grand ambitions. In 1385 the country had formed a personal union with Lithuania that greatly expanded its territory. However, Jagiellonian plans to win control over the kingdoms of BOHEMIA and HUNGARY suffered a serious setback in 1526, when invading Ottoman Turks* triumphed at the Battle of Mohács. Although advances by the Turks gradually restricted Poland's access to the Black Sea, the country's commerce continued. To protect its trade, Poland pursued a policy of peaceful relations with the Ottoman Empire from 1533 to 1620.

Politics, Government, and Economics. In 1569 Poland and Lithuania made their union formal and became a commonwealth. They

186

THE RENAISSANCE

SIGISMVNDVS III. 45

Ioanne Suecorum Rege, et Catharinâ Iagellonâ natus inter gliscentes factiones Regno Poloniarum præficitur An. 1587. Indè post Patrem Suecico diademate insignitur. Reuocatus in Poloniam, Patrueles, Ericum in Suecia, Carolum in Lithuaniâ, Gustauum in Prussiâ primos hostes expertus est. Verum Ericus elisus, Carolus delusus, Gustauus acceptâ clade in Germaniam remissus est. Ducis subinde Moschi exercitum maximâ strage affecit. Moldauum etiam edomuit. In Rasciano, et Gaborio Hungariæ iras attriuit. Scythas octo validis prælijs percussit: denique ex quadrin: gentis millibus Turcarum, et centum viginti millibus Tartarorum, sexaginta millibus in acie cæsis, cæterisque fugatis, Asiam, Africam, Europam bello unico superauit. Tandem An. æta: tis 66, Regni 45, florentissimus relicto regno, vitam clausit An. 1632.

Sigismund III ruled Poland from 1587 to 1632. He founded the Vasa dynasty, which won major military victories that secured the nation's borders.

* **principality**   independent state ruled by a prince or count

* **Jesuit**   refers to a Roman Catholic religious order founded by St. Ignatius Loyola and approved in 1540

shared a common ruler, parliament, and foreign policy. Monarchs were chosen from the Jagiellon family. After the last Jagiellon ruler died in 1572, an assembly of nobles elected the Polish king. Sigismund III (ruled 1587–1632) established the Vasa dynasty, which placed three kings on the throne. Under the Vasa, Poland won military victories over Sweden and the principality* of Muscovy in the early 1600s. The victories secured Poland's borders but did not end the threats posed by its neighbors. The nobles tried to keep Poland out of European conflicts, fearing that war would strengthen royal power.

Poland had a mixed monarchy. Privileges granted to the nobles restricted the power of the king. In 1493 these privileges were transferred to the Chamber of Deputies, which represented the nobles in parliament. Limiting the power of the king prevented the rise of absolutism in Poland. The nobles protected their own rights and backed the supremacy of law over the authority of individual rulers. These developments encouraged a national culture of tolerance and respect for human rights.

Grain agriculture, forest products, and the raising of oxen formed the core of Poland's economy. The nation had enough grain to feed its population and to export to western Europe. Large landowners profited the most from this trade. Because Poland had a small population for its size, nobles could require peasants to perform compulsory labor. This practice reinforced the system of serfdom, which tied peasants permanently to the land.

Culture and Society. The University of Cracow, founded in 1364, was the intellectual center of Poland. It produced many outstanding scholars in the fields of law, mathematics, literature, history, and geography. Nicolaus COPERNICUS, who gained fame for developing a new model of the universe, headed a school of astronomy. In time a network of Polish schools was established. Some followed Protestant models, and some were Jesuit* schools based on Italian and Spanish models. The schools flourished despite the religious disputes of the time.

Poland was closely connected to intellectual and artistic developments in the rest of Europe. Ties with Italy grew stronger in the 1500s because many Polish students attended Italian universities. The influence of Italy can be seen on Polish thought, art, and architecture. The writings of northern humanists, such as Desiderius ERASMUS, also had a broad following in Poland. In turn, works by Polish humanists appeared in cities across Europe. Poland enjoyed considerable prestige in the fields of legal and political thought, literature, and architecture. Writings on public affairs were popular in the country because so many citizens took part in political life.

During the 1500s various historical works encouraged the self-awareness of Poles and their sense of national identity. These works tried to promote the creation of an eastern Europe based on Roman ideals. Scholars borrowed humanist ideas from Italy and the Netherlands to support their vision, which would incorporate the religious and cultural diversity of the region. Latin was generally used for public speech in

Poland in the early part of the Renaissance. However, the Polish language dominated poetry and gained wider acceptance in public life throughout the 1500s.

The Protestant Reformation* affected all social classes in Poland, but it did not lead to conflict as elsewhere in Europe. A notable feature of Polish life was religious tolerance. The Polish nobility used the threat of Protestantism as a tool against the political power of the Catholic Church. But the nobles returned to the Church in large numbers during the late 1500s. At first the nobles looked out for religious freedom, but in 1573 religious freedom became a formal part of the state system. Poland established itself as a strong defender of Catholicism without persecuting those who followed other faiths. Catholics, Protestants, Orthodox Christians, Jews, Muslims, and others lived together peacefully. The country remained a refuge for all persons persecuted for their beliefs. (*See also* **Catholic Reformation and Counter-Reformation; Protestant Reformation.**)

* **Protestant Reformation** religious movement that began in the 1500s as a protest against certain practices of the Roman Catholic Church and eventually led to the establishment of a variety of Protestant churches

Renaissance writers and philosophers engaged in lively debates on questions of politics and statecraft. They wrestled with such fundamental issues as determining the best form of government and the proper use of power. In Italy, schools of political thought emerged in the mid-1300s that were inspired by ancient Greek and Roman texts. Italian political ideas spread into northern and western Europe from about 1450. Scholars in these regions developed their own theories, adding various legal and religious concepts to the Italian ideas. This process continued until the early 1600s, when new intellectual trends brought an end to the distinctive Renaissance approach to political questions.

ITALY

* **humanism** Renaissance cultural movement promoting the study of the humanities (the languages, literature, and history of ancient Greece and Rome) as a guide to living

The development of humanism* in the 1300s influenced many Italian political thinkers. They studied the works of ancient authors, such as the Greek philosopher PLATO and the Roman orator CICERO. They also considered the benefits and drawbacks of the various governments—including republics* and monarchies—found in Italy at the time.

* **republic** form of Renaissance government dominated by leading merchants with limited participation by others

Civic Humanism. In the early Renaissance, humanists debated whether scholars should dedicate themselves to study or should use their wisdom for the public good by participating in politics. The Italian writer PETRARCH (1304–1374) argued in favor of a life of quiet contemplation. Yet, he noted that Cicero had played an active role in Roman politics. Petrarch believed that the prince* had responsibility for maintaining order in society. In his view, only a strong prince could guarantee the freedom and security of his subjects. Pier Paolo VERGERIO (1370–1444) echoed this idea, but held that wise men have a role to play in educating and advising rulers.

* **prince** Renaissance term for the ruler of an independent state

Many other authors viewed republican government as the best way to ensure the liberty of citizens. Writers such as Coluccio SALUTATI

Political thinker Jean Bodin of France published *Six Books of the Commonwealth* in 1576. In this work, he argued that a successful government must concentrate power in the hands of a single person and limit the role of the citizens.

(1331–1406) and Leonardo BRUNI (ca. 1370–1444) thought that liberty came from active participation of citizens in the government and defense of the state. This idea came to be known as civic humanism. Scholars from Florence often pointed to the republican system in their city as an example of civic humanism.

Princely Rule. In the 1400s, the rise of the house of MEDICI led to the end of republicanism in Florence and ushered in an era of princely rule. Other major Italian states—except the republic of Venice—were also ruled by dukes, princes, and kings. For this reason, many political thinkers, such as Niccolò MACHIAVELLI (1469–1527) and Baldassare CASTIGLIONE (1478–1529) wrote about the characteristics of effective rulers and the role of courtiers and counselors.

Machiavelli's vision of government is based on the individual power of a prince or other ruler. In *The Prince* (1513) he argues that a ruler must be willing to defy ordinary morality, if necessary, to preserve the state. In his view, the prince must be ready to rule by fear rather than love and to focus on military capability.

Machiavelli preserves some aspects of republican thought in *The Prince*—claiming, for example, that princes should rely on citizen-soldiers rather than hired foreign troops. Moreover, in some of his other works he states that a strong republic has the best chance of success in an unstable world. However, he argues that even a strong republic depends on a balance between social forces for its survival. This balance ensures the liberty of all by limiting the dominance of any single group. Machiavelli's works, though influential, met with mixed reactions.

NORTHERN AND WESTERN EUROPE

As Renaissance ideas spread north of the Alps, political writers in northern and western Europe dealt with some of the same issues debated in Italy. By the mid-1400s, many diplomats and government officials in France, Germany, Spain, and England had acquired a humanist education. They applied this learning to the political situations of their own states and societies.

Christian Humanism. In some ways, northern Europeans placed more emphasis on religious issues than Italians. Humanist biblical scholarship, such as new translations of the Scriptures, encouraged this emphasis, which came to be known as Christian humanism. Writers such as the Dutch scholar Desiderius ERASMUS (ca. 1466–1536) considered many political issues in light of Christian belief. In *Education of a Christian Prince* (1516), for example, Erasmus points out that the Bible (Matthew 20:25–28) says the ruler should not be the lord and master of his subjects, but their servant. Erasmus states that a Christian prince has a duty to rule wisely for the common good, not for personal gain. He also condemns warfare and argues that political authority should be exercised to promote the well-being of the state's citizens, rather than to exploit* populations.

* **exploit**   to take advantage of

A celebrated example of Christian humanist writing is *Utopia* (1516), by the English writer Thomas MORE (1478–1535). The book describes life on the fictional island of Utopia, which offers a sharp contrast with the Europe of the time. More uses the story to criticize Renaissance society for its focus on warfare, lack of justice, and disregard for the poor.

Other Political Theories. *Utopia* inspired works by other English authors who proposed their own plans for reform. Thomas Starkey's *Dialogue between Pole and Lupset* (1535) defends the idea of an aristocracy*, claiming that members of the ruling class can learn to accept their responsibility to maintain order and protect the public good. Having lived for a time near Venice, Starkey admired the Venetian system of government and distrusted monarchs. However, because he wrote the *Dialogue* for an English audience accustomed to monarchy, he discussed the role of the king and included suggestions for restraining royal power. Starkey's book highlights one of the main concerns of Renaissance political thinkers: reconciling the ideas of republicanism with the widespread presence of monarchy.

* **aristocracy** privileged upper classes of society; nobles or the nobility

Like Starkey, other writers of the early 1500s called for mixed systems that included a monarchy and limits on royal power. The French humanist Claude de Seyssel (ca. 1450–1520) accepted the need for a strong monarch, but he advised using religion, justice, tradition, and custom to control the king's authority. English author John Ponet (1516–1556) proposed a mixed monarchy in his *Shorte Treatise of Politike Power*. Thomas Smith (1513–1577), also of England, argued that while the king exercises final authority, he does so under the guidance and advice of Parliament, which serves to "consult and show what is good and necessary for the commonwealth."

THE LATE RENAISSANCE

Northern European political thought often drew on legal principles. It was also influenced by political and religious conflicts arising from the Protestant Reformation* and the Counter-Reformation*. These movements raised questions about sovereignty—the supreme authority in a state—and whether absolute power lay with the state or the church. Concerned about maintaining order in the face of religious and social divisions, some Europeans used "reason of state"—doing whatever was considered necessary for the public good—as the justification for policies.

* **Protestant Reformation** religious movement that began in the 1500s as a protest against certain practices of the Roman Catholic Church and eventually led to the establishment of a variety of Protestant churches

* **Counter-Reformation** actions taken by the Roman Catholic Church after 1540 to oppose Protestantism

Sovereignty and Reason of State. The French writer Jean BODIN (1530–1596) argued that, in any society, power must be located in a specific person or office—such as the monarchy—and firmly maintained. He believed that questions about authority were certain to undermine the stability of the state. In *Six Books of the Commonwealth* (1576), Bodin rejects the idea of citizen participation in government in favor of the sovereign power of the king. He sees a place for aristocrats and for citizens in carrying out royal policies, but not in formulating those policies.

Classical Roots

The main political debates of the Renaissance had roots in ancient Greece and Rome. Renaissance thinkers looked to the Roman authors Livy and Sallust to define the relationship between rulers and their subjects. Some later Renaissance scholars took as their guide the Latin historian Tacitus, who wrote about several of the most powerful Roman emperors. Although the circumstances of the ancient world and the Renaissance differed, states and citizens in the two periods faced many of the same political issues.

---

* **Flemish** relating to Flanders, a region along the coasts of present-day Belgium, France, and the Netherlands

Other thinkers focused on the concept of reason of state. The German writer Christoph Besold (1577–1638) took it to be the basis for a monarch's ability to overrule ordinary law. The concept of reason of state was also widespread among political writers in Italy, who defended the prince's use of extraordinary measures to defend the state. For many, these ideas were uncomfortably close to those expressed in Machiavelli's *The Prince.* The hardheaded practicality of Machiavelli's ideas aroused criticism, and many writers were reluctant to endorse them openly. As a result, theorists took pains to distinguish legitimate uses of reason of state from what was seen as the illegitimate use in the works of Machiavelli. Flemish* scholar Justus Lipsius (1547–1606) outlined several degrees of reason of state. These range from recommended actions and actions that might be tolerated to those that should be condemned. Others drew a line between justifiable policies that promoted the common good and policies based on a "false reason of state" that served the self-interest of the ruler.

Neo-Stoicism and Other Views. In the late 1500s, another school of political thought—Neo-Stoicism—emerged in northern Europe. Writers who adopted this philosophy include Justus Lipsius, Michel de MONTAIGNE (1533–1592) of France, and the Scottish humanist George Buchanan (1506–1582). Members of this group drew inspiration from some ancient Greek and Roman writers known as Stoics.

The debate over the relative merits of scholarly contemplation versus political participation surfaced again in the works of the Neo-Stoics. Lipsius lived in and wrote about areas of political conflict, but Montaigne deliberately removed himself from public life. In general, the Neo-Stoics took a realistic and accepting view of politics. Montaigne, for example, argued that laws gain force and must be obeyed, not because they are just but simply because they are the laws. Neo-Stoics also believed that citizens should accept the authority of their rulers, and rulers should be guided by true reason of state.

By the early 1600s other ideas were competing with Renaissance humanism. Meanwhile, new legal, political, scientific, and philosophical ideas appeared across Europe, based on the work of thinkers such as Hugo GROTIUS and Galileo GALILEI. Although these ideas arose from humanist roots, they marked the beginning of a new intellectual era. (*See also* **Constitutionalism; Government, Forms of; Humanism; Ideas, Spread of; Law; Monarchy; Philosophy; Princes and Princedoms; Representative Institutions; Utopias.**)

Poliziano, Angelo

1454–1494
Italian scholar and poet

* **classical** in the tradition of ancient Greece and Rome

Angelo Poliziano was one of the leading classical* scholars of Renaissance Italy. He gained fame both for his scholarly works and for his poetry. Born in Siena, Poliziano later settled in Florence, where he studied ancient Greek. The year 1473 marked a turning point in his life. That year Poliziano translated the *Iliad,* an ancient Greek epic*, into Latin. He dedicated the work to Lorenzo de' MEDICI, a wealthy statesman and patron* of learning. In response, Lorenzo invited Poliziano to live

POMPONAZZI, PIETRO

* **epic**   long poem about the adventures of a hero

* **patron**   supporter or financial sponsor of an artist or writer

1462–1525
Italian philosopher

* **treatise**   long, detailed essay

in his palace. There the scholar continued his studies while serving as Lorenzo's private secretary and the tutor of his son.

In 1475 Poliziano began writing a poem in honor of Giuliano de' Medici, Lorenzo's brother, who had just won a jousting match. He called the work *Stanzas Begun for the Jousting Match of the Magnificent Giuliano di Piero de' Medici*. Poliziano kept adding to the poem until Giuliano's death in 1478. Scholars have described the unfinished work as the most extraordinary work of Italian poetry from the late 1400s.

Poliziano later became a priest and took up an academic career. In the early 1480s he served as a professor at the University of Florence. His major scholarly work, known as the *Miscellanea,* appeared in 1489. The work included revolutionary new ideas on how to determine which version of an ancient text was the most accurate. Although many people admired the work, others attacked it. (*See also* **Classical Scholarship; Italian Language and Literature.**)

Pietro Pomponazzi was an important Italian philosopher who explored the theories of the ancient Greek thinker Aristotle. His most famous and controversial work, *Treatise* on the Immortality of the Soul,* examined the idea of whether the human soul lived on after the death of the body. In other works, he examined the idea of fate and the cause of miracles.

Pomponazzi became famous for his claim that reason could not prove that a person's soul lived on after death. In *Treatise on the Immortality of the Soul* he argued that the soul was the same as the intellect, and that the intellect could not function without the body's senses. Without input from the senses, he claimed, the mind is unable to form images and ideas, and therefore it cannot survive after the body dies.

Pomponazzi realized that his theory presented a problem. By stating that reason showed the soul was mortal, he contradicted the doctrines of the Catholic Church, which taught that people who lived a moral life would be rewarded after death and that those who sinned would suffer punishment. He knew some people might argue that without fear of punishment beyond the grave, no one would have any reason to live a virtuous life. Pomponazzi responded to this argument by claiming that moral behavior was a reward in itself.

Treatise on the Immortality of the Soul set off a large controversy. Clergy members throughout Italy attacked Pomponazzi, and in Venice some publicly burned his book. Philosophers and religious thinkers, including one of Pomponazzi's pupils, wrote works attacking him. The author responded with two pieces defending his work. He claimed that he had based his arguments on reason and on Aristotle's ideas, and that he had said nothing against the religious belief that the soul is immortal.

Pomponazzi's works on fate and miracles appeared in print after his death. In *On Fate,* he explored the hidden causes behind human decision-making. In his work on miracles, *On Incantations,* Pomponazzi searched for natural reasons to explain so-called miracles. He also defined religion itself in terms of nature and the cycle of the planets.

Although many of his claims conflicted with those of Christianity, Pomponazzi stressed that philosophy and religion were two different subjects, and that his attacks on certain ideas did not apply to religious beliefs. (*See also* **Aristotle and Aristotelianism; Philosophy.**)

Popes and Papacy

In the early Christian church, people referred to all priests as *pope,* from the Greek and Latin words for "father." Over time, this term became the title of one specific priest—the bishop of ROME. Western Europeans came to view the pope as the earthly representative of Christ and as the head of the entire Roman Catholic Church. Throughout most of Christian history, popes have ruled the Catholic Church in all matters of faith and morals. They have also led the church government and had the final say on matters of doctrine.

In addition to these spiritual duties, Renaissance popes ruled over a secular* realm called the Papal States. This large territory stretched over much of central and northern Italy. Its economy focused on farming and some manufacturing. By the mid-1600s about 1.7 million people lived in the Papal States. Rome and BOLOGNA were the realm's largest cities.

ROLES AND RESPONSIBILITIES

As head of the Roman Catholic Church and ruler of the Papal States, the pope had many responsibilities. These included defending the faith, supporting missionary activities, and supervising military action against enemies. With their great wealth and power, popes also served as patrons* of learning and the arts.

Secular and Spiritual Authority. Popes sought to rule in both spiritual and secular matters. They claimed the right to approve the election of the Holy Roman Emperor* and to crown him personally. Although the pope had no power to overthrow a monarch, he could excommunicate* a king or queen who opposed him and urge other rulers to conquer the monarch's lands. In the 1400s, the popes urged the rulers of Spain and Portugal to win back lands captured by the Moors* and to take over new territories in Africa. They acknowledged the Christian rulers' authority over these newly won territories and encouraged them to establish churches there.

Meanwhile, popes continued to exercise their time-honored role as the final judges in matters of faith. They condemned heresy (teachings that went against church doctrine) and issued decrees on religious topics. To deal with suspected cases of heresy, Sixtus IV granted the Spanish monarchs the power to set up the Spanish Inquisition* in 1479. Paul III later created a Roman Inquisition to combat Protestant ideas in Italy and elsewhere. In 1559 Paul IV issued the first INDEX OF PROHIBITED BOOKS to ban unacceptable views in print.

Some popes faced more immediate threats to the faith. Throughout the Renaissance, the papacy* played a major role in defending Christian

* **secular** nonreligious; connected with everyday life

* **patron** supporter or financial sponsor of an artist or writer

* **Holy Roman Emperor** ruler of the Holy Roman Empire, a political body in central Europe composed of several states that existed until 1806

* **excommunicate** to exclude from the church and its rituals

* **Moor** Muslim from North Africa; Moorish invaders conquered much of Spain during the Middle Ages

* **Spanish Inquisition** court established by the Spanish monarchs that investigated Christians accused of straying from the official doctrine of the Roman Catholic Church, particularly during the period 1480–1530

* **papacy** office and authority of the pope

* **Ottoman Turks** Turkish followers of Islam who founded the Ottoman Empire in the 1300s; the empire eventually included large areas of eastern Europe, the Middle East, and northern Africa

* **Byzantine Empire** Eastern Christian Empire based in Constantinople (A.D. 476–1453)

* **heretic** person who rejects the doctrine of an established church

* **theology** study of the nature of God and of religion

* **classical** in the tradition of ancient Greece and Rome

* **humanist** Renaissance expert in the humanities (the languages, literature, history, and speech and writing techniques of ancient Greece and Rome)

* **aqueduct** structure for channeling large amounts of water

See color plate 2, vol. 3

Europe from the threat of Muslim invasion. Popes tried to persuade Christian rulers to supply military forces and participate in crusades. They also provided money for the campaigns and sent their own troops, sailors, and ships to join in the expeditions. Advances by the Ottoman Turks* into eastern Europe posed a serious threat to the Christian world. To combat this danger, the Roman Catholic Church joined forces with leaders of the Orthodox Church, based in the Byzantine Empire*. In 1453 the Turks captured Constantinople, the capital of the Byzantine Empire. Several popes tried to drive them out, but rivalries between Christian rulers undercut most of their efforts.

Popes also promoted crusades against heretics*, including a failed effort against a group known as the Hussites in the 1400s. They used diplomacy and missionary activities to try to win back lands that had become Protestant. Gregory XIII failed to bring Sweden back into the Catholic ranks, while Clement VIII allowed the French king HENRY IV to rejoin the Catholic Church after several years as a Protestant. Other popes established seminaries (schools for priests) to train missionaries for work in Protestant lands.

After the voyages of Christopher COLUMBUS between 1492 and 1504, popes took a strong interest in spreading the Catholic faith to non-Christian lands. In this task they relied on the rulers of Spain and Portugal, whose exploration of the AMERICAS was opening up new areas for missionary activity. To encourage the spread of the faith, popes granted privileges to these monarchs, who bore the costs of building churches and supporting the priests they sent overseas. Popes also established rules regarding the treatment of people in the new lands. LEO X permitted the training of native peoples as priests in 1519. Paul III condemned the practice of SLAVERY in 1537.

Papal Patronage. Although most Renaissance popes were trained in theology* and church law, few had any classical* learning. Nevertheless, they often hired humanists* as secretaries and administrators. They also supported humanist writers and theologians. As part of their patronage, popes founded new schools and helped maintain existing ones. They provided aid to universities in the Papal States, especially the one in Rome. In addition, several popes worked to reorganize and enlarge the Vatican LIBRARY.

The Renaissance popes were major patrons of the arts, especially in Rome. They sought to make Rome a prosperous and attractive center of culture. To achieve this goal, they repaired the city's walls and aqueducts*, reorganized streets and built new ones, constructed fountains, and opened up new areas for development. To encourage the construction of palaces, Pope Sixtus IV changed church law to allow high-ranking members of the clergy to leave property to their heirs instead of to the church. Many popes built palaces of their own as well.

Popes also collected and commissioned artworks, especially religious ones. They called to Rome the leading artists and architects of the day to restore old churches, build new ones, and decorate chapels, churches, and palaces. Artists such as Fra ANGELICO, Sandro BOTTICELLI, Donato

Pope Julius II (ca. 1445–1513) was known as the warrior pope because he involved himself in several wars in defense of the church and its land.

* **faction** party or interest group within a larger group

BRAMANTE, RAPHAEL, and MICHELANGELO BUONARROTI worked on projects for various popes. Renaissance popes served as patrons of the musical arts as well. They funded choirs to sing in the great chapels and cathedrals of Rome and hired great composers such as Giovanni Pierluigi da PALESTRINA and JOSQUIN DES PREZ to write sacred music.

Popes shaped artistic tastes through their patronage. Through the art they commissioned, popes sought to honor God and the saints, promote the faith, and display the authority of the papacy. Their patronage transformed Rome into the capital of the Christian world.

CHURCH OFFICIALS, ADMINISTRATION, AND FINANCES

The pope stood at the top of the church chain of command. Beneath him served cardinals, bishops, and other officials who played important roles in the workings of the church. To support its spiritual and secular activities, the church needed vast revenues.

Popes and Cardinals. The college of cardinals, the group of high church officials who elected the pope and served as his advisers and administrators, went through major changes during the Renaissance. Two church COUNCILS in the 1400s had passed decrees attempting to limit the number of cardinals to 24, with no more than 8 from any one nation. However, popes claimed that they needed more cardinals and increased their numbers to 70 by 1586. Many cardinals were qualified for their work, but others reached their positions through family or political connections or bribes.

Cardinals enjoyed a great deal of power and authority in the early years of the Renaissance. They ran the church administration and protected the interests of their favorite nations, RELIGIOUS ORDERS, and factions*. As the number of cardinals increased, however, their power declined.

In the 1530s and 1540s Paul III set the college of cardinals on a new course. He appointed many reform-minded cardinals and established committees to deal with specific issues. Sixtus V refined this system into 15 permanent groups, or "congregations"—6 for secular affairs and the rest for spiritual matters. Each congregation had its own specific tasks and members. Such measures reduced the cardinals to administrators who also fulfilled ceremonial roles in the church.

Although cardinals lost power during the Renaissance, they maintained their wealth. Many cardinals had revenue from monasteries, landholdings, or church offices. Cardinals who came from noble families enjoyed private sources of income as well. Moreover, all cardinals received a share of papal revenues. Cardinals used their wealth to advance the fortunes of their relatives and to maintain lavish palaces.

Popes and Bishops. Popes asserted their authority over bishops in a number of ways. They insisted on the right to approve the election of bishops and to collect revenues from them. Popes often joined with

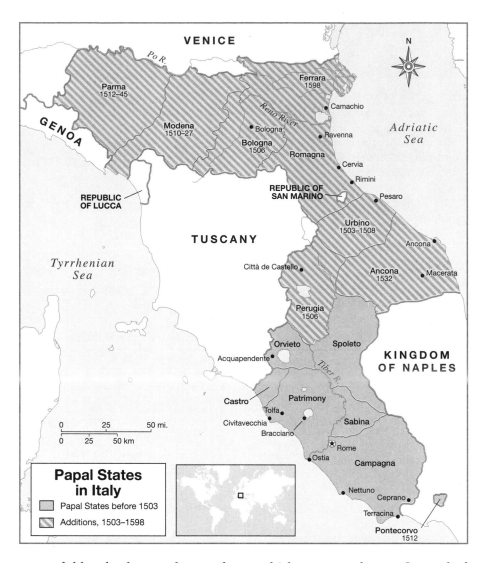

Papal States in Italy

- Papal States before 1503
- Additions, 1503–1598

powerful local rulers to change the way bishops were chosen. Instead of having local officials elect bishops, rulers selected candidates and the pope appointed them. Bishops appointed in this way tended to be very loyal to their rulers.

The Council of TRENT raised the education level of bishops by requiring them to hold advanced degrees in theology or law. It also required them to live within their dioceses*. However, to strengthen their ties to the pope, bishops had to visit Rome once every 3 to 10 years, depending on how far away they lived. The bishops also had to submit regular written reports about their dioceses to the pope.

The Roman Curia. The administrative arm of the papacy was called the Roman Curia. Cardinals ran most of the departments in the Curia with the help of large staffs. The Curia also handled the judicial and financial needs of the church.

Renaissance popes sought to increase their income by adding offices to the Curia and selling the new positions for high prices. Those who

* **diocese** geographical area under the authority of a bishop

The Restorer of Rome

Pope Sixtus IV used the power of his office for two main purposes: to grant favors to his family and to surround the papacy with an image of power and splendor. Sixtus made six of his relatives cardinals and created many new offices in the Curia to generate income. His efforts at magnificence, however, brought lasting cultural benefits. Sixtus reorganized and expanded the Vatican Library and built or repaired many Roman churches. Among these was the Sistine Chapel, an imposing setting for papal ceremonies. His projects earned Sixtus the nickname "Restorer of Rome."

* **tribute** payment made by a smaller or weaker party to a more powerful one, often under threat of force

invested in these lifetime offices received an annual payment from the church, even though many of them did no actual work. Some officials tried to gain extra revenues by engaging in questionable practices, earning the Curia much ill will.

Several councils attempted to reform the Curia during the 1400s, but with little success. Popes resisted their efforts, claiming that they would improve the Curia themselves. Cardinals and members of the Curia fought the changes as well. Still, by the early 1600s a reorganization of the Curia had ended the worst abuses.

Papal Finances. Many popes struggled to manage their finances during the Renaissance. The popes received no annual revenue from church members. Instead, they depended on a patchwork of traditional sources of revenue. These included fees charged for producing documents and other services, fines for violating church laws, the sale of church offices, and the annual tribute* paid by the Papal States. After the early 1500s, church revenues began to decline, due in part to the loss of income from lands that had become Protestant.

Meanwhile, papal expenditures continued to grow. About one-third of the annual budget went toward annual payments to church officials. Salaries of administrators in Rome and the Papal States accounted for another 20 percent. The papacy had to finance an army, the college of cardinals, embassies, and the papal court in Rome. Popes also spent large sums on their relatives in gifts, money, and lands. Wars drained papal revenues, as did the support of crusades against the Ottoman Turks and Protestant governments throughout Europe.

CHALLENGES TO PAPAL AUTHORITY

In the late Middle Ages and early Renaissance, the papacy faced a number of challenges that threatened the stability of the church and the Papal States. In time, the popes resolved these crises and expanded their powers.

The Great Western Schism. During the 1300s, the papacy faced a crisis that threatened to divide its authority and break the ancient tradition of Rome as the seat of the pope and the Christian faith. In 1309 Clement V (reigned 1305–1314), a native of France, moved the papal residence from Rome to the city of Avignon in southern France. Over the next 70 years the papacy remained in Avignon, dominated by the French.

* **depose** to remove from high office, often by force

Following the death of Gregory XI in 1378, the cardinals of the church elected an Italian pope, Urban VI. They later deposed* him and elected a new French pope, Clement VII, who ruled from Avignon. However, Urban VI continued to lay claim to the papacy. The rival popes excommunicated each other and imprisoned each other's supporters. All attempts to resolve this split, or schism, within the church failed. Most cardinals became convinced that only a general council had the authority to impose a solution. In 1409 they deserted the popes and

Leading Renaissance Popes, with Dates of Reign

Eugenius IV (1431–1447)
Nicholas V (1447–1455)
Sixtus IV (1471–1484)
Alexander VI (1492–1503)
Julius II (1503–1513)
Leo X (1513–1521)
Paul III (1534–1549)
Pius IV (1559–1565)
Pius V (1566–1572)
Gregory XIII (1572–1585)
Sixtus V (1585–1590)
Clement VIII (1592–1605)

called the Council of Pisa, at which they deposed both rival popes and elected a new one, Alexander V.

The new pope won the support of most of Europe, and his army captured Rome. However, both of the deposed popes still had supporters and claimed papal authority. At the Council of Constance (1414–1418), the cardinals once again deposed all those who claimed to be pope and elected a new one, Martin V. The council's actions ended the schism and restored the unity of the papacy. However, the schism had weakened papal authority in both secular and spiritual matters.

The Papal States. During the Great Western Schism, the pope's hold on the Papal States weakened. Martin V reasserted control over the Papal States, enabling him to gain badly needed revenues from them. Decisions made by the Council of Constance had greatly reduced revenues from spiritual activities, creating a need for other sources of income.

Martin and his successors broke the power of leading families in various parts of the Papal States. Some popes, such as JULIUS II, deposed local lords and placed their territories under direct papal rule. Others, such as ALEXANDER VI, gave the conquered lands to their relatives. In 1567, however, Pius V declared that all lands in the Papal States that had lost their lords would remain under the direct control of the papacy. By the early 1600s, the papacy had gained near-total control over the territories of the Papal States.

Restoring Spiritual Authority. Renaissance popes also worked to restore the spiritual authority they had lost during the Great Western Schism. They saw church councils as the most serious threat to this goal because councils often issued decrees that limited papal authority. Eugenius IV so strongly opposed the work of the Council of Basel that the council deposed him, although its decree had no effect. When Paul III called the Council of Trent (1545–1563), he made sure that his representatives controlled its agenda. This council proved so willing to allow the pope to interpret its decrees that in 1564 the pope established a body called the Congregation of the Council for that purpose. Its rulings strengthened papal power and eliminated the need for another major church council for three centuries. (*See also* **Art; Art in Italy; Borgia, House of; Catholic Reformation and Counter-Reformation; Factions; Missions, Christian; Music.**)

Popular Culture

* **elite** privileged group; upper class

The term "popular culture" is the modern name for the rituals, customs, and entertainments of ordinary people. During the Renaissance, this term did not exist. People of the time did not draw clear lines between high culture and popular, or "low," culture. However, this line was beginning to appear as Renaissance elites* separated themselves from the common people. For example, readers who closely followed the guidelines for elegant behavior in Baldassare CASTIGLIONE's *The Courtier* (1528) learned to look down on popular tradi-

* **humanist** referring to a Renaissance cultural movement promoting the study of the humanities (the languages, literature, and history of ancient Greece and Rome) as a guide to living

* **literacy** ability to read

tions. At the same time, religious reform movements frowned on elements of popular culture that seemed non-Christian, immoral, or common. The humanist* movement, with its focus on ancient cultures, also encouraged the elites to withdraw from the culture of ordinary people.

Several barriers kept the common people from enjoying forms of high culture such as art and literature. The first of these was language. Much of high culture centered on Latin, a language that the vast majority of the population never learned. A second barrier was literacy*. Only a limited number of people—mostly urban males—could read and write. Finally, money posed a barrier for most people, who could not afford to buy books and paintings. Some could afford other forms of art, however, such as inexpensive prints, engravings, and ceramics.

POPULAR ENTERTAINMENT AND TRADITION

The culture of ordinary people was in many ways a culture of the spoken word. At home, children learned songs, stories, and proverbs. Beyond the household, rumor and gossip were the main sources of information. In addition to this "homemade" culture, people had access to professional communicators such as preachers and actors, especially in towns.

Popular culture also expressed itself through religious beliefs and practices, such as the widespread faith in saints. Many people viewed saints as powerful protectors and healers and associated certain saints with particular situations. For example, Saint Margaret offered protection against the dangers of childbirth, while Saint Blaise guarded against sore throats. Cities, guilds*, and individuals also looked to specific saints for help. The faithful made offerings to these saints or took images of them on processions through the city. The people believed that their saints would punish them if they did not give them enough attention. However, if the people did not get the help they wanted, they sometimes "punished" their saints by dunking their images in water.

* **guild** association of craft and trade owners and workers that set standards for and represented the interests of its members

Events such as fairs and festivals marked the change of seasons and other important events in the lives of ordinary people. Various popular traditions marked these events. For example, during the rowdy annual festival of Carnival, people across Europe overturned the normal rules of society. The most popular activities included overeating, sex, and violence.

RELATIONSHIP BETWEEN HIGH AND LOW CULTURE

Popular culture often imitated the subjects and forms of high culture. For example, upper-class knights and ladies were the first people to enjoy tales of chivalry* during the Middle Ages, but by the 1500s these stories appealed to ordinary people as well. Many popular traditional folktales and ballads dealt with the courts of Charlemagne and King Arthur. Some modern scholars think that these tales of Roland, Lancelot, and other heroes may have had different meanings for listeners from

* **chivalry** rules and customs of medieval knighthood

Several artists and writers of the Renaissance focused on popular culture in their works. Pieter Brueghel the Elder, for instance, showed peasant festivities in his painting *Peasant Dance*.

high and low society. However, the stories themselves were neither "high" nor "low." They were a form of culture that different social groups shared and enjoyed in different ways.

Many people lived somewhere between the popular and elite worlds, or had a foot in both. Craftspeople, shopkeepers, and other townsfolk in large towns had access to schools, plays, and public works of art. Some individuals, such as servants in upper-class households and priests who worked in the community, moved from the popular to the elite world and back again. They played important roles in the interaction between popular culture and the high culture of the Renaissance.

High Culture and the Common People. Some ordinary people knew of at least a small part of the classical* tradition. Publishers printed works by ancient Roman writers in the vernacular*, and stories from Roman history became the subjects of songs, plays, and woodcuts*. Ludovico ARIOSTO's long poem *Orlando Furioso* (Mad Roland, 1516) is an example of how high culture traveled into popular culture. Written by a noble for nobles, it was fairly expensive in its published form. But during the 1500s inexpensive booklets containing sections or summaries of the poem became available, and visitors to Italy reported hearing verses of it in the streets.

Although most Renaissance artists were middle-class crafts workers, only members of the educated elite could afford to buy their works. However, the general public could view their artworks in the form of woodcuts, prints, and engravings. Ordinary people could not afford marble or bronze sculptures, but they could and did buy ceramic plates and jugs, many of which featured painted scenes from classical mythology or ancient history.

Drama also introduced the general population to Renaissance culture. Actors performed plays in the new commedia dell'arte* style in

* **classical**   in the tradition of ancient Greece and Rome

* **vernacular**   native language or dialect of a region or country

* **woodcut**   print made from a block of wood with an image carved into it

* **commedia dell'arte**   improvisational comedy that began in Italy during the Middle Ages and featured stock characters such as a boastful captain, pairs of lovers, and bumbling servants

cities as well as in royal or noble courts. Ordinary folk as well as elites attended the permanent public theaters that opened in the late 1500s in cities such as London, Paris, and Madrid.

Popular Influences on High Culture. Low or popular culture also influenced the high culture of the Renaissance. For example, Giovanni BOCCACCIO was a learned man who wrote scholarly works in Latin. However, he took many of the stories in his *Decameron* (completed in the early 1350s) from the popular tradition of spoken folktales. Several of the plots turn on practical jokes, a central element of popular culture in Tuscany, Boccaccio's home.

The Dutch painter Pieter BRUEGHEL the Elder, active in the 1500s, linked high and low culture in his paintings. He was part of a circle of learned men and was familiar with at least some elements of classical tradition, yet his art frequently shows peasants dancing, working, or enjoying games or Carnival activities. One of Brueghel's biographers wrote that he attended peasant weddings to gather material for his art.

English playwright William SHAKESPEARE included peasants and craftsmen as comic figures in some of his plays. In addition, his comedies draw on popular festive traditions. The play *A Midsummer Night's Dream*, for example, reflects the customs of May Game, a traditional English spring festival. (*See also* **Art; Commedia dell'Arte; Decorative Arts; Fairs and Festivals; Parades and Pageants; Social Status.**)

* **demography** statistical study of characteristics of population, such as size, distribution, growth, birthrates, and death rates

* **plague** highly contagious and often fatal disease that wiped out much of Europe's population in the mid-1300s and reappeared periodically over the next three centuries; also known as the Black Death

How many people lived in Europe during the Renaissance—and in various regions or cities of the continent? Although modern historians do not have exact answers to such questions, they have come up with estimates based on population counts made during the period. By applying the techniques of demography* to information about population size in various places at various times, scholars have concluded that the overall population of Europe reached about 89 million by 1600. Population growth during the Renaissance was unsteady, interrupted by periods of decline caused by the plague* and other disasters, and population trends differed from region to region.

Renaissance Censuses. The primary source of information about population size and characteristics is the census, a survey that counts citizens and may include information about their gender, age, marital status, education, and profession. By the 1300s the cities of western Europe began counting their populations, usually for tax purposes. Some counts simply recorded households or heads of families. Other lists, especially those related to military service, included the ages and genders of individuals. From the census-related documents that survive, historians can estimate the total population of Renaissance urban centers and sometimes of the surrounding rural areas. Few sources cover large territories or whole countries before 1500.

One unusually thorough census is the *catasto* (land register) made in the Italian city of Florence in 1427. It describes the property and real

Population of European Countries (in millions)

	ca. 1400	ca. 1500	ca. 1600
Balkans	4	4.5	6
British Isles	3.5	5	7
France	11	16	18
Germany	6.5	9	12
Italy	7	11	13
Low Countries*	1	2	3
Poland	3	4	5
Russia	9	12	15
Spain and Portugal	7	9	11
Scandinavian Countries	1	2	2
Switzerland	0.8	0.8	1

Sources: Cipolla, *Before the Industrial Revolution;* McEvedy and Jones, *Atlas of World Population History.*

*"Low Countries" refers to the region of present-day Belgium and the Netherlands.

estate of each taxpayer as well as the entire population under the control of the Florentine republic: 60,000 families and more than 260,000 individuals. Venice, another Italian city, also produced detailed censuses. The first complete survey of the city's population was taken in 1338. In 1440 Venetians designed a census project to classify people by age, gender, profession, social condition, and nationality. Although this seemingly modern census was not carried out, Venice continued to take surveys. In 1607 its census takers received the first printed forms on which to record information.

Interesting and valuable as they are, Renaissance urban censuses fall short of providing full information. Not only do they cover limited areas, but they also tend to exclude certain groups, especially those that did not pay taxes. Young children, single widows, vagabonds and poor people, patients in welfare institutions, and members of the clergy or religious orders are probably undercounted. For example, the 1427 *catasto* lists 37,246 inhabitants for the city of Florence, but historians believe that the city's population was larger.

Demographic Patterns. Demography helps historians fill in gaps and expand the population picture. In addition to census counts, demographers study a variety of written records, such as registers of marriages, births, and deaths. They also use archaeological information. For example, the cultivation of new fields and the enlargement of city walls indicate population growth, while deserted villages or large empty areas within cities can be signs of a major drop in population.

From A.D. 1000 to 1300, the population of Europe grew slowly but steadily. Then, in the mid-1300s, Europe was struck by the Black Death, the first and deadliest of the many waves of the plague that swept across

Population of Europe

Year	Population (in millions)	Period	Annual population growth (per 1,000 people)
1200	49	1200–1250	3.0
1250	57	1250–1300	4.1
1300	70	1300–1340	1.4
1340	74	1340–1400	-5.9
1400	52	1400–1500	2.5
1500	67	1500–1600	2.8
1600	89	1600–1700	0.7
1700	95	—	—
		1340–1700	0.7

Source: Biraben, "Essai sur l'evolution du nombre des hommes. *Population*, 1979."
Does not include territories of the former Soviet Union.

the continent over the next several centuries. The Black Death killed large numbers of people at once. It also launched a era in which periods of zero population growth, or even of population decline, alternated with periods of rapid growth. Europe's overall population was an estimated 74 million in 1340, just before the outbreak of the plague. By 1400 it had fallen to 52 million. During the next century it rose to 67 million, still lower than before the Black Death. Only in the late 1500s did the continent's population surpass the level it had reached before the plague.

Europeans reacted to large-scale population decline in a variety of ways. People who had lost spouses remarried. Those who had lost children had more children. Marriage customs changed—women married younger and bore their first children at a younger age. Cities encouraged skilled laborers and productive workers to come from other areas.

Aside from the effects of the plague cycle, two overall, long-term trends shaped demographic patterns in the Renaissance. One was a shift toward greater population density in northern Europe, probably as a result of new agricultural techniques that made farmlands more productive. In 1200, northern Europe had only 12 million people, compared with 33 million in southern Europe. By 1500, northern Europe's population had nearly doubled to 23 million, while southern Europe's had reached only 39 million. Over the next 150 years, European population continued to expand at a faster rate in the north than in the south.

The other major demographic trend of the age was the growth of cities. The cities earned the nickname "man eaters," a reference to the floods of people migrating from the countryside to the urban centers. Cities welcomed skilled and qualified workers as immigrants. During times of famine and hardship, however, many immigrants were poor people in search of food and help.

Urban growth had limits. For example, cities could not outgrow the ability of the surrounding countryside to feed them. Even in Italy, where urbanization began, only about 10 percent of the population lived in

cities by 1500. The century that followed brought increasing urbanization, especially as the new centralized states of Europe developed their capital cities. In some places, however, the rate of urban growth slowed when the cities encountered economic problems. In Italy, for example, manufacturing shifted from some of the cities to smaller towns. No population trend of the Renaissance applied equally to all parts of Europe. (*See also* **Agriculture; Plague.**)

Portugal

* **exploit**   to take advantage of; to make productive use of

* **Black Death**   epidemic of the plague, a highly contagious and often fatal disease, which spread throughout Europe from 1348 to 1350

Portugal led Europe's overseas expansion during the early Renaissance. It established colonies and exploited* the riches of Africa and Asia. Stories of Portuguese exploration and military conquests in the Muslim world dazzled people throughout Europe. However, successes abroad could not make up for the domestic problems that brought an end to Portugal's Golden Age by the late 1500s.

Roots of Portuguese Power. Portugal's great achievements were made possible by its response to the social, political, and economic conditions in Europe at the end of the Middle Ages. The Black Death* and other epidemics, constant warfare, and shortages of food and precious metals affected all European nations at this time. Although the revenues of European monarchs declined, the cost of supporting a royal lifestyle grew. This led to much discontent among members of the nobility, who relied on royal gifts and grants of land as part of their income.

Portugal suffered from these same problems. However, its small size, sense of identity, and strong royal family enabled the country to respond more effectively than most kingdoms. The Avis dynasty arose when Dom João (ruled 1385–1433) won a power struggle after the death of the king Dom Fernando in 1383. However, war with Portugal's powerful neighbor, the Spanish kingdom of Castile and Leon, began soon after Dom João took the throne.

Rather than weaken Portugal, the war actually helped strengthen it. The need to raise money for armies led Dom João to impose a sales tax within the country. Over time this tax became a source of regular revenue. The war also expanded the crown's power and freedom of action. The monarchy grew stronger because its opponents appeared to be traitors and Dom João was able to reward nobles with grants of captured land and riches plundered from the enemy. These developments helped the Avis dynasty centralize power and authority in Portugal to a greater extent than in most other European states.

The war with Castile and Leon had turned in Portugal's favor by 1389. However, the nations did not stop fighting until 1411. The end of hostilities presented Dom João with a new problem—how to keep the nobility satisfied without being able to reward them with land and revenue seized in war. Four years after the conflict ended, Dom João attacked the North African city of Ceuta. The campaign's success increased Dom João's prestige and provided new sources of wealth with which to reward Portuguese nobles. This conquest marked the beginning of Europe's overseas expansion.

The capital city of Lisbon played a major role in the growing power of Portugal during the 1400s and early 1500s. Improvements to Lisbon's seaport, shown here, helped the country's economy by increasing trade with northern and Mediterranean cities.

Troubles at Home. Despite foreign successes, economic and social conditions in Portugal led to discontent at home. The crown and nobles had to look abroad for new income opportunities. Some members of the upper class left the country to settle elsewhere in Europe; others sought their fortunes in overseas ventures. Between the 1420s and the 1460s, Portugal explored and colonized several island groups, including the Azores, Madeiras, and Cape Verde Islands, and gained control of the northern coast of Morocco. Its gold and slave trade in western Africa brought great riches.

These successes relieved some internal pressures but increased others. Men who served the crown overseas often received titles or became knights, but the king had little land or money with which to reward those he honored. As a result, lawless bands of knights began to roam the countryside, serving as private armies for large landholders who protected them from royal authority. Even relatives of the king who received land grants were not always loyal, and splits within the royal family threatened the power of the crown.

In the 1480s Dom João II (ruled 1481–1495) tried to reassert his power and rebuild the nation's economic base. He suppressed a revolt by the nobles and took back some of the land he had given them. His succes-

sor, Dom Manuel (ruled 1495–1521), continued the policy of centralizing power but used more subtle tactics. He won the support of nobles by increasing their gifts and restoring lands taken away by Dom João II. He could afford to do so because income from trade in Africa and Asia more than doubled the state's revenue. Although these policies reduced tensions at home, about 80 percent of Portugal's budget went to supporting the nobility.

Triumph and Decline. The reigns of Dom João II and Dom Manuel marked the high point of the Avis dynasty's power and prestige. Dom João II promoted trade with Africa and supported the first major effort to reach Asia by sea. In 1494 the Treaty of Tordesillas, which divided lands in the New World between Spain and Portugal, ensured Portugal's access to the African and Asian markets. Under Dom Manuel, the navigator Vasco da GAMA pioneered a new route to Asia. This opened the door to trade, conquest, and a Portuguese empire in east Africa and Asia. During the next 20 years the Portuguese extended their reach to Brazil, southeast Asia, and China. They dominated the shipping lanes of the Indian Ocean and controlled the profitable spice trade. Despite these accomplishments, Dom Manuel was most interested in fighting the Muslims. He considered the conquest of Morocco his most important accomplishment, and he hoped to drive the Muslims from the Holy Land.

Dom Manuel also came very close to uniting the Iberian Peninsula* under his rule. In 1525 his son, Dom João III, married the sister of CHARLES V, the Holy Roman Emperor*. The next year the emperor wed Dom João's sister. The two unions were a major diplomatic victory for Portugal. However, Dom João III's death in 1557 put the young and sickly Dom Sebastião on the throne. Dom Sebastião produced no heirs of his own and was killed in battle in Morocco in 1578. His elderly uncle struggled to rule the country, but his death two years later led to a brief war of succession*. PHILIP II, the king of Spain and the most powerful European monarch of the time, had little trouble enforcing an old claim to the throne in 1580. Portugal remained under Spanish rule for the next 60 years.

Union with Spain was merely the conclusion of a long period of slow decline in Portugal. Overseas expansion had benefited most Portuguese, but it did not cure the social and political problems left over from the late Middle Ages. The Protestant Reformation* triggered a wave of religious conformity in Catholic Portugal. The INQUISITION, a court established to investigate charges of heresy*, drove many converted Jews out of Portugal. This cost the country some of the most talented individuals in the areas of business and government. The Inquisition also led to repression of new ideas and a decline in higher education. Later Portuguese rulers struggled to match the achievements of Dom João II and Dom Manuel. A sense of pessimism about the future and a longing for the heroic past took root. (*See also* **Africa; Art in Spain and Portugal; Asia, East; Conversos; Exploration; Lisbon; Portuguese Language and Literature; Spain.**)

* **Iberian Peninsula** part of western Europe occupied by present-day Spain and Portugal

* **Holy Roman Emperor** ruler of the Holy Roman Empire, a political body in central Europe composed of several states that existed until 1806

* **succession** determination of person who will inherit the throne

* **Protestant Reformation** religious movement that began in the 1500s as a protest against certain practices of the Roman Catholic Church and eventually led to the establishment of a variety of Protestant churches

* **heresy** belief that is contrary to the doctrine of an established church

Portuguese Language and Literature

* **classical**   in the tradition of ancient Greece and Rome

* **humanist**   referring to a Renaissance cultural movement promoting the study of the humanities (the languages, literature, and history of ancient Greece and Rome) as a guide to living

* **colloquy**   dialogue

* **satiric**   involving the use of satire, the ridicule of human wickedness and foolishness in a literary or artistic work

During the Renaissance, Portuguese scholars stressed the ties between the Portuguese language and classical* Latin. For example, author João de Barros (ca. 1496–1570) composed poetry that could be read as either language. The appearance of dictionaries and grammar books in the mid-1500s shows that the Portuguese language was fully developed by this time. It was also spreading to Portugal's colonies in Asia and Africa. The nation's efforts to explore and colonize unfamiliar lands had a strong effect on its literature. Exposure to foreign cultures helped give rise to new, humanist* viewpoints that clashed with the country's church-centered traditional values.

Writings Related to Exploration.   One of the most important writers inspired by the subjects of exploration and conquest was Barros. He produced a range of prose writings that include a flattering history of Portuguese royalty, a Portuguese grammar book, and writings on morality. Barros is most famous for his four-part *Decades of Asia*. In it, he compared the history of Portuguese expansion in Asia to the tales of classical heroes.

Descriptions of the lands, peoples, and cultures that the Portuguese encountered in India, China, and Japan were popular topics for prose writers. The major work of this kind is Fernão Mendes Pinto's account of his adventures in Asia, *Travels* (1614), which became one of the most widely read books of the 1600s. In it, Pinto's narrator learns to see himself and his fellow Portuguese through the eyes of the Asians. Although *Travels* includes details that seem incredible, recent investigations have shown that much of Pinto's work is accurate.

Portuguese exploration also fueled a variety of other writings, including letters, travel diaries, and reports of shipwrecks. Some texts, such as the ship's log from the voyage of explorer Vasco da GAMA, dealt with the subject of navigation. Others, like Garcia da Orta's *Colloquies* * *on the Simples* [plants] *and Drugs of India* (1563), focused on the natural sciences.

Other Writings.   Although exploration had a great impact on Portuguese prose, it was far from the only topic writers addressed. Essayists of the mid-1500s discussed religion and art. Fiction writers from the same period, such as Jorge de Montemayor and Francisco de Morais, produced comedies and novels. Religious letters and biographies also made up a great deal of Renaissance Portuguese prose.

Portuguese drama took various forms during the Renaissance. Court theater featured popular characters and moral messages. Portugal's major Renaissance playwright, Gil Vicente, wrote and produced 45 plays of various types for the court between 1502 and 1536. Many of his plays are satiric*, and they target people from all levels of society. Playwright António Ferreira produced dramas in a classical style, such as his tragedy *Castro* (1587). Another form of theater was the religious dramas staged on ships at sea.

In the field of poetry, elements of Portuguese oral traditions blended with the new forms of the European Renaissance. Poet Garcia de Resende used a variety of local forms in his collection *General Songbook*

* **epic** long poem about the adventures of a hero

(1516). Luíz Vaz de CAMÕES, by contrast, perfected Italian forms of poetry in Portugal. Camões's epic* *The Lusiads* (1572) is one of the classic works of Western literature, full of rich imagery and musical rhythm. Its hero is Vasco da Gama, who recites the history of Portugal as he makes his voyage to India. On the way, he encounters magic, the gods of classical mythology, and a variety of natural oddities. Camões used his epic to blend the diverse elements of his country into a vision of a united Portugal. (*See also* **Art in Spain and Portugal; Inquisition; Spanish Language and Literature.**)

Poverty and Charity

During the Renaissance, cities and towns tried many methods to deal with the widespread problem of poverty. Urban centers, which tended to attract many poor people, usually provided better care for the poor than rural areas. However, even in larger cities, public authorities did not take a direct part in poor relief until the later Renaissance.

Extent of Poverty. Between 50 and 70 percent of the people in Europe's largest cities were poor in some sense. A very small proportion of the population depended on poor relief at all times. These people, known as the helpless poor, included invalids, the young, the aged, and the mentally ill. Their numbers grew during times of famine as refugees from the countryside came to the cities and towns in search of food or alms—charity given freely to the poor.

Just above the helpless poor on the social scale was a large group of people who relied on poorly paid seasonal or irregular work. This group, known as the *miserabili* or "have-nothings," included people such as laborers, porters, journeymen*, and out-of-work servants. They made up about 20 percent of the urban population. In normal times they could scrape by, but they had no savings. Sudden increases in the price of bread or downturns in the economy could make them dependent upon charity.

* **journeyman** person who has completed an apprenticeship and is certified to work at a particular trade or craft

A third group of poor people included craft workers, shopkeepers, and minor officials. Society thought of them as respectable in normal times, but an illness, personal loss, or public disaster such as an epidemic could put them at risk of poverty. These people would not beg openly like other groups of poor people, but they would not turn down charitable gifts if offered.

* **hierarchy** organization of a group into higher and lower levels

Types of Poverty. Renaissance Europe recognized a hierarchy* of poverty, based on the circumstances that had brought an individual to poverty. The shamefaced poor were nobles or influential citizens who had fallen on hard times and could no longer maintain a lifestyle fitting their class. Although more likely to lose their honor than to starve, the shamefaced poor enjoyed the best treatment from charitable organizations.

The "poor of Christ" included widows and orphans who patiently accepted their misfortune. In the eyes of those who dispensed charity,

Renaissance cities worked to provide relief for the increasing number of poor residents. In this painting from the mid-1400s by Domenico di Bartolo, beggars line up to receive food.

See color plate 10, vol. 3

the poor of Christ best represented Christ's suffering on earth, and a gift to them would gain the donor God's favor. A related group that appeared in Catholic countries was those who voluntarily gave up worldly goods. Begging RELIGIOUS ORDERS such as the Franciscans fell into this category. Protestants frowned on such orders and the religious poor because they believed that people earned entrance into heaven solely through faith, not through actions such as charitable actions.

The laboring poor, those who worked but had no assets to fall back on in hard times, made up the largest body of poor people. Below the laboring poor fell the outcast poor. These included vagrants, idlers, false cripples, prostitutes, and others who received charity through deception. By the 1500s, most people regarded the outcast poor as habitual sinners who had little hope for salvation.

Brotherhoods of the Poor

Most confraternities that performed charitable works were made up of people from the upper and middle classes. However, some cities had confraternities of approved beggars. The more skillful and attractive beggars, often the blind and the lame, would collect alms on the street. Elected officers of the confraternity then distributed the money evenly among the members. Some groups had rules that barred certain people from membership, while others included everyone who lived in a town or church district. The Spanish town of Zamora boasted 150 confraternities, about one for every 14 households.

* **patronage**   support or financial sponsorship

* **laypeople**   those who are not members of the clergy

* **plague**   highly contagious and often fatal disease that wiped out much of Europe's population in the mid-1300s and reappeared periodically over the next three centuries; also known as the Black Death

* **Low Countries**   region bordering on the North Sea, made up of present-day Netherlands and Belgium

See color plate 11, vol. 2

Types of Poor Relief. A great deal of poor relief was personal. Almsgivers donated money to beggars, neighbors supported one another, and landlords and farmers gave grain to the local poor. Shopkeepers often extended credit to those who could not pay for goods at the time of purchase. Cities developed some formal structures to deal with the poor, such as religious organizations, hospitals, and banks. Wealthy individuals often ran these organizations as a way to provide patronage* or improve their social standing.

In Catholic cities, organized groups of religious brotherhoods called CONFRATERNITIES provided many services for the poor. These were groups of laypeople* who believed that they could earn God's favor by performing good works. They banded together to perform charitable works such as giving alms, caring for the sick, visiting prisoners, and taking in strangers. Many towns and cities relied on confraternities to provide these types of public services. Some groups provided burials or offered Masses (religious services) for the souls of the dead. Confraternities directed much of their effort toward their own members and their families, but over time more of them provided help to outsiders as well.

As their name suggests, hospitals provided hospitality rather than medical care. They took in orphans and abandoned children, sheltered people traveling to religious sites, and cared for widows and the aged. Medical attention became a concern of hospitals because the poor often became sick and because sickness often led to poverty. People who could afford medical care usually received it in their homes. Early hospitals were small, but some cities later established large hospitals, often to deal with outbreaks of plague*. These hospitals served as places to hold and observe visitors or goods suspected of infection before allowing them to enter the city.

Some towns tried to provide small, low-interest loans to the poor. They might license a Jewish pawnbroker for this service. After 1460, people turned to cut-rate Christian pawnshops, which operated as nonprofit banks that charged a very low interest rate. These became popular in Italy, but similar banks arose in Spain, the Low Countries*, and France. The pawnshops also served as disaster banks from which local people could borrow in times of emergency.

Reform of Poor Relief. In the early 1500s, many towns and some nations tried to coordinate their systems of poor relief. They made efforts to restrict begging, conduct a census of the local poor, and provide training and work for the unemployed. Protestant cities that had sold off Catholic institutions, such as monasteries, often used the assets from the sale for poor relief and education. In some Catholic cities, officials used poor relief as a way to collect information on local residents. For example, officials in the French town of Ypres visited the poor and assembled records about their financial condition, health, and habits.

Some cities passed laws to raise money for the poor when voluntary charity proved insufficient. Many of these cities adopted the practice of rating, or examining each citizen's relative wealth to determine how much he should contribute to poor relief. City leaders then pressed the

citizens to contribute more if they were not being generous enough. Over time, public authorities became even more directly involved in providing poor relief. For example, in Venice the Board of Health took charge of preventing begging, vagrancy, and prostitution. (*See also* **Hospitals and Asylums; Orphans and Foundlings; Social Status.**)

Prague

* **Holy Roman Empire** political body in central Europe composed of several states; existed until 1806

* **diocese** geographical area under the authority of a bishop

See color plate 15, vol. 3

* **artisan** skilled worker or craftsperson

* **Counter-Reformation** actions taken by the Roman Catholic Church after 1540 to oppose Protestantism

Duning the Renaissance, Prague was the capital of the kingdom of BOHEMIA and a leading city of the Holy Roman Empire*. At various times, the city served as an imperial power base, a stronghold for certain religious groups, and a center of intellectual and cultural activity.

Early Renaissance. The city of Prague rose to prominence in the middle of the 1300s. It engaged in an extensive building program. In 1344, the pope raised the diocese* of Prague from a bishopric to an archbishopric. Four years later, the University of Prague, the first university in central Europe, was founded.

In the early 1400s, a religious movement inspired by the teaching of reformer Jan Hus developed in Prague. In 1419 supporters of the movement, known as Hussites, led an uprising and seized control of the city. The rebels of Prague defied the authority of the emperor, the nobles, and the Roman Catholic Church. By 1421 they controlled most of Bohemia, but they fell from power in 1434. This period of turmoil took a toll on the city's economy.

Rise to Prominence. In the mid- to late 1400s, Prague gradually regained economic and political power. Under kings George Podebrady (ruled 1458–1471) and Vladislav II (ruled 1471–1516), foreign trade improved and various public buildings went through major renovations. This process continued during the reign of FERDINAND I (ruled 1526–1564), who made the city a powerful financial and political center. Ferdinand established a glittering royal residence in Prague, adding a summer palace and splendid gardens to the castle.

Under RUDOLF II (ruled 1575–1612), Prague reached a peak of cultural development. Both the court and the university attracted writers and scientists from throughout the empire. Rudolf took a serious interest in the arts, amassing one of the largest art collections in Europe. He hired Italian masons and artisans* to transform Prague Castle into a magnificent Renaissance palace. Following his example, local nobles also supported the arts and commissioned architects to build stately homes.

Throughout the 1500s, religious conflicts continued to surface around Prague. The city became a center for the Counter-Reformation*, which created opposition from Protestants. In 1618 a group of Protestant noblemen threw two ministers of the Catholic king out of a window in Prague Castle. This event helped spark the THIRTY YEARS' WAR (1618–1648), a series of battles fought across much of central Europe. During the war, invading armies attacked Prague repeatedly, looting many of its treasures. The city did not fully recover until the end of the

1600s. (*See also* **Art in Central Europe; Catholic Reformation and Counter-Reformation; Holy Roman Empire; Protestant Reformation.**)

Preaching and Sermons

Preaching means communicating the word of God in human speech to awaken faith. Most Christians base the call for preaching on passages in the Gospels, the four books of the Bible that tell of Christ's life and teachings. These passages describe Christ proclaiming the "Good News" about the Kingdom of God and commanding his followers to spread the faith to all nations.

In the Middle Ages and the Renaissance, preaching commonly took place during the Roman Catholic religious service, or Mass, after the reading of the Gospel. There were many other opportunities for preaching, such as sermons during the Christmas and Easter seasons, funerals, and in times of sickness or hunger. Officially, the right to preach belonged to bishops, who extended it to priests. Laypeople* sometimes preached as well—although church leaders did not always approve of this practice and sometimes forbade it.

The Importance of Preaching. During the Renaissance, many people claimed that the quality of preaching had fallen into decline. Catholic leaders sought to address this problem at church councils. As early as 1215, a council declared that bishops were responsible for preaching and religious education. Another council in 1516 warned the faithful about incompetent preachers and advised bishops to keep watch over their preachers.

The Council of TRENT (1545–1563), called to address the concerns raised by Protestant reformers, issued the strongest statements about preaching. The council reaffirmed the idea that preaching was the "special duty of bishops." It instructed them to use plain language to describe the vices Catholics should avoid and the virtues to which they should aspire. Both Catholics and Protestants began to view preaching in a new light. Several RELIGIOUS ORDERS made preaching a priority, and some—especially the Jesuits*—applied new methods of rhetoric* to preaching.

Preaching Styles. In the early days of the church, speakers simply rose whenever they felt moved to preach. But by the time of the Renaissance, church officials had regulated preaching. They stressed that preaching required much preparation and training in Scripture. Also, most importantly, it called for holiness in the preacher. In addition, all aspects of the sermon—the theme, length, language, subject matter, and style—should fit the occasion.

Two forms of preaching became common during the Catholic Mass. The homily, a flexible form of preaching, began with an opening address followed by a discussion of a passage from Scripture read at that Mass. Then came an appeal for good moral behavior and praise to God. During the Renaissance the homily became more attractive to scholarly

* **laypeople** those who are not members of the clergy

* **Jesuit** refers to a Roman Catholic religious order founded by St. Ignatius Loyola and approved in 1540

* **rhetoric** art of speaking or writing effectively

Formal sermons became a popular form of preaching during the Renaissance. This painting from the early 1600s shows a group of churchgoers, including the English king James I, gathered to listen to a sermon at St. Paul's Cathedral in London.

* **humanist** referring to a Renaissance cultural movement promoting the study of the humanities (the languages, literature, and history of ancient Greece and Rome) as a guide to living

* **classical** in the tradition of ancient Greece and Rome

clergymen, who felt they could apply the methods of rhetoric used so effectively by early Greek and Roman church leaders.

The other common type of preaching was the sermon, a more formal speech. Preachers used their sermons to teach moral and spiritual lessons based on texts from Scripture. Sometimes the sermon differed little from the homily, but during the Middle Ages it took on a more formal structure. Many religious scholars of the time argued that the sermon should teach and convince listeners of the truths of their faith. They developed handbooks with specific rules for each aspect of the sermon—from invention and arrangement to delivery and use of rhetoric.

By the 1500s handbooks for preaching fell out of favor, especially in Italy. Humanist* clergy members came to view preaching in light of the three main aims of classical* rhetoric: to move, to teach, and to delight.

The Dutch humanist Desiderius ERASMUS wrote a book explaining how to apply classical rhetoric to Catholic preaching. His work inspired countless preaching manuals, which became popular with both Catholics and Protestants.

Jewish Preaching and Sermons. Despite their differences in theology*, Jewish and Christian preachers shared similar styles. During the Renaissance some Jews used rhetoric to improve their preaching. For example, the Italian scholar Judah Messer Leon turned to the works of the ancient Roman authors CICERO and Quintilian. In his best-known work, Leon praised the ideal of eloquence. He argued that the Hebrew Bible provided a model of eloquent speech.

Leon's ideas had an immediate impact. In the 1500s, training in the preparation and delivery of sermons became part of the schooling for Jewish males. However, drawing on classical models sometimes caused problems for Jewish preachers. In 1598 Jewish leaders criticized David Del Bene for referring to myths in a sermon.

The Italian rabbi Judah Moscato often used Greek myths in his sermons. He avoided criticism by comparing Greek and Roman philosophers and Christian scholars to Jewish thinkers and Scripture. Moscato may also have been the first Jewish preacher to give his sermons titles. (*See also* **Catholic Reformation and Counter-Reformation; Councils; Humanism; Jewish Language and Literature; Jews; Philosophy; Religious Literature; Religious Thought.**)

* **theology** study of the nature of God and of religion

Princes and Princedoms

* **duchy** territory ruled by a duke or duchess

* **Holy Roman Emperor** ruler of the Holy Roman Empire, a political body in central Europe composed of several states that existed until 1806

Renaissance princes were the heads of independent states. The territory ruled by a prince might be a kingdom, a duchy*, a city-state, or some other type of self-governing realm. Originally the term *prince* referred to the emperor of ancient Rome. In the Middle Ages it was applied to the Holy Roman Emperor*. During the Renaissance, however, the meaning of *prince* changed, as princedoms—states governed by strong and effective rulers—emerged.

Renaissance princes ranged from monarchs of large kingdoms to rulers of minor cities. They could be legitimate or illegitimate, depending on their position with regard to the law. The prince's right to rule might or might not be recognized by long tradition, by local authorities, or by a superior power such as the Holy Roman Emperor or the pope. The most important characteristic of a prince was effective power—the ability to make and enforce laws, impose taxes, command armies, form alliances, and declare war.

The Rise of Princedoms. Renaissance princedoms developed in three stages. The first stage was the formation of self-governing towns, or communes, in northern and central Italy in the late 1200s. In the absence of any authority from the emperor or pope, these cities began to exercise powers usually held by such rulers. The second stage in the development of princedoms came with the transfer of powers from community institutions (the commune) to an individual signore (lord).

The individual was usually, but not always, a leading member of a prominent and powerful local family.

The third, and perhaps most crucial, stage in the development of princely power involved a basic change in the relationship between the commune and the signore. The key to this change was the recognition of the hereditary nature of the signore's authority. This right of succession gave the rulers legitimacy as princes. It also represented a strengthening of the power and resources of princes and gave them significant military and political advantages over rivals.

Powers of the Prince. For many years, historians viewed the Renaissance prince as a sort of all-powerful ruler who could impose his will on society. However, most recent scholars have shifted away from that view. Research has shown that the Renaissance princedom involved a complex web of power-sharing relationships among the prince, prominent members of society, governing bodies, and other groups. Even Renaissance princes with far-reaching power, such as Lorenzo de' MEDICI of Florence, did not possess absolute authority. In such cases, the city's republican* institutions continued to function alongside the governing bodies controlled by the prince.

A prince's power sometimes depended on his relationship with other authorities, such as the Holy Roman Emperor. In 1395 Emperor Wenceslas recognized the rise to power of Giangaleazzo Visconti by naming him duke of Milan. However, when the Sforza family gained control of Milan in the 1450s, the emperor refused for decades to give them the title *duke*. Similarly, the pope could influence the extent of a prince's power. Popes often granted princely titles to noble families, such as the ESTE of Ferrara, that supported papal* causes. (*See also* **City-States; Government, Forms of; Holy Roman Empire; Machiavelli, Niccolò.**)

* **republican** refers to a form of Renaissance government dominated by leading merchants with limited participation by others

* **papal** referring to the office and authority of the pope

Note: Volume numbers precede each page number, separated by a colon. Page numbers in boldface type refer to main discussions of a topic.